How Change Happens

How Change Happens

Cass R. Sunstein

The MIT Press
Cambridge, Massachusetts
London, England

This book was set in Stone by Toppan Best-set Premedia Limited. Printed and bound in the United States of America.

Library of Congress Cataloging-in-Publication Data

Names: Sunstein, Cass R., author.
Title: How change happens / Cass R. Sunstein.
Description: Cambridge, MA : MIT Press, [2019] | Includes bibliographical references and index.
Identifiers: LCCN 2018026995 | ISBN 9780262039574 (hardcover : alk. paper)
Subjects: LCSH: Social change. | Social groups. | Common good. | Decision making
Classification: LCC HM831 .S86 2019 | DDC 303.4--dc23 LC record available at https://lccn.loc.gov/2018026995

10 9 8 7 6 5 4 3 2 1

Opposition? How would anybody know? How would anybody know what somebody else opposes or doesn't oppose? That a man *says* he opposes or doesn't oppose depends upon the circumstances, where, and when, and to whom, and just how he says it. And then you still must guess *why* he says what he says. So, too, even in action.

—Carl Klingelhofer, former Nazi[1]

If I had known that not a single lunch counter would open as a result of my action I could not have done differently than I did. If I had known violence would result, I could not have done differently than I did. I am thankful for the sit-ins if for no other reason than that they provided me with an opportunity for making a slogan into a reality, by turning a decision into an action. It seems to me that this is what life is all about.

—Sandra Cason[2]

We are all Expressionists part of the time. Sometimes we just want to scream loudly at injustice, or to stand up and be counted. These are noble motives, but any serious revolutionist must often deprive himself of the pleasures of self-expression. He must judge his actions by their ultimate effects on institutions.

—Herbert Simon[3]

Contents

Preface

A few decades ago, I testified in Congress about President Bill Clinton's "don't ask, don't tell" policy, which allowed gays and lesbians to serve in the US military, but only on condition that they did not disclose their sexual orientation. After my testimony, a member of Congress came up to me and said to me, with evident nostalgia, "In my day, we didn't have any homosexuals." He paused and added, "Well, maybe we had one. There was a guy who lived by himself, up on a hill."

How does social change happen? One answer points to the role of social norms, which can be both powerful (in the sense that they greatly affect behavior) and fragile (in the sense that they can collapse in a short time). If norms lead people to silence themselves, a status quo can persist—even if some or many people hate it, and even if those who seem to support it are actually pretty indifferent to it. One day, someone challenges the norm. Maybe it's a child who says that the Emperor has no clothes. Maybe it's a guy who lives by himself, up on a hill. After that small challenge, others may begin to say what they think. Once that happens, a drip can become a flood.

Most of us live, at least some of the time, in accordance with norms that we abhor. We might not think about them; they are part of life's furniture. But in our heart of hearts, we abhor them. The problem is that none of us can change a norm on our own. To be sure, we can *defy* a norm, but defiance comes at a cost, and it may end up entrenching rather than undermining existing norms. What is needed is some kind of movement, initiated by people who say that they disapprove of the norm, and succeeding when some kind of tipping point is reached, by which time it is socially costless, and maybe beneficial, and maybe even mandatory, to say: *Me Too*.

That's a stylized version of what has happened with respect to sexual orientation in many nations. But the same dynamics help capture a host of social movements, including those that involve Catholicism, the French Revolution, the creation of Israel, the Universal Declaration of Human Rights, the collapse of the Soviet Union, disability discrimination, age discrimination, animal rights, the rise of Barack Obama and Donald Trump, Brexit, nationalism, white supremacy, and the abolition of slavery. These movements are of course different in important ways. Some of them are unambiguously good, while others are harder to evaluate, and still others are deeply troubling. But in all of them, suppressed beliefs and values, including suppressed outrage, started to get some oxygen. Once they did, change was inevitable.

It was also hard or perhaps impossible to anticipate those social movements. A central reason is that *because people falsified their preferences, individuals did not know what their fellow citizens actually thought.* In the face of preference falsification, the circumstances are right for unleashing social change—but because preferences are falsified, few people may be aware of that fact.

Another reason for the unpredictability is the overriding importance of social interactions. For change to occur, interactions need to produce, at just the right times and places, a growing sense that an existing norm is vulnerable, and that may or may not happen. Serendipity might be crucial. Who talks to whom at the right point? What is covered in the right newspaper? Who retweets what, and exactly when?

Science fiction writers like to explore "counterfactual history"—historical arcs in which the South won the Civil War, Hitler devoted his entire life to painting, John F. Kennedy wasn't assassinated, or Donald Trump decided to ramp up his real estate activities rather than to run for president. At their most intriguing, counterfactual histories emphasize small shifts (or nudges) that produced massive changes; they make it plausible to think that with a little push or pull, whole nations might have ended up looking radically different.

Because history is only run once, we can't know when that's true. But we do observe large shifts in short time frames. If we have a sense of the mechanisms that account for those shifts, we might be newly aware of the extent to which things we now take for granted were not exactly predestined, and of how with a little pressure at the right time, the coming decades might take startlingly different courses. (I know that these claims raise many questions; I will explore them in due course.)

This book consists of sixteen chapters. While they do not make for a unitary narrative, they are connected by an effort to connect findings in behavioral science with enduring issues in law and policy, and by an effort to show how seemingly small perturbations can often produce big shifts. The first three chapters explore the power of social norms; the importance of social cascades; the phenomenon of group polarization; and the expressive function of law. I emphasize that in many cases, people are unleashed, for better or for worse, and that in other cases, something very different happens, as people end up holding views that they would not have entertained before. A general theme is the shift from the unsayable, and even the unthinkable, to the conventional wisdom (and vice-versa).

Chapters 4–11 explore the uses and limits of "nudges" as tools for change. The question here is how public or private institutions might shift behavior, and sometimes unleash it, through seemingly small steps.

Nudges are choice-preserving interventions, informed by behavioral science, that can greatly affect people's choices. There is nothing new about nudging. In Genesis, God nudged: "You may freely eat of every tree of the garden; but of the tree of knowledge of good and evil you shall not eat, for in the day that you eat of it, you shall die." The serpent was a nudger as well: "God knows that when you eat of it your eyes will be opened, and you will be like God, knowing good and evil." With a threat and a promise, and distinctive framing, God and the serpent preserved freedom of choice.

In recent years, public officials have started to become quite disciplined about the project of nudging, often drawing on the latest behavioral research. Sometimes they have gone beyond nudges, enlisting findings about human error, including "present bias" and unrealistic optimism, to justify mandates and bans (or taxes, as in the case of soda, alcohol, and cigarettes). Here I attempt to explore the most pressing current issues, which turn out to raise deep questions in multiple fields, including law, economics, and political philosophy. For example: (1) What are the criteria for evaluating nudges? (2) Which way should we nudge? (3) When do nudges fail? (4) When nudges fail, what should we do instead? (5) Are nudges ethical? (5) What about people's desire to control their own destiny?

In the process of answering these questions, I emphasize two points that are in some tension with each other. The first involves the importance of human agency. People often say: *Don't tell me what I can't do!* That plea, a cry of the human spirit, demonstrates that people place a premium on their ability to control the course of their lives. It should be understood, appreciated, and (I think) cherished.

The second point involve the legitimate use of coercion. In some cases, a mandate or a ban is well-justified, at least if we care about human welfare. Consider bans on trans fats; social security programs; energy efficiency requirements; and cigarette taxes. For the last decade, nudges have dominated official discussions of the use of behavioral science. Because of the importance of freedom and agency, that's nothing to lament. But we are at the early stages of thinking more carefully about more aggressive tools—and of defining the circumstances in which they make sense, if we really care about human welfare (and I shall have something to say about that disputed concept).

Chapters 12–16 explore issues at the intersection of public policy, behavioral science, and political philosophy. I argue that transparency is often crucial, because it promotes accountability and also allows people to obtain information that they can use to improve their own lives. Transparency can be a terrific nudge, and it often fuels change.

I suggest that the Precautionary Principle, popular in many nations, is a conceptual mess, because it forbids the very steps that it requires—and that we can best understand its popularity, and its apparent lack of messiness, by reference to behavioral science. Perhaps most controversially, I suggest that some of our thinking about human rights is best understood as a product of "moral heuristics"—simple rules of thumb, and generally sensible, but a crude way to get at what most matters, which is human welfare. I conclude with discussions of the rise of "partyism" in the United States. In some ways, partyism is a large obstacle to social change, certainly at the level of national legislation. But as we shall see, it is nonetheless possible to identify promising paths forward.

I Norms and Values

1 Unleashed

In the late 1980s, when I was a visiting professor at Columbia Law School, I happened to pass, in the hallway near my office, a law student (female) speaking to an older law professor (male). To my amazement, the professor was stroking the student's hair. I thought I saw, very briefly, a grimace on her face. It was a quick flash. When he left, I said to her, "That was completely inappropriate. He shouldn't have done that." Her response was dismissive: "It's fine. He's an old man. It's really not a problem."

Thirty minutes later, I heard a knock on my door. It was the student. She was in tears. She said, "He does this all the time. It's horrible. My boyfriend thinks I should make a formal complaint, but I don't want to do that. Please—I don't want to make a fuss. Do not talk to him about it and do not tell anyone." (What I did in response is a tale for another occasion.)

Social norms imposed constraints on what the law student could say or do. She hated what the professor was doing; she felt harassed. After hearing my little comment, she felt free to tell me what she actually thought. But because of existing norms, she did not want to say or do anything.

I am interested here in two different propositions. The first is that that when norms start to collapse, people are unleashed, in the sense that *they feel free to reveal what they believe and prefer, to disclose their experiences, and to talk and act as they wish*. (Bystanders can of course be important here.) New norms, and laws that entrench or fortify them, may lead to the discovery of preexisting beliefs, preferences, and values. The discovery can be startling. In various times and places, the women's movement has been an example. The same is true for the civil rights movement of the 1960s, the movement for LGBT rights, and the disability rights movement. It is also true for the pro-life movement.

The second is that revisions of norms can construct preferences and values. New norms, and laws that entrench or fortify them, can give rise to beliefs, preferences, and values that did not exist before. No one is unleashed. People are changed. Something like this can be said for the antismoking movement, the rise of seatbelt-buckling, and the rise of Nazism.

Begin with the phenomenon of unleashing: When certain norms are in force, people falsify their preferences or are silent about them. As a result, strangers and even friends and family members may not be able to know about them.[1] People with certain political or religious convictions might just shut up. Once norms are revised, people will reveal preexisting preferences and values, which norms had successfully suppressed. What was once unsayable is said, and what was once unthinkable is done.

In the context of sexual harassment, something like this account is broadly correct: Women disliked being harassed, or even hated it, and revision of old norms was (and remains) necessary to spur expression of their feelings and beliefs.[2] (This account is incomplete, and I will complicate it.) As we shall see, law often plays a significant role in fortifying existing norms or in spurring their revision.[3] Part of the importance of judicial rulings that forbid sexual harassment is that they contributed to the revision of norms.[4] The election of a new leader or the enactment of new legislation[5] can have a crucial and even transformative signaling effect, offering people information about what other people think. If people hear the signal, norms may shift, because people are influenced by what they think other people think.[6]

But some revisions of norms, and some laws that entrench those revisions, do not liberate anything. As norms begin to be altered, people come to hold, or to act as if they hold, preferences and values that they did not hold before. Revisions of norms, and resulting legal reforms, do not uncover suppressed desires; they produce new ones, or at least statements and actions that are consistent with new ones.

Politically Correct

Consider in this regard the idea of "political correctness," which is standardly a reference to left-leaning social norms, forbidding the expression of views that defy the left-of-center orthodoxy and so silencing people.

Political correctness means that people cannot say what they actually think; they are forced into some kind of closet. (The very term should be seen as an effort to combat existing norms. Part of the cleverness of the term is that it describes those who follow certain views as cowardly conformists, rather than people who are committed to hard-won principles.[7]) That is often what happens. On many university campuses, those who are right of center learn to shut up. What a terrible lesson: they are leashed. But in other environments, the norms are different, and they can say what they think. Sometimes their friends and associates are surprised, even stunned: "Does he really think that? I had no idea."

In the educational setting, one problem is that left-of-center students will have no idea about the actual distribution of views within the community. They might think that everyone thinks as they do. Another problem is that people will be less able to learn from one another. And when people say what they actually think, large-scale changes might occur. I taught at the University of Chicago Law School in the early 1980s, when a group of terrific students created the Federalist Society, an organization dedicated to the exploration and defense of conservative views about the American legal system. The Federalist Society has had a massive effect on American political and legal life because it creates a kind of forum, or enclave, in which people can say what they think.

But whether left or right, political correctness can go beyond the suppression of views. It can also reconstruct preferences and values, making certain views unthinkable (for better or for worse). If some view is beyond the pale, people will stop expressing it. Eventually the unthinkable might become unthought. Is that chilling? Sometimes, but sometimes not; it is not terrible if no one thinks pro-Nazi thoughts.

A stunning study of the power of political correctness comes from Saudi Arabia.[8] In that country, there remains a custom of "guardianship," by which husbands are allowed to have the final word on whether their wives work outside the home. The overwhelming majority of young married men are privately in favor of female labor force participation. But those men are profoundly mistaken about the social norm; they think that other, similar men do not want women to join the labor force. When researchers randomly corrected those young men's beliefs about what other young men believed, they became far more willing to let their wives work. The result was a significant impact on what women actually did. A full four months after the intervention, the wives of men in the experiment were more likely to have applied and interviewed for a job.

The best reading of this research is that because of social norms, men in Saudi Arabia are in a sense leashed, and as a result, their wives are leashed as well. Most young men privately support female labor force participation, but they will say what they think, even to their own wives, only after they learn that other young men think as they do. It is fair to say that after the researchers revealed what young men actually thought, both men and women ended up more liberated.

What Matters

Does it matter whether revisions of norms free people to say what they think or instead construct new preferences and values? For purposes of understanding social phenomena, it certainly does. If preferences and values are hidden, rapid social change is possible and nearly impossible to predict.[9] When people are silent about their preferences or values, and when they falsify them, it can be exceedingly difficult to know what they are. Because people conceal their preferences, outsiders cannot readily identify them. If people are discontent but fail to say so, and if they start to talk and act differently once norms are challenged and changed, then large-scale shifts in behavior are possible—but no one may have anticipated them.[10]

The rise of norms against sex discrimination and sexual harassment is an example (which is hardly to say that either has disappeared). The partial collapse of norms authorizing or promoting discrimination against transgender people can be seen in similar terms: For (many) transgender people, the effect is to prevent self-silencing and preference falsification. Similar dynamics help account for the rise of religions,[11] the fall of Communism,[12] the Arab Spring,[13] and the election of Donald Trump.[14]

When revisions in norms produce new preferences and beliefs, rapid change is also possible, but the mechanics are different. Those who produce such change do not seek to elicit preexisting preferences, beliefs, and values. As norms shift, people are not liberated. Influenced and informed by new or emerging norms, they develop fresh thoughts and feelings, or at least act as if they have them.[15] The rise of Nazism is famously complicated and highly disputed, but it can be understood in these terms.[16] From one view, of course, it had a great deal to do with the longstanding geographical segregation of Jews and the emergence of suppressed hatred: "In this separation the devil slumbered and in slumber built sinew before Hitler was born."[17] From another view, Hitler was able to spur hatred that did not really exist before. As one former Nazi put it, he was not anti-Semitic "until [he] heard anti-Semitic propaganda."[18]

We can also find intermediate cases, in which people do not exactly have antecedent preferences that norms silence, but in which they hear a stubborn, uneasy voice in their heads that they ignore, thinking, *Why bother to listen to that?* But as norms start to shift, that question has an answer: *Maybe it is telling me something important, or something that reflects my real feelings and beliefs.* There is a kind of intrapersonal tipping point at which that answer becomes louder and people's statements and actions change.

My principal examples involve discrimination, but the general points hold more broadly. Consider, for example, cigarette smoking, seatbelt buckling, alcohol consumption, uses of green energy, purchases of organic food, considerateness,[19] veganism, the use of new languages,[20] polyamory, religious beliefs and practices,[21] drug use, and crime. In all of these cases, norms can constrain antecedent preferences; new norms can liberate them or instead help construct new ones (or at least the appearance of new ones). In all of these cases, revisions in norms can result in large-scale changes in an astoundingly short time, including legal reforms, which can entrench and fortify those revisions.

Preference Falsification and Norm Entrepreneurs

Let's begin with an intuitive account, offered by Jon Elster, who emphasizes that social norms are "shared by other people and partly sustained by their approval and disapproval. They are also sustained by the feelings of embarrassment, anxiety, guilt, and shame that a person suffers at the prospect of violating them."[22] Elster's quartet is worth underlining: embarrassment, anxiety, guilt, and shame are different from one another. The student at Columbia Law School felt all four. In cases of sexual harassment, that is not uncommon.

Because violations of social norms create such negative feelings, they impose costs on those who violate them. In that sense, they operate in the same way as taxes,[23] and the costs might turn out to be low or high. Importantly, however, some people are rebels, by nature or circumstance, and for them defiance of social norms, taken as such, might be a benefit rather than a cost. I will have something to say shortly about the importance of rebels.

In the simplest and most common cases, the objects of discrimination have an antecedent preference, and the norm prevents them from stating or acting on it. The preference may even be falsified (as it was when the law student initially assured me that she did not object to what the professor was doing). In that respect, the objects of discrimination are like actors in a play; they are reciting the expected lines. In cases of sex and race discrimination, that is a familiar phenomenon. The legitimation of the antecedent preference brings it out of the closet; recall here the young men in Saudi Arabia, who had no objection to female labor force participation.

In circumstances of this kind, large-scale change is possible. Suppose that many people within a population object to discrimnation, but because of existing norms they do not say or do anything. Suppose that the objectors have different thresholds for raising an objection. A few people will do so if even one person challenges or defies the norm; a few more will do so if a few people challenge or defy the norm; still more will do so if more than a few people challenge or defy the norm; and so on. Under the right conditions, and with the right distribution of thresholds, a small spark can ignite a conflagration, eventually dismantling the norm.[24]

There is an important role here for *norm entrepreneurs*,[25] operating in the private or public sector, who oppose existing norms and try to change them. Norm entrepreneurs draw attention to what they see as the stupidity, unnaturalness, intrusiveness, or ugliness of current norms. They may insist that many or most people secretly oppose them (and thus reduce pluralistic ignorance, understood as ignorance about what most people actually think).[26] They may describe their experiences. Norm breakers—those who simply depart from existing norms, and refuse to speak or act in accordance with them—may or may not be norm entrepreneurs, depending on whether they seek to produce some kind of social change, or instead wish merely to do as they like.

Norm entrepreneurs might turn out to be effective, at least if the social dynamics, discussed below, work out in their favor. They might be able to signal not only their personal opposition to the norm, but also the existence of widespread (but hidden) opposition as well. The idea of a "silent majority" can be a helpfully precise way to signal such opposition. Importantly, norm entrepreneurs might also change the social meaning of compliance with the norm: if they succeed, such compliance might suggest a lack of independence and look a bit pathetic, whereas those who defy the norm might seem courageous, authentic, and tough.

What Happens

It is important to emphasize that with small variations in starting points and inertia, resistance, or participation at the crucial points, social change may or may not happen. Suppose that a community has long had a norm in favor of discrimination based on sexual orientation; that many people in the community abhor that norm; that many others dislike it and that many others do not care about it; that many others are mildly inclined to favor it; and that many others firmly believe in it. If norm entrepreneurs make a public demonstration of opposition to the norm, and if the demonstration reaches those with relatively low thresholds for opposing it, opposition will immediately grow. If the growing opposition reaches those with relatively higher thresholds, the norm might rapidly collapse. But if the early public opposition is barely visible or if it reaches only those with relatively high thresholds, it will fizzle out and the norm might not even budge.

These are the two extreme cases. We could easily imagine intermediate cases in which the norm suffers a slow, steady death or in which the norm erodes but manages to survive. It is for this reason that otherwise similar communities can have multiple equilibria, understood here as apparently or actual stable situations governed by radically different norms. In some communities, people may recycle; in others, they may not. In some communities, people might drink a lot of liquor; in others, they might not.

After the fact, it is tempting to think that because of those different norms, the communities are not otherwise similar at all, and to insist on some fundamental cultural difference between them. But that thought might be a product of an illusion in the form of a failure to see that some small social influence, shock, or random event was responsible for the persistence of a norm in one community and its disintegration in another. History plays tricks, but because it is only run once, we do not see them.

Cascades

Some of the most interesting work on social influences involves the existence of informational and reputational "cascades"; this work has obvious relevance to the revision of norms and eventually legal reform.[27]

For informational cascades, a starting point is that when individuals lack a great deal of private information (and sometimes even when they have such information), they are attentive to the information provided by the statements or actions of others. If A is unaware whether genetic modification of food is a serious problem, he may be moved in the direction of alarm if B seems to think that alarm is justified. If A and B believe that alarm is justified, C may end up thinking so too, at least if she lacks independent information to the contrary. If A, B, and C believe that genetic modification of food is a serious problem, D will need a good deal of confidence to reject their shared conclusion. The result of this process can be to produce cascade effects, as large groups of people eventually end up believing something, simply because other people seem to believe it too. It should be clear that cascade effects may or may not occur, depending on seemingly small factors, such as the initial distribution of beliefs, the order in which people announce what they think, and people's thresholds for abandoning their private beliefs in deference to the views announced by others.

Though social cascades have been discussed largely in connection with factual judgments, the same processes are at work for norms; we can easily imagine norm cascades (information-induced or otherwise), which may well produce legal reform.[28] Some such cascades may be a product of information; some may involve values. In such contexts, many people, lacking firm convictions of their own, may end up believing what (relevant) others seem to believe. Changes in social attitudes toward smoking, drinking, climate change, recycling, and sexual harassment have a great deal to do with these effects. And here as well, small differences in initial conditions, in thresholds for abandoning private beliefs because of reputational pressures, and in who hears what when, can lead to major differences in outcomes.

Availability

The availability heuristic,[29] to which I will frequently return in this book, often plays a major role in norm cascades.[30] The basic idea is that judgments about probability are often made by asking whether relevant events come to mind. If, for example, a particular case of egregious discrimination receives a great deal of public attention, then people might see or come to believe that such discrimination is widespread. In a variation on the availability heuristic, a single event might come to be highly salient, affecting not only probability judgments but also judgments about morality and norms. With respect to sexual harassment, Anita Hill's widely publicized allegations about Clarence Thomas had a significant effect on public perceptions of sexual harassment in the 1980s. The #MeToo movement, which started in 2017, is analogous; prominent women, including the actresses Alyssa Milano, Ashley Judd, and Uma Thurman, drew attention to sexual harassment or sexual assault that many women faced, eventually creating a worldwide cascade.

Some people, including Hill and members of the #MeToo movement, serve as *availability entrepreneurs*; they emphasize particular incidents in an effort to produce an availability cascade, involving facts or norms. In many contexts, the effects of civil disobedience (of norms or law) are greatly magnified by the unduly aggressive responses of official targets; those responses tend to be publicized, and they signal that those who engaged in disobedience may well have been right. Consider the aggressive responses of state and local officials to civil disobedience by civil rights activitists. Martin Luther King Jr. was well aware that such responses could be helpful to the cause.

Thus far the discussion has emphasized purely informational pressures and informational cascades, where people care about what other people think because they do not know what to think, and they rely on the opinions of others, to learn what it is right to think. But with respect to norms, there can be reputational pressures and reputational cascades as well. People speak out or remain silent partly in order to preserve their reputations, even at the price of failing to say what they really think. Suppose, for example, that A believes that climate change is an extremely serious environmental problem; suppose too that B is skeptical. B may keep quiet, or even agree with A, simply to preserve A's good opinion. C may see that A believes that climate change is a serious problem and that B seems to agree with A; C may therefore voice agreement even though privately she is skeptical or ambivalent.

It is easy to see how this kind of situation might occur in political life with, for example, politicians expressing their commitment to gun rights, to capital punishment, to stemming the flow of immigrants, to same-sex marriage, or to eliminating discrimination against transgender persons (even if they are privately skeptical). Here too the consequence can be cascade effects—large social movements in one direction or another—when a number of people appear to support a certain course of action simply because others (appear to) do so.

A "Down Look"

It is too simple, of course, to say that the objects of discrimination are opposed and silence themselves. Often that is true. But when discrimination is widespread and when norms support it, its objects might see discrimination as part of life's furniture. In some cases, they might not even feel that their preferences and values have been constrained. Some preferences are *adaptive*; they are a product of existing injustice. If a victim of sexual harassment genuinely believes that "it's not a big deal," it might be because it's most comfortable or easiest to believe that it's not a big deal.

Consider Gordon Wood's account of the pre-Revolutionary American colonies, when "common people" were "made to recognize and feel their subordination to gentlemen," so that those "in lowly stations ... developed what was called a 'down look,'" and "knew their place and willingly walked while gentlefolk rode; and as yet they seldom expressed any burning desire to change places with their betters."[31] In Wood's account, it is impossible to "comprehend the distinctiveness of that premodern world until we appreciate the extent to which many ordinary people *still accepted their own lowliness.*"[32]

Wood argues that as republicanism took hold, social norms changed, and people stopped accepting their own lowliness. His account is one of a norm cascade, but not as a result of the revelation of preexisting preferences. Something different happened; people changed. With amazement, John Adams wrote that "Idolatry to Monarchs, and servility to Aristocratical Pride, was never so totally eradicated from so many Minds in so short a Time."[33] David Ramsay, one of the nation's first historians (himself captured by the British during the American Revolution), marveled that Americans were transformed "from subjects to citizens," and that was an "immense" difference because citizens "possess sovereignty. Subjects look up to a master, but citizens are so far equal, that none have hereditary rights superior to others."[34] Thomas Paine put it this way: "Our style and manner of thinking have undergone a revolution more extraordinary than the political revolution of a country. We see with other eyes; we hear with other ears; and think with other thoughts, than those we formerly used."[35]

Adams, Ramsay, and Paine are speaking of new preferences, beliefs, and values, rather than the revelation of suppressed ones. How this happens remains imperfectly understood. While the idea of preference falsification captures much of the territory I am exploring, it is complemented by situations in which adaptive preferences are altered by new or revised norms.

Partially Adaptive Preferences

There are also intermediate cases, involving what might be called *partially adaptive preferences*. These cases are especially interesting, not only because they are common but also because they create promising circumstances for rapid change.

Objects of discrimination, and others suffering from injustice or deprivation, may not exactly accept discrimination, injustice, or deprivation. They might live with it, and do so with a degree of equanimity, thinking that nothing can be done. It is not a lot of fun to beat your head against the wall. In cases of partially adaptive preferences, objects of discrimination are not like actors in a play; they are not falsifying their preferences. But they have a sense that something is wrong. They hear a small voice in their heads. The question is whether they try to silence that voice or instead try to find out exactly what it is saying.

Once norms change, some inchoate belief or value might be activated that was formerly suppressed or that was like that small voice in the head. It is fair enough to speak of liberation, but the case is not as simple as that of the law student at Columbia, who was entirely clear about what she thought. Partially adaptive preferences should be familiar. The task of norm entrepreneurs is to try to bring them out of the closet.

Discriminators

Thus far my focus has been on objects of discrimination. But as the case of the young men in Saudi Arabia suggests, discriminators are also affected by social norms. With respect to those who discriminate on the basis of sex and race (or other characteristics), we can imagine four kinds of cases:

1. Those in which discriminators want to discriminate, and norms allow them to do so
2. Those in which discriminators want to discriminate, but norms discourage or forbid them from doing so

3. Those in which discriminators do not want to discriminate, and norms allow them not to do so

4. Those in which discriminators do not want to discriminate, but norms encourage or require them to do so

In cases 1 and 3, there is no conflict between preferences and norms. Case 2 is the familiar one; norms are operating as leashes or constraints. Note that in such cases, discrimination will not be observed, at least if the relevant norms are effective. Discriminators will falsify their preferences, or at least not reveal them. They will act as if they do not want to discriminate, even though they do. At the same time, they might hope to change the norm, at least in their community, and the question is whether they can succeed. To do so, they might well have to act collectively. Their efforts are far more likely to succeed if they are highly publicized. (To be sure, some discriminators will simply defy the norm.)

Case 4 may be the most interesting one. Here too, many discriminators will falsify their preferences. As in the case of Saudi Arabian men, they will act as if they are sexist, even though they are not. (In human history, that has often happened.) Faced with the stated conflict, what can discriminators do, short of defying the norm?

Here as well, norm entrepreneurs can act to alter the norm. They can also ask for or enlist law. Consider a revealing fact: *Some of the restaurants and hotels that that were regulated by the Civil Rights Act of 1964 actually lobbied vigorously for the legislation.*[36] Why, you might ask, would such companies affirmatively seek to be forbidden by law from discriminating on the basis of race? If they did not want to discriminate on the basis of race, they certainly could have stopped doing so. Why did they need the law?

Norms help to explain what happened. The relevant companies had an antecedent preference: they wanted to make money. The best way to make money was to serve anyone who was willing to pay. For that reason, they did not want to discriminate. In fact, they wanted *not* to discriminate, because discrimination was costly on their part. But in light of prevailing norms, they would incur a high cost for not discriminating, which would provoke a hostile reaction in their community. As Lawrence Lessig writes, "For a white to serve or hire blacks was for the white to mark him or herself as having either a special greed for money or a special affection for blacks."[37] In these circumstances, the force of the law was needed to alter the social meaning of nondiscrimination. Once the Civil Rights Act of 1964 was enacted, nondiscrimination was a matter of compliance. Profit-making companies were liberated.

We can see related phenomena in other domains in which revised norms, or new laws, work to counteract discrimination. No one should doubt that many men who have engaged in sex discrimination did not want to do so, in the sense that they acted in accordance with norms that they did not endorse (and might have abhorred). As norm entrepreneurs began their work, norms started to change, and as law prohibited discriminatory behavior, such men could do what they wanted to do. Of course, this is far from a full picture of the consequence of new antidiscrimination norms. But it is part of it.

The phenomenon holds more broadly. Many people are glad that the law requires them to buckle their seatbelts because it enables them to do as they wish, and buckle up, without seeming to accuse people of being risky drivers. Many people support laws that forbid drug use in part because such laws make it easier for them to decline to use drugs. Many people support drunk-driving laws, in part because it enables them to decline to drive when they should not. New norms and norm revisions, and laws that codify them, can operate as precommitment strategies. They can help people to do what they want; previous norms stopped them from doing so.

Liberating Isms

Some norms reduce discrimination, but others increase it. Suppose that people have antecedent hostility toward members of social groups; suppose that social norms constrain them from speaking or acting in ways that reflect that hostility. This is a good side of "political correctness"; it prevents people from expressing ugly impulses. But norms that constrain sexism and racism are of course stronger in some times and places than in others, and they can be relaxed or eliminated. In the aftermath of the election of Donald Trump, many people feared that something of this kind had happened (and as of this writing, are fearing that it continues to happen). The concern is that President Trump is a norm entrepreneur; he is shifting norms in such a way as to weaken or eliminate their constraining effects.

It is difficult to test that proposition in a rigorous way, but let's consider a highly suggestive experiment.

Leonardo Bursztyn of the University of Chicago, Georgy Egorov of Northwestern University and Stefano Fiorin of the University of California at Los Angeles attempted to test whether Trump's political success affected Americans' willingness to support, in public, a xenophobic organization.[38] Two weeks before the 2016 election, Bursztyn and his colleagues recruited 458 people from eight states that the website PredictWise said that Trump was certain to win (Alabama, Arkansas, Idaho, Nebraska, Oklahoma, Mississippi, West Virginia and Wyoming). Half the participants were told that Trump would win. The other half received no information about Trump's projected victory.

All participants were then asked an assortment of questions, including whether they would authorize the researchers to donate one dollar to the Federation for American Immigration Reform, accurately described as an anti-immigrant organization, the founder of which has written, "I've come to the point of view that for European-American society and culture to persist requires a European-American majority, and a clear one at that."[39] If participants agreed to authorize the donation, they were told that they would be paid an additional one dollar. Half the participants were assured that their decision to authorize a donation would be anonymous. The other half were given no such assurance. On the contrary, they were told that members of the research team might contact them, thus suggesting that their willingness to authorize the donation could become public.

For those who were not informed about Trump's expected victory in their state, giving to the anti-immigration group was far more attractive when anonymity was assured: 54 percent authorized the donation under cover of secrecy as opposed to 34 percent when the authorization might become public. But for those who were informed that Trump would likely win, anonymity did not matter at all! When so informed, about half the participants were willing to authorize the donation regardless of whether they received a promise of anonymity. The central point is that information about Trump's expected victory altered social norms, making many people far more willing to give publicly and eliminating the comparatively greater popularity of anonymous endorsements.

As an additional test, Bursztyn and his colleagues repeated their experiment in the same states during the first week after Trump's 2016 election.

They found that Trump's victory also eliminated the effects of anonymity: again, about half the participants authorized the donation regardless of whether the authorization would be public. The general conclusion is that if Trump had not come on the scene, many Americans would refuse to authorize a donation to an anti-immigrant organization unless they were promised anonymity. But with Trump as president, people feel liberated. Anonymity no longer matters, apparently because Trump's election has weakened the social norm against supporting anti-immigrant groups. It is now more acceptable to be known to agree "that for European-American society and culture to persist requires a European-American majority, and a clear one at that."

The central finding can be seen as the mirror image of the tale of the law student and the law professor. For a certain number of people, hostility to anti-immigrant groups is a private matter; they do not want to voice that hostility in public. But if norms are seen to be weakening or to be shifting, they will be willing to give voice to their beliefs. The case of the Saudi Arabian men is essentially the same.

We can easily imagine much uglier versions of the central finding. When police brutality increases, when hateful comments or action are directed at members of certain religious groups, when white supremacy marches start, when ethnic violence breaks out, when mass atrocities occur, and when genocide is threatened, one reason is the weakening or transformation of social norms that once made the relevant actions unthinkable.[40] In some such cases, what was akin to a tax has been eliminated; in other cases, what was akin to a tax has been transformed into something like a subsidy. The subsidy might be necessary to spur the destructive behavior, but for some participants, removal of the tax is enough.

Internalized Norms

My emphasis has been on situations in which people have an antecedent preference or value, whose expression a norm blocks; revision of the norm liberates them so that they can talk or act as they wish. Sexual desires may be the most obvious example, where people may be startled to find out what they like, though in that context, there can be a complex interplay between discovery and construction of preferences. (The 2017 Netflix television series *Gypsy* is a brilliant exploration of that topic.) For sexual desires, the weakening of norms can and does produce a kind of unleashing, as people feel free to acknowledge to others, and to express, preferences that had been hidden. Sometimes people do not even acknowledge those preferences to themselves, and it takes a comment, an image, or a partner to unleash them.

But I have also noted that some norms are internalized, so that people do not feel chained at all. Once the norm is revised, they speak or act differently, either because they feel constrained by the new norm to do that, or because their preferences and values change. Orwell's Nineteen Eighty-Four is a chilling tale of something like that, with its terrifying closing lines: "But it was all right, everything was all right, the struggle was finished. He had won the victory over himself. He loved Big Brother."[41]

That is the dark side. But let's return to the case of sexual harassment. Many men are appalled by the very thought of sexual harassment. For them, norms and legal rules against sexual harassment are not a problem, any more than norms and legal rules against theft and assault are a problem. If they are older, some of these men might have experienced a shift over the course of their lives. If they are younger, some of these men might not be able to imagine a context in which sexually harassing someone would be a fun or good experience.

For such men, we do not have cases of preference falsification. For some of them, it might be helpful and clarifying to speak of adaptive preferences. But it is better to say that the relevant people are deeply committed to the norm in principle, so that defying it would not merely be costly; it would be unthinkable.

Something similar can be said for many actions that conform to social norms. Most people are not bothered by the social norm against dueling. For many people, seatbelt buckling and recycling are not properly characterized as costs; they are a matter of routine, and for those who buckle their seatbelts or recycle, the relevant actions may well feel like a benefit. When the social norm is one of considerateness, those who are considerate usually do not feel themselves to be shackled; they want to be considerate. When this is so, the situation will be stable. Norm entrepreneurs cannot point to widespread, but hidden, dissatisfaction with the norm. But for both insiders and outsiders, it will often be difficult to distinguish between situations in which norms are internalized and situations in which they merely seem to be. That is one reason that stunning surprises are inevitable.

2 The Law of Group Polarization

Consider the following:

• A group of citizens is concerned about immigration. The citizens think that illegal immigrants are committing serious crimes. They are also fearful that legal immigration has "gone too far" and that it is "taking our jobs." The group decides to meet every two weeks to focus on common concerns. After a year, is it possible to say what its members are likely to think?

• After a nationally publicized shooting at a high school, a group of people in the community—most of them tentatively in favor of greater gun control—come together to discuss the possibility of imposing new gun control measures. What, if anything, will happen to individual views as a result of this discussion?

• Affirmative action is under attack in the state of Texas. Most professors at a particular branch of the University of Texas are inclined to be supportive of affirmative action; they meet to exchange views and to plan further action, if necessary. What are these professors likely to think and to do after they talk?

My principal purpose in this chapter is to investigate a striking statistical regularity—group polarization—and to relate that phenomenon to underlying questions about the role of deliberation in the "public sphere" of a heterogeneous democracy. In brief, group polarization means that members of a deliberating group predictably move toward a more extreme point in the direction indicated by the members' predeliberation tendencies. "Like polarized molecules, group members become even more aligned in the direction they were already tending."[1] Thus, for example, members of the first group will become deeply hostile to immigration; members of the second group will probably end up favoring gun control quite enthusiastically; members of the third group will become more firmly committed to affirmative action.

Notably, groups consisting of individuals with extremist tendencies are more likely to shift, and likely to shift more; the same is true for groups with some kind of salient shared identity (like conservatives, socialists, Catholics, Jews, and lawyers, but unlike jurors and experimental subjects). When like-minded people are participating in "iterated polarization games"—when they meet regularly, without sustained exposure to competing views—extreme movements are all the more likely.

Three principal mechanisms underlie group polarization. The first emphasizes the role of information—in particular, the limited "argument pools" within any group and the directions in which those limited pools lead group members. The second points to social influences on behavior and in particular to people's desire to maintain their reputation and their self-conception. The third emphasizes the relationships among confidence, corroboration, and extremism. The basic idea is that when people find their views corroborated by others, they become confident—and thus more extreme. Radical movements can be fueled in that way.

An understanding of the three mechanisms provides many insights into social change and democratic institutions. It illuminates a great deal about likely processes within political parties, legislatures, and multimember courts—not to mention ethnic and religious groups, extremist organizations, terrorists, criminal conspiracies, student associations, faculties, institutions engaged in feuds or "turf battles," workplaces, and families.

One of my largest purposes is to evaluate the social role of *enclave deliberation*, understood as deliberation within small or not-so-small groups of like-minded people. I suggest that enclave deliberation is, simultaneously, a potential danger to social stability, a source of social fragmentation, and a safeguard against social injustice and unreasonableness. As we will see, group polarization helps explain an old point, with clear foundations in constitutional law in many nations, to the effect that social homogeneity can be quite damaging to good deliberation. An understanding of group polarization thus illuminates social practices designed to reduce the risks of deliberation limited to like-minded people.

How and Why Groups Polarize

Group polarization is among the most robust patterns found in deliberating bodies, and it has been found in many diverse tasks. As a result, groups often make more extreme decisions than would the typical or average individual in the group (where *extreme* is defined solely internally, by reference to the group's initial dispositions). There is a clear relationship between group polarization and cascade effects. As we will see, the former, like the latter, has a great deal to do with both informational and reputational influences. A key difference is that group polarization involves the effects of deliberation.

Although standard within psychology, the term *group polarization* is somewhat misleading. It is not meant to suggest that group members will shift to two poles. Instead, the term refers to a predictable shift *within* a group discussing a case or problem. As the shift occurs, groups and group members move and coalesce not toward the middle of antecedent dispositions, but toward a more extreme position in the direction indicated by those dispositions. The effect of deliberation is both to decrease variance among group members, as individual differences diminish, and to produce convergence on a relatively more extreme point among predeliberation judgments.

Consider a few examples of the basic phenomenon, which has been found in over a dozen nations:[2]

1. A group of moderately profeminist women will become more strongly profeminist after discussion.[3] (This finding is obviously relevant to the dynamics of #MeToo.)
2. After discussion, citizens of France become more critical of the United States and its intentions with respect to economic aid.[4] (This finding is obviously relevant to skepticism about the United States in various nations.)
3. After discussion, whites predisposed to show racial prejudice offer more negative responses to the question whether white racism is responsible for conditions faced by African-Americans in American cities.[5] (This finding is obviously relevant to increases in racial antagonism.)
4. After discussion, whites predisposed not to show racial prejudice offer more positive responses to the same question.[6] (This finding is obviously relevant to the softening of ethnic and racial divisions.)

As statistical regularities, it follows, for example, that that those moderately critical of an ongoing war effort will sharply oppose the war after discussion; that those who believe that climate change is a serious problem are likely to hold that belief with considerable confidence after discussion; that people tending to believe in the inferiority of a certain racial group will become more entrenched in this belief as a result of discussion.

The phenomenon of group polarization has conspicuous relevance to social media and the communications market—where groups with distinctive views and identities often engage in within-group discussion—and also to the operation of many deliberating bodies of relevance to law and politics, including legislatures, commissions, multimember courts, and juries. I will return to this point shortly; for now, notice a few obvious possibilities. If the public is sharply divided, and if different groups design their own preferred communications packages, the consequence may be further division, as group members move one another toward more extreme points in line with their initial tendencies. Different deliberating groups, each consisting of like-minded people, may be driven increasingly far apart, simply because most of their discussions are with one another.

In a similar vein, members of a political party, or of the principal political parties, may polarize as a result of internal discussions; party-line voting is sometimes explicable partly on this ground. Extremist groups will often become more extreme. A set of judges with similar predilections on a three-judge panel may well produce a more extreme ruling than any individual member would write if he were judging on his own. As we will soon see, the largest group polarization typically occurs with individuals already inclined toward extremes.

Risky Shifts and Cautious Shifts

Group polarization was first found in a series of experiments involving risk-taking decisions. Before 1961, conventional wisdom held that as compared with the individuals who compose it, a group of decision-makers—for example, a committee or board—would be likely to favor a compromise and thus to avoid risks. But the relevant experiments, originally conducted by James Stoner, found otherwise; they identified what has become known as the *risky shift*.[7] Deliberation tended to shift group members in the direction of greater risk-taking, and deliberating groups, asked to reach a unanimous decision, were generally more risk-inclined—sometimes far more risk-inclined—than the mean individual member predeliberation.

It is important to distinguish at this point between two aspects of these findings, both of relevance to law and policy. The first involves the movement of deliberating groups, when a group decision is necessary, toward the group's extreme end; this is sometimes described as a *choice shift*. This means that if a group decision is required, the group will tend toward an extreme point, understood against the background set by the original distribution of individual views. In other words, the group will be more extreme than the median or average member. Undoubtedly, the group's decision rule will matter here; majority rule might produce a different outcome from a requirement of unanimity. If those with the most extreme views are least tractable and most confident, a unanimity requirement might produce a shift toward the most extreme points.

The second involves the movement of (even private) individual judgments as a result of group influence; this is the standard meaning of the term *group polarization*. To the extent that the private judgments of individuals are moved by discussion, the movement will be toward a more extreme point in the direction set by the original distribution of views. It is possible to have one kind of movement without the other, though ordinarily the two accompany one another.

A possible (and contemporaneous) reading of Stoner's early studies would be that group dynamics usually move people—both groups and individuals within them—in the direction of greater risk-taking. But this conclusion would be much too simple. Later studies showed that under certain conditions, it was possible, even easy, to induce a *cautious shift* as well. Indeed, certain problems reliably produced cautious shifts.[8] The principal examples involved the decision whether to marry and the decision whether to board a plane despite severe abdominal pain possibly requiring medical attention. In these cases, deliberating groups moved toward caution, as did the members who composed them. Burglars, in fact, show cautious shifts in discussions with one another, though when they work together, the tendency is toward greater risk-taking.[9]

Later researchers noticed that in Stoner's original data, the largest risky shifts could be found when group members "had a quite extreme risky initial position," in the sense that the predeliberation votes were weighted toward the risky end, whereas the items "that shifted a little or not at all started out near the middle of the scale."[10] Thus the direction of the shift seemed to turn on the location of the original disposition, and the size of the shift depended on the extremeness of that original disposition. A group of very cautious individuals would produce a significant shift toward greater caution; a group of individuals inclined toward risk-taking would produce a significant shift toward greater risk-taking; and groups of individuals in the middle would produce smaller shifts in the direction indicated by their original disposition.

Similar results have been found in many contexts with relevance to law and democracy, involving, for example, questions about economic aid, architecture, political leaders, race, feminism, and judgments of guilt or innocence. Polarization has been found for questions of obscure fact (e.g., how far Sodom on the Dead Sea is below sea level), as well as for evaluative questions, including political and legal issues and even the attractiveness of people in slides.

The Outrage Heuristic

A number of years ago, I was involved in a series of studies of outrage, punitive intentions, and monetary punishments. Our basic finding was that when ordinary people are thinking about how much to punish people, they use the *outrage heuristic*.[11] They begin by deciding how outrageous the underlying conduct was, and their judgments about punishment build on that decision. We found that people's outrage judgments, on a bounded numerical scale, almost exactly predicted their punitive intentions on the same scale. That means that people are *intuitive retributivists*. They believe that people should be punished for wrongdoing, as a way of reflecting the outrage of the community. Unless prompted, they do not think about optimal deterrence (and even when prompted, they resist the idea).

One of our studies tested the effects of deliberation on both punitive intentions and monetary judgments.[12] The study involved about three thousand jury-eligible citizens; its major purpose was to determine how individuals would be influenced by seeing and discussing the punitive intentions of others. Our central goal was to explore how social interactions heighten outrage.

People initially were asked to record their individual judgments privately, on a bounded scale, and then asked to join six-member groups to generate unanimous "punishment verdicts." Subjects were asked to record, in advance of deliberation, a "punishment judgment" on a scale of 0 to 8, where 0 indicated that the defendant should not be punished at all and 8 indicated that the defendant should be punished extremely severely. (Recall that outrage judgments on such scales are mirrored by punishment judgments, so we were essentially measuring outrage.) After the individual judgments were recorded, jurors were asked to deliberate to reach a unanimous punishment verdict. It would be reasonable to predict that the verdicts of juries would be the median of punishment judgments of jurors—but that prediction would be badly wrong.

The finding that I want to emphasize here is that deliberation made the lower punishment ratings *decrease* when compared to the median of predeliberation judgments of individual jurors—whereas deliberation made the higher punishment ratings *increase* when compared to that same median. When the individual jurors favored little punishment, the group showed a *leniency shift*, meaning a rating that was systematically lower than the median predeliberation rating of individual members. This means that when people began with low levels of outrage, deliberation produced lower levels still. But when individual jurors favored strong punishment, the group as a whole produced a *severity shift*, meaning a rating that was systematically higher than the median predeliberation rating of individual members. In groups, outrage grows—a reflection of group polarization in action.

Mechanisms

There are three main explanations for group polarization.[13] Significant support has been found for all of them.

Information

The first explanation, emphasizing the role of information, starts with a simple claim: any individual's position will be affected by what information she ends up hearing, and by which arguments presented within the group seem most convincing. People's positions therefore move to fit with the information and arguments shared within the group, taken as a whole. Because (and this is the critical point) a group whose members are already inclined in a certain direction will have a disproportionate number of arguments supporting that same direction, the result of discussion will be to move individuals further in the direction of their initial inclinations.

The key is the existence of limited information and a limited argument pool, one that is skewed (speaking purely descriptively) in a particular direction. Members of a group will have thought of some, but not all, of the arguments that justify their initial inclination. In discussion, the arguments of different people may be stated and heard, but the total argument pool will be tilted in one direction or another, depending on the predispositions of the people who compose the group. Hence there will be a shift in the direction of the original tilt.

Social Comparison

The second explanation begins with the claim that people want to be perceived favorably by other group members and to perceive themselves favorably. Once they hear what others believe, they adjust their positions in the direction of the dominant position. They may want to signal, for example, that they are not cowardly or cautious, especially in an entrepreneurial group that disparages these characteristics, and hence they will frame their position so that they do not appear as such by comparison to other group members.

With respect to risk-taking activities, people want to occupy a certain position in comparison to others; before they hear what other people think, they might well assume that they do in fact occupy that position. But when they hear what other people think, they often find that they occupy a somewhat different position, and they might shift accordingly. The result is to press the group's position toward one extreme or another and to induce shifts in individual members.

Something similar happens in other contexts. People may wish, for example, not to seem too enthusiastic or too restrained in their enthusiasm for affirmative action, feminism, or an increase in national defense; hence their views may shift when they see what other group members think. The result will be both choice shifts and group polarization. Thus individuals move their judgments to preserve their image for others and for themselves. A key claim here is that information alone about the actual positions of others—without discussion—will produce a shift. Evidence has confirmed this fact; mere exposure induces a substantial risky shift (though it is less substantial than that produced by discussion—about half as large).[14] This effect helps explain a shift toward caution (the *cautious shift*) as well.

Corroboration and Confidence

The third explanation points to the relationship among corroboration, confidence, and extremism.[15] Those who lack confidence and who are unsure what they should think tend to moderate their views. It is for this reason that cautious people, not knowing what to do, are likely to choose the midpoint between relevant extremes. But if other people seem to share your view, you might become more confident that your view is right—and hence move in a more extreme direction.

Refinements

I now turn to some refinements, complicating the basic account of group polarization. For purposes of understanding the relationship among that phenomenon, organizations, and democracy, the central points are two-fold. First, it matters a great deal whether people consider themselves part of the same social group as other members; a sense of shared identity will heighten the shift, and a belief that identity is not shared will reduce and possibly eliminate it. Second, deliberating groups will tend to "depolarize" if they consist of equally opposed subgroups and if members have a degree of flexibility in their positions.

Statistical Regularities

Of course, not all groups polarize; some groups end up in the middle, not toward either extreme. Note that in Stoner's original experiments, one of the twelve deliberating groups showed no polarization at all. Nor is it hard to understand why this might be so. If the people defending the original tendency are particularly unpersuasive, group polarization is unlikely to occur. If the outliers are especially convincing, groups may even shift away from their original tendency and in the direction held by few or even one. (*Twelve Angry Men* is a vivid exploration of this possibility.)

Moreover, external constraints or an external "shock" sometimes may prevent or blunt group polarization. Group members with well-defined views on a certain issue (gun control, separation of church and state, intervention in foreign nations) may be prone to polarize, but to maintain political effectiveness—and even basic credibility—they will sometimes maintain a relatively moderate face, publicly or even privately. Groups that have started to polarize in an extreme direction may move toward the middle to promote their own legitimacy or because of new revelations of one kind of another. In some times and places, political parties have done exactly that.

Affective Factors

Affective factors are quite important in group decisions, and when manipulated such factors will significantly increase or decrease polarization. If group members are linked by affective ties—if they know and like each other—dissent is significantly less frequent. The existence of affective ties thus reduces the number of divergent arguments and also intensifies social influences on choice. Hence people are less likely to shift if the direction advocated is being pushed by unfriendly group members; the likelihood of a shift and its likely size are increased when people perceive fellow members as friendly, likeable, and similar to them.[16] A sense of common fate and intragroup similarity tend to increase group polarization, as does the introduction of a rival out-group.[17]

The confidence of particular members also plays an important role. Indeed, part of the reason for group polarization appears to be that as a class, extreme positions tend to be less tractable and more confidently held. This point is an important complement to explanation based on information and persuasive arguments: the persuasiveness of arguments, not surprisingly, depends not simply on the grounds given, but also on the confidence with which they are articulated. (Consider here both juries and multimember courts.) Group polarization can also be fortified through *exit*, as members leave the group because they reject the direction in which things are heading. If exit is pervasive, the tendency to extremism will be greatly increased.

Identity and Solidarity

In a refinement of particular importance to politics and daily life, it has been found to matter whether people think of themselves, antecedently or otherwise, as part of a group having a degree of connection and solidarity. If they think of themselves in this way, group polarization is all the more likely, and it is also likely to be more extreme.[18] Thus when the context emphasizes each person's membership in the social group engaging in deliberation, polarization increases.

This finding is in line with more general evidence that social ties among deliberating group members tend to suppress dissent and thus to lead to inferior decisions.[19] This should not be surprising. If ordinary findings of group polarization are a product of social influences and limited argument pools, it stands to reason that when group members think of one another as similar along a salient dimension, or if some external factor (politics, geography, race, sex) unites them, group polarization will be heightened.

Depolarization and Deliberation without Shifts

Is it possible to construct either groups that will depolarize—that will tend toward the middle—or groups whose members will not shift at all? Both phenomena seem to be real in actual deliberating bodies. In fact, the persuasive arguments theory implies that there will be depolarization if and when new persuasive arguments are offered that are opposite to the direction initially favored by group members. Depolarization, rather than polarization, will also be found when the relevant group consists of individuals drawn equally from two extremes.[20] Thus if people who initially favor caution are put together with people who initially favor risk-taking, the group judgment will move toward the middle.

Group members with extreme positions generally change little as a result of discussion or shift to a more moderate position. Consider a study[21] consisting of six-member groups specifically designed to contain two subgroups (of three persons each) initially committed to opposed extremes; the effect of discussion was to produce movement toward the center. One reason may be the existence of partially shared persuasive arguments in both directions.[22] Interestingly, this study of opposed subgroups found the greatest depolarization with obscure matters of fact (e.g., the population of the United States in 1900)—and the least depolarization with highly visible public questions (e.g., whether capital punishment is justified). Matters of personal taste depolarized a moderate amount (e.g., preference for basketball or football, or for colors for painting a room).[23]

These findings fit well with the account of group polarization that stresses information and persuasive arguments. When people have a fixed view of some highly salient public issue, they are likely to have heard a wide range of arguments in various directions, producing a full argument pool, and an additional discussion is not likely to produce movement. With respect to familiar issues, people are simply less likely to shift at all. And when one or more people in a group know the right answer to a factual question, the group is likely to shift in the direction of accuracy. For "eureka" problems—where the right answer produces a kind of click or spark of recognition—we will not find group polarization. That is one reason that groups tend to be good at solving crossword puzzles.

Regularities

These remarks suggest some simple conclusions about how and when group discussion will move predeliberation opinions. Views based on a great deal of thought are least likely to shift; depolarization can occur with equal subgroups tending in opposite directions; groups will usually shift in the direction of an accurate factual judgment if one or more members knows the truth; if views are not firmly held but there is an initial predisposition, group polarization is the general rule. The effects of discussion are also likely to depend on members' perception of the group and of their relationship to it. If a group consists of "people," less polarization is likely than if it consists of "Republicans" or "defenders of the Second Amendment" or "opponents of American imperialism."

Depolarization may well occur in groups with equal subgroups having opposite tendencies. But this is less likely and less pronounced (1) if subgroup members have fixed positions and (2) if subgroup members know that they are members of identifiable groups and that their codiscussants are members of different identifiable groups.

Life's Polarization Games

Studies of group polarization involve one-shot experiments. We will turn shortly to group polarization in the real world, but first let us examine an intriguing implication of the experiments, one with special importance for democratic deliberation involving people who meet with each other not once, but on a regular basis.

If participants engage in repeated discussions—if, for example, they meet each month, express views, and take votes—there should be repeated shifts toward, and past, the defined pole. Thus, for example, if a group of citizens is thinking about genetic engineering of food, the minimum wage, or Islamic terrorism, the consequence of their discussions over time should be to lead in quite extreme directions. In these repeated *polarization games*, deliberation over time should produce a situation in which individuals hold positions more extreme than those of any individual member before the series of deliberations began. In fact, the idea of iterated polarization games seems far more realistic than the processes studied in one-shot experiments.

There appears to be no study of such repeated polarization games, but the hypothesized outcome is less fanciful than it might seem. In the jury study referred to earlier, deliberating groups frequently came up with punishment ratings as high as or even higher than that any individual held predeliberation. And it is not difficult to think of real-world groups in which the consequence of deliberation over time appears to be to shift both groups and individuals to positions that early on they could not possibly have accepted. Iterated polarization games are an important real-world phenomenon.

But this raises two questions: (1) Why and when do groups stop polarizing? (2) Why and when do they end up at a certain point and go no further, or even shift in the opposite direction? Nothing in the literature on group polarization adequately answers these questions, but it is possible to speculate that polarization often ends or reverses as a result of some *external shock*—as, for example, when new members add new arguments or when the simple self-interest of political leaders produces a shift in direction or when new circumstances, of fact or value, alter the perspectives and incentives of group members. Social cascades often change direction as a result of such external shocks, as through the release of new information; the same processes seem to terminate or to reverse group polarization.

Polarizing Events

Group polarization has a large effect on many deliberating groups and institutions. Consider, for example, the political and social role of religious organizations. Such organizations tend to strengthen group members' religious convictions, simply by virtue of the fact that like-minded people are talking to one another.[24] Religious groups amplify the religious impulse, especially if group members are insulated from other groups, and on occasion the result can be to lead people in quite bizarre directions. Whether or not this is so, political activity by members of religious organizations is undoubtedly affected by cascade-like effects and by group polarization. In a related vein, survey evidence shows that dramatic social events, like the assassination of Martin Luther King and civil rights disturbances, tend to polarize attitudes, with both positive and negative attitudes increasing within demographic groups.[25] More generally, discussion will often harden attitudes toward outsiders and social change; thus proposals "for establishment of a halfway house or a correctional facility have typically elicited private apprehensions which, after discussion, become polarized into overt paranoia and hostility."[26]

It is easy to produce examples of *professional polarizers* or *polarization entrepreneurs*—political activists who have as one of their goals the creation of spheres in which like-minded people can hear a particular point of view from one or more articulate people and participate, actually or vicariously, in a deliberative discussion in which a certain point of view becomes entrenched and strengthened. For those seeking to promote social reform, an extremely promising strategy is to begin by promoting discussions among people who tend to favor the relevant reform; such discussions are likely to intensify the underlying convictions and concerns. As an example from a few decades ago, consider the extraordinary success of Lois Marie Gibbs, a Love Canal resident who became the principal force behind the national concern over abandoned hazardous waste dumps.[27] Gibbs engaged self-consciously in efforts to mobilize citizens around that issue, partly by promoting discussions of like-minded people—first in small groups, then in larger ones. The areas of environmental protection and civil rights are filled with leaders who took advantage of cascade-like processes and group polarization.

Polarization is also likely to be produced by outlets or hosts with distinctive positions, generally shared by the relevant audience. Because the results of group polarization cannot be evaluated in the abstract, nothing need be dishonorable in these efforts. What can be said, in the abstract, is that attempts to ensure discussion among people with similar predispositions may be strikingly successful in increasing the confidence of individual participants and in moving them toward more extreme positions. In any society, would-be social reformers do well to create forums, whether in-person, over-the-air, in cyberspace, or in print, in which people with similar inclinations speak frequently with one another and can develop a clear sense of shared identity.

Out-Groups

Group polarization has particular implications for insulated out-groups; these might be political groups, ethnic groups, or groups defined in any other identifiable way. Recall that polarization increases when group members identify themselves along some salient dimension—and especially when the group can define itself by contrast to another group. Out-groups are in this position—of self-contrast to others—by definition. Excluded by choice or coercion from discussion with others, such groups may become polarized in quite extreme directions, often in part because of group polarization. In the midst of Communist rule, for example, the anticommunist underground was subject to polarization—sometimes undoubtedly for the better, but sometimes for the worse. Whenever an outgroup is isolated, its members often will have a feeling of shared identity and a sense of humiliation. Extremism on the part of outgroups (including murders and suicides, as by terrorists) is a possible result, especially if we consider the fact that extreme groups show comparatively greater polarization.

The tendency toward polarization among outgroups helps explain special concern about hate speech. There is indeed reason to fear the consequences of such speech; group polarization shows why. An understanding of group polarization simultaneously raises some questions about the idea that certain group discussions produce "consciousness raising." It is possible, at least, that the consequence of discussion is not only or mostly to raise consciousness (an ambiguous idea to be sure), but to produce group polarization in one direction or another—and at the same time to increase confidence in the position that has newly emerged. This does not mean that consciousness is never raised; undoubtedly group discussion can identify and clarify problems that were previously repressed or understood as an individual rather than social product (see chapter 1). But nothing of this sort is established by the mere fact that views have changed and coalesced and are held, post-discussion, with a high degree of confidence.

An understanding of group polarization also casts light on the imposition of liability for criminal conspiracy, which in most jurisdictions can be added to the penalty for the substantive offense. It is tempting to think that this kind of "doubling up" is indefensible, a form of overkill. But if the act of conspiring leads people moderately disposed toward criminal behavior to be more than moderately disposed, precisely because they are conspiring together, it makes sense, on grounds of deterrence, to impose extra, independent penalties. Some courts have come close to recognizing this point in discussing the imposition of distinct sanctions on conspiracies.[28]

Feuds and Strife

Group polarization is at work in feuds of all kinds. One of the characteristic features of feuds is that members of feuding groups tend to talk only to one another, fueling and amplifying their outrage and solidifying their impression of the relevant events. Informational and reputational forces are very much at work here, typically producing cascade effects, and group polarization can lead members to increasingly extreme positions.

It is not too much of a leap to suggest that these effects are sometimes present within ethnic groups and even nations, notwithstanding the usually high degree of national heterogeneity. In the United States, sharp divergences between whites and African-Americans, on particular salient events or more generally, can be explained by reference to group polarization. Often people are speaking or listening mostly to like-minded others. Racial and ethnic strife, or hostility amid "multiculturalism," is often affected by the same process.

The economist Timur Kuran has explored the broader international phenomenon of *ethnification*.[29] Kuran's basic claim is that in many nations, including Turkey and the former Yugoslavia, ethnic strife is not a reawakening of long-suppressed resentments, but instead a product of reputational cascades. In this process, a failure to engage in ethnically identified activity produces reputational sanctions, which grow in intensity over time as increasing numbers of people join the cascade. Initially people may be asked to dress in an ethnically identifiable way; later people who shared their ethnic identify may ask them to engage in certain celebrations and to participate in meetings; still later they may be asked to segregate themselves. Hence "the fears and antagonisms that accompany high levels of ethnic activity may be a result of ethnification rather than its root cause."[30]

Kuran does not refer to group polarization. But an understanding of this phenomenon would much fortify his analysis, by showing how within-group discussion (which is, under conditions of ethnification, an increasingly large percentage of total discussion) can ensure that ethnic groups, and individual members of ethnic groups, end up with a far stronger ethnic identification than the median member held before discussions began. Informational and reputational pressures have undoubtedly had effects in the Middle East. In the extreme case, the result might be war. And when a war begins, group polarization, if it operates at the national level, can help ensure continued hostility and antagonism.

Enclave Deliberation and Suppressed Voices

I have mentioned but not yet explored the potential vices of heterogeneity and the potentially good effects of deliberating "enclaves" consisting of groups of like-minded individuals. It seems obvious that such groups can be extremely important in a heterogeneous society, not least because members of some demographic groups tend to be especially quiet when participating in broader deliberative bodies. In this light, a special advantage of "enclave deliberation" is that it promotes the development of positions that would otherwise be invisible, silenced, or squelched in general debate.

In numerous contexts, this is a great advantage. Many social movements have been made possible through this route (consider feminism, the civil rights movement, Reaganism, environmentalism, and the movement for LBGT rights). The efforts of marginalized groups to exclude outsiders, and even of political parties to limit their primaries to party members, can be justified in similar terms. Even if group polarization is at work—perhaps *because* group polarization is at work—enclaves can provide a wide range of social benefits, not least because they greatly enrich the social "argument pool."

The central empirical point here is that in deliberating bodies, high-status members tend to initiate communication more than others and their ideas are more influential—partly because low-status members lack confidence in their own abilities, partly because they fear retribution.[31] For example, women's ideas are often less influential and are sometimes "suppressed altogether in mixed-gender groups,"[32] and in ordinary circumstances, cultural minorities have disproportionately little influence on decisions by culturally mixed groups.[33] It makes sense to promote deliberating enclaves in which members of multiple groups may speak with one another and develop their views—a point that bears on the constitution of multicultural societies.

But there is a serious danger in such enclaves. The danger is that through the mechanisms of social influence and persuasive arguments, members will move to positions that lack merit but are predictable consequences of the particular circumstances of enclave deliberation. In the extreme case, enclave deliberation may even put social stability at risk (for better or for worse). And it is impossible to say, in the abstract, that those who sort themselves into enclaves will move generally in a direction that is desirable for society at large or even for its own members. It is easy to think of examples to the contrary—for example, in the rise of Nazism, hate groups, and numerous "cults" of various sorts.

There is no simple solution to the dangers of enclave deliberation. Sometimes the threat to social stability is desirable. As Jefferson wrote, turbulence can be "productive of good. It prevents the degeneracy of government, and nourishes a general attention to ... public affairs. I hold ... that a little rebellion now and then is a good thing."[34] Turbulence aside, any judgments about enclave deliberation are hard to make without a sense of the underlying substance—of what it is that divides the enclave from the rest of society. From the standpoint of institutional design, the problem is that any effort to promote enclave deliberation will ensure group polarization among a wide range of groups, some necessary to the pursuit of justice, others likely to promote injustice, and some potentially quite dangerous.

In this light we should be able to see more clearly the sense in which Edmund Burke's conception of representation—rejecting "local purposes" and "local prejudices" in favor of "the general reason of the whole"[35]— is not accidentally but instead *essentially* conservative (speaking purely descriptively, as a safeguard of existing practices). The reason is that the submersion of "local purposes" and "local prejudices" into a heterogenous "deliberative assembly"[36] will inevitably tend to weaken the resolve of groups—and particularly low-status or marginalized groups—whose purely internal deliberations would produce a high degree of polarization.

Hence James Madison—with his fear of popular passions producing "a rage for paper money, for an abolition of debts, for an equal division of property, or for any other improper or wicked project"[37]—would naturally be drawn to a Burkean conception of representation, favoring large election districts and long length of service to counteract the forces of polarization. By contrast, those who believe that "destabilization" is an intrinsic good or that the status quo contains sufficient injustice that it is worthwhile to incur the risks of encouraging polarization on the part of diverse groups will, or should, be drawn to a system that enthusiastically promotes insular deliberation within enclaves.

In a nation suffering from widespread injustice, or mistaken in various ways, enclave deliberation may be the only way to develop a sense of clarity or justice—at least for some. It may have large benefits for those within the enclave, precisely because it helps them to develop that sense. Enclaves may have different norms from those outside of them; people may feel unleashed, often for better. Civil rights movements have often needed enclaves. Although enclaves may reduce diversity among those within them, they may increase diversity throughout society—at least if there are plenty of enclaves. One advantage of multiple enclaves is that they may produce *second-order diversity*—that is, diversity across society— potentially to the benefit of all.[38]

But even in such a nation, enclave deliberation is unlikely to produce change unless its members are eventually brought into contact with others. In constitutional democracies, the best response is to ensure that any such enclaves are not walled off from competing views and that, at certain points, there is an exchange of views between enclave members and those who disagree with them. It is total or near-total self-insulation, rather than group deliberation as such, that carries with it the most serious dangers, often in the highly unfortunate (and sometimes deadly) combination of extremism with marginality.

An appreciation of group polarization helps show why a constitutional democracy takes steps to protect deliberation within enclaves, to ensure that those inside enclaves hear alternative views, and to ensure as well that those outside of particular enclaves are exposed to what enclave members have to say. Above all, it is important to avoid a situation in which people are exposed to echoes of their own voices. In a diverse society, this form of self-insulation can create serious deliberative trouble, in the form of mutual incomprehension or much worse. Heterogeneity, far from being a source of social fragmentation, can operate as a creative force, helping to identify problems and even solutions that might otherwise escape notice.

3 The Expressive Function of Law

Actions are expressive; they carry meanings. This is true for nearly everything we do, from the most mundane to the most significant. A lawyer who wears a loud tie to court signals something distinctive about his self-conception and his attitude toward others; so too a professor who teaches in blue jeans; so too a student who comes to class in a business suit. What can be said for nonverbal acts applies to purely verbal statements as well. A bank president who uses the terms *Miss* and *Mrs.*, or who refers to African Americans as *Negroes*, shows a wide range of things about his attitudes on matters of gender and race.

In these and other cases, what the agent communicates, or will be taken to mean, may or may not have a great deal to do with his intentions. In this sense, the meanings of actions are not fully within the agent's control. Indeed, some agents may not even be aware of the relevant meanings. Consider a foreigner whose very foreignness is often signaled by obliviousness to the social meanings of his actions. What he says may be very different from what he means.

The social meanings of actions are very much a function of existing social norms. When a social norm tells people not to smoke in public places, the social meaning of smoking is obtuseness, discourtesy, or worse. When a social norm requires people to dress casually for dinner, formal attire "means" something bad, like a desire to seem superior or a manifestation of an odd social rigidity. And when social norms change, social meaning changes too. Thus the social meanings of lighting up a cigarette, engaging in an act of sexual harassment, using a condom, or refusing to eat meat are very different now from what they were in 1961 because of dramatic shifts in underlying norms.

What can be said for actions can also be said for law. Many people support law because of the statements made by law, and disagreements about law are frequently debates over the expressive content of law, rather than its consequences. Much of the debate over school segregation, for example, was about the meaning of laws calling for segregation. *Plessy v. Ferguson* asserted that such laws did not "mean" black inferiority;[1] *Brown v. Board of Education*[2] tried to respond to this assertion with empirical work suggesting the contrary.

So too debates over immigration may not be mostly about economic growth and employment. They have a large expressive dimension. Those who seek to reduce immigration want to make a statement: *It is our country, not theirs*. Those who seek to increase immigration want to make a statement: *We are open to outsiders*. Of course both sides also care about consequences, but the expressive content of immigration policy looms very large.

In the 1980s, the enormously lengthy and heated debate over whether flag burning is protected by the Constitution was permeated by expressive concerns. By seeking to outlaw flag burning, people wanted to make a statement about patriotism and love of country. If we ask whether the debate is about how best to deter flag burning, we will find the debate unintelligible. In the 1980s, the number of people who burned the American flag was not exactly high, and it is reasonable to suppose that a constitutional amendment making it possible to criminalize flag burning would have among its principal consequences a dramatic increase in annual acts of flag burning. In fact, adopting a constitutional amendment may be the best possible way to promote the incidence of flag burning: people might burn the flag to show that they abhor the amendment!

In these circumstances, it seems clear that those who supported the amendment were motivated not so much by consequences as by expressive concerns. They wanted to make a statement about the venality of the act of flag burning—perhaps to affect social norms, perhaps because they thought that making the statement is intrinsically good. For a more recent example, consider President Donald Trump's efforts to encourage the National Football League to punish its players for refusing to kneel during the national anthem. To be sure, Trump did not argue that the refusal to kneel should be a crime. But he did want the players to be punished. The debate over his efforts was intensely expressive. Did the refusal to kneel show a disrespect for one's country? Or was it an acceptable way of protesting injustice?

In many nations, the debate over regulating hate speech is similar. It is above all about the social meaning of such regulation. Do bans on hate speech "mean" that victims of hate speech require special paternalistic protections, are weak and thin-skinned, and are unable to take care of themselves? Or do they "mean" that bigotry is utterly unacceptable in a liberal society? Debates of this kind could not plausibly be focused on consequences, for the stakes are usually low (we are not dealing with action, after all) and thus cannot justify the amount of time and energy devoted to the issue. In this way, debates over flag burning and debates over hate speech have a great deal in common: they are expressive in character.

Consider, too, a subject far afield from constitutional law but bearing directly on the role of law in a democracy: risk regulation. In environmental protection, public debate often is focused on the perceived social meaning of law. Thus the Endangered Species Act has a special salience as a symbol of a certain conception of the relationship between human beings and their environment. Efforts to "weaken" the Endangered Species Act may or may not have large consequences for endangered species; but people who oppose such efforts are insisting on certain values. In the same way, mandatory recycling (as opposed to curbside charges, which seem far better from an economic standpoint) may well receive public support on expressive grounds. In the legal profession, the same may also be true of mandatory pro bono work (as opposed to compulsory donations from lawyers who refuse to do such work).

In this chapter, I explore the expressive function of law—the function of law in "making statements" as opposed to controlling behavior directly. Statements can be seen as nudges, at least if they are unaccompanied by sanctions (see part II). I focus on the particular issue of how legal "statements" might be designed to change social norms. I catalog a range of possible (and in my view legitimate) efforts to alter norms through legal expressions about appropriate evaluative attitudes. I also argue that the expressive function of law makes most sense in connection with efforts to change norms and that if legal statements produce bad consequences, they should not be enacted even if they seem reasonable or noble.

Making Statements

We might understand the expressive function of law in two different ways. First, and most straightforwardly, the law's "statement" about, for example, the risks of distracted driving may be designed to affect social norms and in that way ultimately to affect both judgments and behavior. The goal is to reduce distracted driving and thus to save lives. On this view, an expressive approach to law depends on an assessment of social consequences; certain expressions are favored because they will (ultimately) have good consequences.

Here there is a prediction about the facts: an appropriately framed law may influence social norms and push them in the right direction. If the law mandates recycling, perhaps it will affect social norms about the environment in a desirable way. Or people might think that if the law treats something—say, sexual capacities—as a commodity for sale and exchange, social norms may be affected in a troublesome way. People might start to see such capacities in a way that will demean and disparage them; the legitimation of prostitution might spill over into ordinary relationships (in a destructive way).

Sometimes the claim that the law affects norms is plausible. Prevailing norms, like preferences and beliefs, are usually not a presocial given but a product of a complex set of social forces, sometimes including law. Laws designed to change norms will be my focus here. But sometimes people support a law not because of its effects on norms but because they believe that it is intrinsically valuable for the relevant "statement" to be made. And sometimes law will have little or no effect on social norms.

Thus a second understanding of the expressive function of law does not concern itself with effects on norms at all. Instead, its grounding is connected with the individual interest in integrity. In a brief but suggestive discussion, Bernard Williams notes that people often refuse to perform offensive or objectionable actions even though their refusal will result in worse consequences.[3] Williams argues that our actions are determined not only by consequences but by judgments related to personal integrity, commitment, the narrative continuity of a life, and the individual and social meaning of personal conduct. The expressive dimension of action can be an important reason for action. Williams offers cases that might be understood in these terms. Someone might refuse to kill an innocent person at the request of a terrorist, even if the consequence of the refusal is that many more people will be killed. Or a pacifist might refuse to take a job in a munitions factory, even if the refusal has no effect on the factory itself.

People's responses to these cases are not adequately captured in terms that ignore expressive considerations—and Williams thinks that people's responses are right. To be sure, it is possible that the refusal to kill an innocent person is consequentially justified on balance, for people who refuse to commit bad acts may cultivate attitudes that lead to value-maximizing behavior. But this is a complex matter, and it is not Williams' point, nor is it the view of those who defend law for expressive reasons.

In my view, Williams's argument is not convincing; he is using a moral heuristic for what counts, which is welfare (see chapters 14 and 15 for details). My point here is only that human behavior is sometimes a function of expressive considerations. We might agree on this point even if we also believe that consequences count and that people should not be fanatical.

There is an analog at the social and legal level. A society might identify the norms to which it is committed and insist on those norms via law, even if the consequences of the insistence are obscure or unknown. A society might insist on a constitutional right against racial discrimination, or a civil rights law, for expressive reasons even if it is unsure to what extent the right or the law will actually help members of minority groups. A society might endorse or reject capital punishment because it wants to express a certain understanding of the appropriate course of action when one person takes the life of another. A society might protect animal welfare for the same reason.

The point bears on the cultural role of law, adjudication, and even Supreme Court decisions. The empirical effects of those decisions are highly disputed. If the Supreme Court holds that that segregation is unlawful, that certain restrictions on hate speech violate the First Amendment, or that students cannot be asked to pray in school, the real-world consequences may be smaller than is conventionally thought. But the close attention American society pays to the court's pronouncements is connected with the expressive or symbolic character of those pronouncements. When the court makes a decision, it is often taken to be speaking on behalf of the nation's basic principles and commitments. The idea that the court's decisions have an expressive function captures what is often at stake.

I do not claim that the expressive effects of law, thus understood, are decisive or that they cannot be countered by a demonstration of more conventional bad consequences. In fact, I will argue otherwise and thus try to vindicate Simon's remark in the epigraph to this book. Recall his words:

"Sometimes we just want to scream loudly at injustice, or to stand up and be counted. These are noble motives, but any serious revolutionist must often deprive himself of the pleasures of self-expression. He must judge his actions by their ultimate effects on institutions."[4] My principal aim is to defend laws that attempt to alter norms, rather than laws that merely "speak." It cannot be doubted, however, that the expressive function is a large part of legal debate. Without understanding the expressive function of law, we will have a hard time getting an adequate handle on public views on such issues as civil rights, free speech, welfare rights, prostitution, the environment, immigration, endangered species, capital punishment, and abortion.

Collective Action Problems

Many social norms solve collective action problems.[5] Some of these problems involve coordination; others involve prisoner's dilemmas. Norms solve such problems by imposing social sanctions on defectors. When defection violates norms, defectors might well feel guilt or shame, important motivational forces. The community may enforce its norms through informal punishment, the most extreme form of which is ostracism. But the most effective use of norms happens before an act is even committed. The expectation of guilt or shame—a kind of social "tax," sometimes a very high one—is usually enough to produce compliance.

Thus, for example, if there is a norm in favor of cooperation, people may be able to interact with one another in a way that is in their mutual interest. Professors write tenure letters and engage in a wide range of tedious administrative tasks that they could refuse to do at little cost (putting to one side guilt or shame—the emotional price of violating institutional norms). Or suppose that a community is pervaded by a strong norm against littering. If the norm is truly pervasive, a problem of environmental degradation can be solved without any need for legal intervention. The norm can do what the law would do at much greater cost. The norms associated with courtesy and considerateness are an especially important source of successful interaction among strangers and friends, and within families.[6]

Sometimes, however, good norms do not exist, and bad ones exist in their stead—where we understand "good" or "bad" by reference to the functions of norms in solving collective action problems. Imagine, for example, that there is no norm in favor of refusing to litter or even that there is a norm in favor of littering. In the face of such norms, the social meaning of littering may be independence and fearlessness, and the social meaning of cleaning up or failing to litter may be fastidiousness or even cowardice or neurosis. In such a situation, a society would, under imaginable assumptions, do well to reconsider and reconstruct its norms. It may be able to do so through voluntary efforts.

We have seen that norm entrepreneurs in the private sphere attempt to change norms by identifying their bad consequences and trying to shift the bases of guilt, shame, and pride. Many norm entrepreneurs are alert to the existence of collective action problems. In the environmental setting, public-interest groups often carry out this role by pressing private conduct in environmentally desirable directions, sometimes by providing new grounds for both pride (a kind of informal social subsidy) and guilt or shame (a kind of informal social tax).

But sometimes these private efforts fail. When this is so, the law might be enlisted as a corrective. In fact, the least controversial use of the expressive function of law operates in this way, as an attempted solution to some kind of collective action problem. Here the goal is to reconstruct existing norms and to change the social meaning of action through a legal expression or statement about appropriate behavior. Insofar as regulatory law is concerned with collective action problems, this is a standard idea—especially in the environmental context, but also in the settings of automobile safety, occupational safety and health, and many other problems. What is perhaps less standard is to see the law as an effort to produce adequate social norms. The law might either do the work of such norms or instead be designed to work directly against existing norms and to push them in new directions. The latter idea is grounded in the view that law will have moral weight and thus convince people that existing norms are bad and deserve to be replaced by new ones.

Sometimes legal mandates take the place of good norms by requiring certain forms of behavior through statutory requirements accompanied by significant enforcement activity. Environmental law, for example, imposes legal mandates to control industrial pollution; it adds a large commitment of enforcement resources.

But there is a subtler and more interesting class of cases of special importance for understanding the expressive function of law. These cases arise when the relevant law announces or signals a change in social norms unaccompanied by much in the way of enforcement activity. Consider, for example, laws that forbid smoking (in public places), laws that forbid littering, and laws that require people to clean up after their dogs. In many localities such laws are rarely enforced through criminal law, but they have an important effect in signaling appropriate behavior and in inculcating the expectation of social opprobrium and hence guilt or shame in those who deviate from the announced norm.

With or without enforcement activity, such laws can help reconstruct norms and the social meaning of action. Someone who fails to clean up after his dog may then be showing disrespect or even contempt for others. Many, most, or all people may see things this way, and large changes in behavior can result. Eventually there can be norm cascades as reputational incentives shift behavior in new directions. It should be unsurprising to find that, in many places, people clean up after their dogs even though doing so is not especially pleasant and even though the laws are rarely enforced.

When legally induced shifts in norms help solve collective action problems, there should be no objection in principle. Here, then, is the least controversial case for the expressive function of law.

Danger

Often the expressive function of law is brought to bear on dangerous behavior, including behavior that is dangerous only or principally to one's self. Of course, all behavior creates risks: driving a car, walking on city streets, volunteering for military service. When government tries to change norms that "subsidize" risk-taking behavior, it must do so because of a judgment that the change will promote overall welfare. This judgment might be rooted in an understanding that the intrinsic utility of the act is relatively low and that reputational incentives are the real source of the behavior. We are dealing, then, with cases in which risk-taking behavior persists because of social norms.

There are numerous examples. Elijah Anderson's vivid sociological analysis of life in an African American ghetto shows how social norms can create a variety of risks.[7] Powerful norms motivate people to use and sell drugs; powerful norms motivate teenagers to engage in sexual activity that may result in pregnancy. Anderson shows that with respect to drugs, pregnancy, and the use of firearms, behavior is driven in large part by reputational effects. For much risk-taking behavior, especially among young people, social norms are the crucial factor. Consider, for example, the existence of powerful norms governing cigarette smoking, alcohol use, the consumption of unlawful drugs, diet and exercise, texting while driving, and carrying and using firearms. It is easy to imagine that a decision to smoke a cigarette or not to buckle a seatbelt would be a function not primarily of the intrinsic utility of the underlying act but instead largely of the reputational effects.

Norm entrepreneurs in the private sector can play an important role here. Thus, for example, there was a dramatic decrease in cigarette smoking among young African Americans in the early 1990s, a decrease apparently fueled by changes in social norms for which private norm entrepreneurs are partly responsible.[8] In the relevant communities, the changes meant that the social meaning of smoking was not attractiveness, independence, and rebelliousness, but dirtiness and willingness to be duped. More broadly, religious leaders often try to change social norms involving risky conduct such as promiscuous behavior.

But here as elsewhere, private efforts may be unsuccessful. In this light, law might attempt to express a judgment about the underlying activity in such a way as to alter social norms. If we see norms as a tax on or subsidy to choice, the law might attempt to change a subsidy into a tax, or vice versa. In fact, this is a central, even if implicit, goal behind much risk regulation policy. Educational campaigns often have the goal of changing the social meaning of risk-taking activity. Going beyond the provision of information and nudging, coercion might be defended as a way of increasing social sanctions on certain behavior. Through time, place, and manner restrictions or flat bans, for example, the law might attempt to portray behavior like smoking, using drugs, or engaging in unsafe sex as a sign of stupidity or weakness.

Are such efforts illiberal or unacceptably paternalistic? Under imaginable assumptions, they should not be so regarded. Choices are a function of norms for which individual agents are not responsible and which, on reflection, many or most agents may not endorse. This is conspicuously so in the context of risk-taking activity involving cigarettes, drugs, unsafe sex, and firearms. Much discussion of whether law should respect "preferences" or "choices" is confused by virtue of its silence on the matter of social norms. People may follow such norms despite the fact that they deplore them.

It is important in this regard that social norms are often a function of existing information. If people start to believe that smoking is dangerous to themselves and to others, it becomes more likely that social norms will discourage smoking. Certainly there has been a dramatic norm cascade in the last fifty years with respect to smoking, a cascade fueled in large part by judgments about adverse health effects. Shifts in norms governing behavior may well be produced by new information about risk (although norms can shift in both directions; sometimes a perception of dangerousness increases the attractiveness of behavior). One can imagine similar information-induced norm cascades with respect to diet, sugar consumption, exercise, and unsafe sex. In fact, people often try to bring norms into accord with existing information.

Because the provision of information, a kind of nudge, is the least intrusive regulatory strategy, it should be the preferred option. Other nudges may also help. Whether more aggressive strategies make sense depends on their costs and benefits (see part II).

Money

A complex network of social norms governs the acceptable uses of money. This is so in two different respects. First, some social norms impose sanctions on using money as a reason for action. Here people are not supposed to engage in certain acts if their reason for doing so is financial gain. Second, some social norms make different kinds of money nonfungible: that is, the prevailing norms require different kinds of money to be used for different purposes.[9] These sets of norms raise many complexities. They are also entangled with the expressive function of law. Finally, they suggest that it is sometimes inappropriate to infer general valuations from particular choices, because those choices are a function of norms that are limited to the context in which they are made.

Let us begin with norms punishing the use of money as a reason for action. An instructive article by Joel Waldfogel, *The Deadweight Loss of Christmas*,[10] will help to introduce the point. Waldfogel finds no less than four million dollars in annual deadweight losses from the fact that people give in-kind presents rather than mere cash on Christmas Day. Waldfogel's analysis is simple. For those who give presents, the cost of Christmas is higher than it would be if they gave cash instead. The cost of gift-giving includes not just the expenditure of money but also the time and effort devoted to deciding what gifts to give. And for those who receive presents, the benefit is typically lower than it would be if they received cash. Many people don't like what they get, and even if they do like it, they don't like it a lot. Recipients would be better off if they received cash, which they could use as they wished—just as food stamps are worth less than their dollar value because, unlike cash, they can be spent only on food. The four-million-dollar "waste" is a result of these sorts of considerations.

Waldfogel's findings are intriguing, but he neglects the role of social norms. In many contexts, norms severely discourage the giving of cash rather than, say, a tie, a book, or a sweater. Under existing norms, a cash present—from a husband to a wife or a father to a son, for example—may reflect contempt or indifference. It might even seem to be a joke. This is precisely because cash is both impersonal and fungible. A tie or a book—whether or not it is a wonderful tie or a wonderful book—fits well with norms that call for a degree of individualized attention on the part of the donor. Waldfogel devotes too little attention to the cluster of Christmas-related norms and the social meaning of diverse forms of gift-giving.

What can be said for Christmas can be said for many areas of social life in which money is deemed an inappropriate basis for action. If someone asks an adult neighbor to shovel his walk or to mow his lawn in return for money, the request will often be regarded as an insult, because it is based on an inappropriate valuation of the neighbor. The request embodies a con-ception of neighborliness that is, under existing norms, judged improper; a neighbor is not a servant. The norm is in place even if the offeree would in some sense be better off if he received the money in return for undertaking the task.

Quite generally it is inappropriate to offer money to one's friends in return for hurt feelings, disappointments, tasks, or favors. If you have been unkind, offering a friend an apology is a good idea; offering a check is not. In fact, the universe of cases in which norms disallow monetary exchange is very large, and unremarked upon only because it is so taken for granted. It would be quite strange to give an adult a certain sum of money after hear-ing that his parent had died or to ask a colleague to clean up your office for, say, $250. This is so even though favors are of course common, and even though there can be in-kind implicit transactions between friends, neighbors, and even spouses.

There is often a connection between norms that block exchanges and ideas about equal citizenship. The exchange can be barred by social norms because of a perception that, though there may be disparities in social wealth, the spheres in which people are very unequal ought not to invade realms of social life in which equality is a social norm or goal. The prohibition on vote trading is one example. So too with certain social taboos on the use of wealth to buy services or goods—for example, organ donation— from other people. (I do not mean to resolve the question whether such taboos are a good idea.) Some part of the intricate web of norms covering the exchange of money among both friends and strangers is connected with the principle of civic equality. Monetary exchange would reflect forms of inequality that are not legitimate in certain spheres.

Familiar objections to "commodification"[11] are part and parcel of social norms banning the use of money. The claim is that people ought not to trade sexuality or reproductive capacities on markets, because market exchange of these "things" is inconsistent with social norms identifying their appropriate valuation. The claim is not that markets value sexuality "too much" or "too little"; rather, it is that markets value these activities in the wrong way. Under existing practice, social norms of course affect the adoption of children and impose severe sanctions on any effort (literally) to sell children even to willing and loving parents. The fact that the adoption market is accompanied by safeguards making any "sale" at most implicit is meant to reaffirm existing norms.

This point very much bears on law. In many ways, law tries to fortify norms regulating the use of money and to prevent new social practices from eroding those norms. This is an important domain for the expressive use of law. It is connected with the effort to create separate social spheres— some in which money is appropriately a basis for action, some in which money cannot be used. Thus the law bans a wide range of uses of money. Votes cannot be traded for cash; the same is true of body parts. In many places, prostitution is illegal. There is a sharp social debate about surrogate motherhood, and those who seek legal proscriptions are thinking in expressive terms. One of their goals may be to fortify existing social norms that insulate reproduction from the sphere of exchange. Or their argument may be less instrumental. They may seek to make a "statement" about reproduction without also seeking to affect social norms.

Equality

Norms of partiality[12] are an important part of social inequality. Social norms may require women to perform the most domestic labor; in some places, women who refuse to do so may incur social sanctions and may even feel guilty or ashamed. The social meaning of a woman's refusal may be a rejection of her appropriate gender role, and the refusal may be interpreted by others as a signal of a range of undesirable traits. In the areas of both race and gender, prevailing norms help constitute inequality. And here, as elsewhere, collective action is sometimes necessary to reconstitute existing norms.

Private norm entrepreneurs may be able to accomplish a great deal. With respect to the division of domestic labor between men and women, private efforts at norm management have played an important role. Individual acts that are expressive in character—a refusal to clean clothes or to make dinner, for example—are an important part of modern feminism. But the expressive function of law is especially important here, and it can move to the fore in public debates. If a discriminatory act is consistent with prevailing norms, there will be more in the way of discriminatory behavior. If discriminators are ashamed of themselves, there is likely to be less discrimination. A large point of law may be to shift social norms and social meaning (see chapter 1).

Recall in this connection that many restaurant owners and innkeepers supported the Civil Rights Act of 1964, which would have prevented them from discriminating. Why would people want the state to act against them? The answer lies in the fact that the law helped shift social norms and the social meaning of nondiscrimination. Whereas nondiscrimination would formerly signal a willingness to act on a race-neutral basis—and hence would trigger social norms that call for discrimination on the basis of race— it would henceforth signal a willingness to obey the law and hence fail to trigger adverse social norms.

Social norms help constitute a wide range of qualitatively different kinds of valuation, and these diverse valuations much affect behavior and the social meaning of behavior. These norms are omnipresent and are usually taken for granted. Imagine, for example, that Jane values a plant in the same way that most people value their children or that Sandy values her car like most people value art or literature. Antidiscrimination law is often designed to change norms so as to ensure that people are treated with a kind of dignity and respect that discriminatory behavior seems to deny.

The point is not limited to race and sex equality. Consider, as an especially interesting example, the movement for animal welfare and animal rights. Some people think that animals should be treated with dignity and respect and not as if they exist solely for human consumption, play, and use. This view is very much about social norms; it need not entail the further claim that animal life is infinitely valuable. It is best taken as a recommendation for a shift in norms governing the treatment of animals, accompanied by a judgment that the new norms will have good consequences for what human beings do. The recommendation may be based on the view that if we see animals (and nature in general) in this way, we will solve collective action problems, ecological in nature, faced by human beings; it may be based on a noninstrumental effort to extend ideals of basic dignity to all living things. In its most powerful form, the goal is to ensure that other living creatures are treated with kindness and respect, and not as if they are mere things. The expressive function of law can be important in making that more likely.

Qualifications

The discussion thus far has certainly not been exhaustive. There are many areas in which law is used in an expressive way, largely to manage social norms. Criminal law is a prime arena for the expressive function of law; as we have seen, the debate over flag burning has everything to do with the statement that law makes. I hope I have said enough to show the wide range of possible "expressions" via law and to see how the law might plausibly be used to manage social norms.

I now qualify the basic argument. The first set of qualifications stems from a hard question: What if the statement seems right but the consequences are unfortunate? The second set of qualifications emerges from the need to impose constraints on the expressive function of law.

Consequences

I have suggested that some expressivists are concerned with norm management, whereas others are concerned with the "statement" law makes entirely apart from its consequences. Expressivists can be both fanatical and ineffectual—a most unfortunate combination.

For those who endorse the expressive function of law, the most important testing cases arise when (a) people support laws because of the statement made by such laws but (b) the effects of such laws seem bad or ambiguous, even by reference to the values held by their supporters. How should such cases be understood? My basic proposition is that any support for "statements" via law should be rooted in plausible judgments about their effects on social norms and hence in "on balance" judgments about their consequences. Here we can bridge the gap between consequentialists and expressivists by showing that good expressivists are consequentialists too. They want to make the world better, not just to say things. If saying things makes the world better, then things should be said; if not, then not.

Consider, for example, the debate over emissions trading in environmental law. With such trading, polluters are allowed to buy and sell pollution rights, with the goal of reducing pollution to the right degree, and at the right cost. Some of the most pervasive objections to emissions trading are expressive in nature.[13] Critics claim that emissions trading has damaging effects on social norms by making environmental amenities seem like any other commodity: a good that has its price, to be set through market mechanisms. They contend that emissions-trading systems may have damaging effects on social norms by making people see the environment as something unobjectionable and without special claims to public protection. To some extent, the suggestion might be taken as an empirical prediction and evaluated as such. Will emissions-trading systems have substantial effects on social norms associated with the environment?

On that issue, we may be able to make some progress. We have an empirical question that is subject, in principle, to empirical resolution. If emissions-trading programs could be shown to have bad effects on social norms, they might be rejected notwithstanding their other virtues; perhaps the overall effects on such programs would be bad. (Compare this to the question whether to require recycling; mandatory recycling might well have better effects on norms than curbside charges.) But in the area of emissions-trading programs, we should be skeptical about the expressivist's concern. There is no evidence that such programs weaken people's commitment to clean air and water. Public attitudes toward the environment do not depend much on whether government has a command-and-control system or instead relies on emissions trading or other economic incentives.

Some people appear to think that it is intrinsically problematic to "say," through law, that environmental amenities are ordinary goods with appropriate prices. Is this a convincing objection to emissions-trading programs if (as we might suppose) such programs can save billions of dollars in return for the same degree of environmental protection? It is hard to see the force of the objection if, in fact, costs are lower, jobs are saved, the air is cleaner, norms are held constant, and fewer people are poor. On what basis should the "statement" made by law be taken to be cause for concern?

Or consider the question whether the minimum wage should be significantly increased. A possible justification for such increases is expressive in nature. Many people think that the government ought to make a statement to the effect that human labor is worth, at a minimum, $X per hour; perhaps any amount less than $X seems like an assault on human dignity. But suppose too that the consequence of the minimum wage is to increase unemployment among the most vulnerable members of society. Why should we care about mere statements, if the overall effects are bad? If a significant increase in the minimum wage would really drive vulnerable people out of the workplace in significant numbers, it is not easy to see why people should support it. I do not mean to take a final stand on the question whether the minimum wage should be significantly increased; that depends on the consequences. The point is that expressive approaches to law verge on fanaticism where effects on norms are unlikely and where the consequences of the "statement" are bad.

Constraints

What barriers should there be to governmental efforts at managing social norms? The simplest answer is simple: the same barriers that apply to any other kind of governmental action.

Thus, for example, government should not be permitted to invade rights, whatever our understanding of rights may be. The rights constraints that apply to government action generally are fully applicable here as well. If government tried to change social norms, through legislation, so as to ensure that women would occupy domestic roles, and men would not, it would violate the Equal Protection Clause. If government tried to change social norms, through legislation, to ensure that everyone would be Protestant, it would violate the right to religious liberty. At least these conclusions would make sense if government action is coercive.

Quite apart from the question of rights, there is always a risk that efforts at norm management will be futile or counterproductive. When government attempts to move social norms in a particular direction, it may fail miserably (see chapter 9). It is necessary to ensure that those who engage in norm management are trusted by the people whose norms are at issue. For this reason, it may be best for government to attempt to enlist the private sector to ensure that people with authority in relevant communities are participating in the process.

Some people would go further than this. From one view, any effort at norm management is illegitimate; this is a project that is off-limits to government. But it is hard to see how this argument might be made persuasive. Effects on social norms are not easily avoided; any system of government is likely to affect norms, including through the creation of the basic systems of contract, tort, and property. With respect to prevention of violent crime, intentional norm management is a conventional and time-honored part of government. To be sure, we could imagine abuses, even unspeakable ones. But the proper response is to insist on a wide range of rights-based constraints on the management of social norms through law.

No system of law can avoid that managerial role. Even markets themselves—which are very much a creation of law—are exercises in norm management. In these circumstances it is best for government to proceed pragmatically and contextually, seeing which norms are obstacles to well-being and using law when it is effective in providing correctives.

II The Uses and Limits of Nudges

4 Nudging: A Very Short Guide

Some policies take the form of *mandates* and *bans*. For example, criminal law forbids theft and assault. Other policies take the form of *economic incentives* (including disincentives), such as subsidies for renewable fuels, fees for engaging in certain activities, or taxes on gasoline and tobacco products. Still other policies take the form of *nudges*—liberty-preserving approaches that steer people in particular directions, but that also allow them to go their own way. In recent years, both private and public institutions have shown mounting interest in the use of nudges, because they generally cost little and have the potential to promote economic and other goals (including public health).

In daily life, a GPS device is an example of a nudge; so is an app that tells people how many calories they ate during the previous day; so is a text message that informs customers that a bill is due or that a doctor's appointment is scheduled for the next day; so is an alarm clock; so is automatic enrollment in a pension plan; so are the default settings on computers and cell phones; so is a system for automatic payment of credit card bills and mortgages. In government, nudges include graphic warnings for cigarettes; labels for energy efficiency or fuel economy; "nutrition facts" panels on food; MyPlate, which provides a simple guide for healthy eating (see choosemyplate.gov); default rules for public-assistance programs (as in "direct certification" of the eligibility of poor children for free school meals); a website like data.gov or data.gov.uk, which makes a large number of datasets available to the public; and even the design of government websites, which list certain items first and in large fonts.

Freedom of Choice

It is important to see that the goal of many nudges is to make life simpler, safer, or easier for people to navigate. Consider road signs, speed bumps, disclosure of health-related or finance-related information, educational campaigns, paperwork reduction, and public warnings. When officials reduce or eliminate paperwork requirements, and when they promote simplicity and transparency, they are reducing people's burdens. Some products (such as cell phones and tablets) are intuitive and straightforward to use. Similarly, many nudges are intended to ensure that people do not struggle when they seek to interact with government or to achieve their goals.

It is true that some nudges are properly described as a form of "soft paternalism," because they steer people in a certain direction. But even when this is so, nudges are specifically designed to preserve full freedom of choice. A GPS device steers people in a certain direction, but people are at liberty to select their own route instead. And it is important to emphasize that some kind of social environment (or "choice architecture"), influencing people's choices, is always in place. Nudges are as old as human history. New nudges typically replace preexisting ones; they do not introduce nudging where it did not exist before.

Transparency and Effectiveness

Any official nudging should be transparent and open rather than hidden and covert. Indeed, transparency should be built into the basic practice. Suppose that a government (or a private employer) adopts a program that automatically enrolls people in a pension program, or suppose that a large institution (say, a chain of private stores or a company that runs cafeterias in government buildings) decides to make healthy foods more visible and accessible. In either case, the relevant action should not be hidden in any way. Government decisions in particular should be subject to public scrutiny and review. A principal advantage of nudges, as opposed to mandates and bans, is that they avoid coercion. Even so, they should never take the form of manipulation or trickery. The public should be able to review and scrutinize nudges no less than government actions of any other kind.

All over the world, nations have become keenly interested in nudges. To take two of many examples, the United Kingdom has a Behavioral Insights Team (sometimes called the "Nudge Unit"), and the United States has had a

White House Social and Behavioral Sciences Team, now called the Office of Evaluation. The growing interest in nudges is not a mystery. They usually impose low (or no) costs; they sometimes deliver prompt results (including significant economic savings); they maintain freedom; and they can be highly effective. In some cases, nudges have a larger impact than more expensive and more coercive tools. For example, default rules, simplification, and uses of social norms have sometimes been found to have even larger impacts than significant economic incentives.

In the context of retirement planning, automatic enrollment has proved exceedingly effective in promoting and increasing savings. In the context of consumer behavior, disclosure requirements and default rules, establishing what happens if people do nothing, have protected consumers against serious economic harm, saving many millions of dollars. Simplification of financial aid forms can have the same beneficial effect in increasing college attendance as thousands of dollars in additional aid (per student). Informing people about their electricity use and how it compares to that of their neighbors can produce the same increases in conservation as a significant spike in the cost of electricity. If properly devised, disclosure of information can save both money and lives. Openness in government, disclosing both data and performance, can combat inefficiency and even corruption.

Testing

For all policies, including nudges, it is exceedingly important to rely on evidence rather than intuitions, anecdotes, wishful thinking, or dogmas. The most effective nudges tend to draw on work in behavioral science (including behavioral economics) and hence reflect a realistic understanding of how people will respond to government initiatives. But some policies, including some nudges, seem promising in the abstract, but turn out to fail in practice. Empirical tests, including randomized controlled trials, are indispensable. Bad surprises certainly are possible, including unintended adverse consequences, and sensible policymakers must try to anticipate such surprises in advance (and to fix them if they arise). Sometimes empirical tests reveal that the planned reform will indeed work—but that some variation on it, or some alternative, will work even better.

Experimentation, with careful controls, is a primary goal of the nudge enterprise. Fortunately, many nudge-type experiments can be run rapidly and at low cost and in a fashion that allows for continuous measurement and improvement. The reason is that such experiments sometimes involve small changes to existing programs, and those changes can be incorporated into current initiatives with relatively little expense or effort. If, for example, officials currently send out a letter to encourage people to pay delinquent taxes, they might send out variations on the current letter and test whether the variations are more effective.

Ten Important Nudges

Nudges span an exceedingly wide range, and their number and variety are constantly growing. Here is a catalog of ten important nudges—very possibly, the most important for purposes of policy—along with a few explanatory comments.

1. *default rules* (e.g., automatic enrollment in programs, including education, health, savings)

Default rules may well be the most effective nudges. If people are automatically enrolled in retirement plans, their savings can increase significantly. Automatic enrollment in health care plans or in programs designed to improve health can have significant effects. Default rules of various sorts (say, double-sided printing) can promote environmental protection. Note that unless *active choosing* (also a nudge) is involved, some kind of default rule is essentially inevitable, and hence it is a mistake to object to default rules as such. True, it might make sense to ask people to make an active choice, rather than relying on a default rule. But in many contexts, default rules are indispensable, because it is too burdensome and time-consuming to require people to choose.

2. *simplification* (in part to promote take-up of existing programs)

In both rich and poor countries, complexity is a serious problem, in part because it causes confusion (and potentially violations of the law), in part because it can increase expense (potentially reducing economic growth), and in part because it deters participation in important programs. Many programs fail, or succeed less than they might, because of undue complexity. As a general rule, programs should be easily navigable, even intuitive. In many nations, simplification of forms and regulations should be a high priority. The effects of simplification are easy to underestimate. In many nations, the benefits of important programs (involving education, health, finance, poverty, and employment) are greatly reduced because of undue complexity.

3. *uses of social norms* (emphasizing what most people do, e.g., "most people plan to vote" or "most people pay their taxes on time" or "nine out of ten hotel guests reuse their towels")

One of the most effective nudges is to inform people that most others are engaged in certain behavior. Such information often is most powerful when it is as local and specific as possible ("the overwhelming majority of people in your community pay their taxes on time"). Use of social norms can reduce criminal behavior and also behavior that is harmful whether or not it is criminal (such as alcohol abuse, smoking, and discrimination). It is true that sometimes most or many people are engaging in undesirable behavior. In such cases, it can be helpful to highlight not what most people actually do, but instead what most people *think* people should do (as in, "90 percent of people in Ireland believe that people should pay their taxes on time").

4. *increases in ease and convenience* (e.g., making low-cost options or healthy foods visible)

People often make the easy choice, and hence a good slogan is this: make it easy. If the goal is to encourage certain behavior, reducing various barriers (including the time that it takes to understand what to do) often helps. Resistance to change is often a product not of disagreement or of skepticism, but of perceived difficulty—or of ambiguity. A supplemental point: If the easy choice is also fun, people are more likely to make it.

5. *disclosure* (e.g., the economic or environmental costs associated with energy use or the full cost of certain credit cards—or large amounts of data, as in the cases of data.gov and the Open Government Partnership; see opengovernmentpartnership.org)

The American Supreme Court Justice Louis Brandeis said that "sunlight is said to be the best of disinfectants," and disclosure can make both markets and governments much "cleaner."[1] For consumers, disclosure policies can be highly effective, at least if the information is both comprehensible and accessible. Simplicity is exceedingly important. (More detailed and fuller disclosure might be made available online for those who are interested in it.) In some settings, disclosure can operate as a check on private or public inattention, negligence, incompetence, wrongdoing, and corruption. The Open Government Partnership, now involving dozens of nations, reflects a worldwide effort to use openness as a tool for promoting substantive reform; nations must produce national action plans containing new policies to increase transparency.

6. *warnings, graphic or otherwise* (as for cigarettes)

If serious risks are involved, the best nudge might be a private or public warning. Large fonts, bold letters, and bright colors can be effective in triggering people's attention. A central point is that attention is a scarce resource, and warnings are attentive to that fact. One virtue of warnings is that they can counteract the natural human tendency toward unrealistic optimism and simultaneously increase the likelihood that people will pay attention to the long term. There is a risk, however, that people will respond to warnings by discounting them ("I will be fine"), in which case it would make sense to experiment with more positive messages (e.g., providing some kind of reward for the preferred behavior, even if the reward is nonmonetary, as in apps that offer simple counts and congratulations). Research also shows that people are far less likely to discount a warning when it is accompanied by a description of the concrete steps that people can take to reduce the relevant risk ("you can do X and Y to lower your risk").

7. *eliciting implementation intentions* ("do you plan to vote?")

People are more likely to engage in activity if someone elicits their implementation intentions. With respect to health-related behavior, a simple question about future conduct ("do you plan to vaccinate your child?") can have significant consequences. Emphasizing people's identity can also be effective ("you are a voter, as your past practices suggest").

8. *precommitment strategies* (by which people commit to a certain course of action)

Often people have certain goals (e.g., to stop drinking or smoking, to engage in productive activity, or to save money), but their behavior falls short of those goals. If people precommit to engaging in a certain action—such as a smoking cessation program—they are more likely to act in accordance with their goals. Notably, committing to a specific action at a *precise* future moment in time better motivates action and reduces procrastination.

9. *reminders* (e.g., by email or text message, as for overdue bills and coming obligations or appointments)

People tend to have a great deal on their minds, and when they do not engage in certain conduct (e.g., paying bills, taking medicines, or making a doctor's appointment), the reason might be some combination of inertia, procrastination, competing obligations, and simple forgetfulness. A reminder can have a significant impact. For reminders, timing greatly matters; making sure that people can act immediately on the information is critical (especially in light of the occasional tendency to forgetfulness). A closely related approach is *prompted choice*, by which people are not required to choose but asked whether they want to choose (e.g., clean energy or a new energy provider, a privacy setting on their computer, or to be organ donors).

10. *informing people of the nature and consequences of their own past choices* (smart disclosure in the United States and the midata project in the United Kingdom)

Private and public institutions often have a great deal of information about people's own past choices—for example, their expenditures on health care or on their electric bills. The problem is that individuals often lack that information. If people obtain it, their behavior can shift, often making markets work better and saving a lot of money. If, for example, people are given information about how much they have spent on electricity in the last year, they can take steps to reduce their spending in the future.

Institutionalizing Nudges

What is the best method for implementing nudges? It is certainly possible to rely entirely on existing institutions. We could imagine a system in which an understanding of nudges is used by current officials and institutions, including leaders at the highest levels. For example, the relevant research could be enlisted by those involved in promoting competitiveness, environmental protection, public safety, consumer protection, and economic growth—or in reducing private and public corruption and combating poverty, infectious diseases, and obesity. Focusing on concrete problems rather than abstract theories, officials with well-established positions might be expected to use that research, at least on occasion.

If the relevant officials have both knowledge and genuine authority, they might be able to produce significant reforms simply because they are not akin to a mere research arm or a think tank. (Even a single person, if given the appropriate authority and mission, could have a large impact.) In one model, the relevant officials would not engage in new research, or at least not in a great deal of it. They would build on what is already known (and perhaps have formal or informal partnerships with those in the private sector who work on these issues). In an important sense, this approach is the simplest because it does not require new offices or significant additional funding, but only attention to the relevant issues and tools, and a focus on the right appointments. In the United States, this kind of approach has proved highly successful with the adoption of numerous nudges.

A quite different approach would be to create a new institution—such as a behavioral insights team or a nudge unit of some sort (as in the United Kingdom, the United States, Australia, the Netherlands, Ireland, Qatar, and increasingly many nations). Such an institution could be organized in different ways and could have many different forms and sizes. In a minimalist model, it would have a small group of knowledgeable people (say, five) bringing relevant findings to bear and perhaps engaging in, or spurring, research on their own. In a more ambitious model, the team could be larger (say, thirty or more), engaging in a wide range of relevant research. A behavioral insights team could be created as a formal part of government (the preferred model to ensure real impact) or could have a purely advisory role.

Whatever its precise form, the advantage of such an approach is that it would involve a dedicated and specialized team, highly informed and specifically devoted to the relevant work and with expertise in the design of experiments. If the team can work with others to conduct its own research, including randomized controlled trials, it might be able to produce important findings (as has in fact happened in the United Kingdom, Australia, Ireland, the Netherlands, and the United States, and similar efforts are occurring elsewhere). The risk is that such a team would be akin to an academic adjunct, a kind of outsider, without the ability to power or initiate real reform. Authority greatly matters. The United Kingdom has had the most experience with this kind of approach, and it has succeeded in part because it has enjoyed high-level support and access.

In this domain, one size does not fit all, but it is noteworthy that a growing number of nations have concluded that it is worthwhile to have a dedicated team. Of course, the two approaches might prove complementary.

5 Forcing Choices

When you enter a taxicab in a large city and ask to go to the airport, you might well be asked: "What route would you like me to take?" If you are like many people, you will not welcome the question. You might even hate it. After all, it is the business of the driver to know how to get to the airport, and in any case the driver almost certainly has access to a GPS device. For you, the question—asking you to choose—is a kind of mental tax, cognitive for sure (because of the need to think) and possibly hedonic as well (because it is not exactly pleasant to ponder how to get to the airport). To be sure, the tax is likely to be small—but it might well be unwelcome.

Whenever a doctor or a lawyer asks a patient or a client a battery of questions, a possible reaction might be: "On some of these questions, why don't you decide for me?" If the emotional stakes are high, and if the issues are difficult, the hedonic and cognitive tax might be very high. And whenever public officials require people to fill out complex forms to qualify for training or for benefits, the tax might turn out to be prohibitive, at least for some people. It might lead them not to apply at all. It is for this result that complex form-filling requirements are not merely a paperwork burden; they can undermine and even undo the underlying programs. Form filling can be a curse.

In this light, consider three problems:

1. An online clothing company is deciding whether to (a) adopt a system of default settings for privacy or (b) require first-time users to specify, as a condition for access to the site, what privacy settings they would prefer.
2. A large employer is deciding among three options: (1) to enroll employees automatically in a health insurance plan; (2) to ask them to opt in if they like; or (3) to say that as a condition for starting work, they must

indicate whether they want health insurance and, if they do, which plan they want.

3. A utility company is deciding whether to adopt a "green default" for consumers, with a somewhat more expensive but environmentally preferable energy source, or instead a "gray default," with a somewhat less expensive but environmentally less desirable energy source—or, alternatively, to ask consumers which energy source they prefer.

In these cases, and countless others, a public or private institution or an individual is deciding whether to use some kind of default rule or to require people to make some kind of active choice. (I shall say a good deal about what the word *require* might mean in this setting.) For those who reject paternalism and who prize freedom of choice, active choosing has evident appeal. Indeed, it might seem far preferable to any kind of default rule. It respects personal agency; it promotes responsibility; it calls for an exercise of individual liberty. It seems to reflect a commitment to human dignity.

In light of these considerations, it is tempting to think that active choosing deserves some kind of pride of place, especially if it is accompanied by efforts to improve or "boost" people's capacities, perhaps by providing them with information, perhaps by increasing their statistical literacy. Some social scientists like to distinguish between System 1, the automatic or intuitive system of the mind, and System 2, the deliberative system.[1] The deliberative system might tell you that air travel is very safe, even if the intuitive system thinks that planes cannot possibly make it over long distances. Perhaps the best approach is to strengthen System 2 and insist on active choosing.

In recent years, there have been vigorous debates about freedom of choice, paternalism, behavioral economics, individual autonomy, and the use of default rules and choice architecture. Invoking recent behavioral findings, some people have argued that because human beings err in predictable ways and cause serious problems for themselves, some kind of paternalism is newly justified, especially if it preserves freedom of choice, as captured in the idea of "nudging" or "libertarian paternalism." Others contend that because of those very errors, some form of coercion is needed to promote people's welfare. They believe that as a result, the argument for denying choice or nonlibertarian paternalism is strengthened.[2]

My central goal here is to unsettle that opposition and to suggest that it is often illusory. The central reason is that people often *choose* not to choose, and forcing them to choose is a kind of tax. In many contexts, insisting on active choosing, or forcing people to choose, is a form of paternalism, not an alternative to it. Under imaginable assumptions, any effort to require active choosing easily fits within the standard definition of paternalism and runs afoul of the most conventional objections to paternalism. Many people believe, in many contexts, that choosing is burdensome and costly. Sometimes they choose not to choose explicitly (and indeed are willing to pay a considerable amount to people who will choose for them). They have actively chosen not to choose.

Sometimes people have made no explicit choice; they have not actively chosen anything. But it is nonetheless reasonable to infer that in particular contexts, their preference is not to choose, and they would say so if they were asked. (Recall the case of the cab ride to the airport or the interaction with a doctor or a lawyer.) They might fear that they will err. They might be busy and lack "bandwidth"[3] and thus have limited cognitive resources and do not want them to be taxed. They might want to focus on some concerns but not others; they might think that choosing would deny them that freedom. They might be aware of their own lack of information or perhaps their own behavioral biases (such as unrealistic optimism). They might find the underlying questions confusing, difficult, painful, and troublesome—empirically, morally, or otherwise. They might not enjoy choosing. They might not want to take responsibility for potentially bad outcomes for themselves (and at least indirectly for others).[4] They might anticipate their own regret and seek to avoid it.

But even when people prefer not to choose, many private and public institutions favor and promote active choosing on the ground that it is good for people to choose. They may have sufficient reasons for that belief. Sometimes active choosing is required as a way of overcoming a collective action problem (people cannot delegate the right to vote), but sometimes it is a means of *protecting those who choose not to choose against their own mistake(s)*. The central idea is that people should be choosing even if they do not want to do so. An institution might think that choice making builds some kind of muscle; it might think that it helps people to learn. To the extent that the institution's preference for choice making overrides that of the chooser (who prefers not to choose), active choosing counts as paternalistic. It overrides people's own judgments about what is good or what best promotes welfare or freedom.

To be sure, nanny states forbid choosing, but they also forbid the choice not to choose. *Choice-promoting* or *choice-requiring paternalism* might be attractive forms of paternalism, but neither is an oxymoron, and they are paternalistic nonetheless.

If people are *required* to choose even when they would prefer not to do so, active choosing counts as a species of nonlibertarian paternalism in the sense that people's own choice is being rejected. We shall see that in many cases, those who favor active choosing are mandating it and may therefore be overriding (on paternalistic grounds) people's choice not to choose. When people prefer not to choose, required choosing is a form of coercion—though it may be a justified form, at least when active choosing does not impose high taxes, when it does not increase the likelihood and magnitude of errors, and when it is important to enable people to learn and to develop their own preferences.

If, by contrast, people are *asked whether they want to choose* and can opt out of active choosing (in favor of, say, a default rule), active choosing counts as a form of libertarian paternalism. In some cases, it is an especially attractive form. A company might ask people whether they want to choose the privacy settings on their computer or instead rely on the default, or whether they want to choose their electricity supplier or instead rely on the default.

With such an approach, people are being asked to make an active choice between the default and their own preference, and in that sense their liberty is fully preserved. Call this *simplified active choosing*. Simplified active choosing has the advantage of avoiding the kinds of pressure that come from a default rule while also allowing people to rely on such a rule if they like. In the future, we should see, and we should hope to see, adoption of this approach by a large number of institutions, both public and private.

But that approach is no panacea. It imposes a tax of its own, even if the tax is small. It is important to acknowledge that whenever a private or public institution asks people to choose, it might be overriding their preference not to do so and in that sense engaging in choice-requiring paternalism. This point applies *even when people are being asked whether they want to choose to choose*. (The passenger must focus her attention even if a cab driver merely asks, "Do you want to tell me how to go, or would you like it better if I choose the route on my own?") After all, they might not want to make that second-order choice (and might therefore prefer a simple default rule). If the point is not obvious, consider the fact that any question—in person, by email, by regular mail—that demands an answer is in effect a tax on people's scarce cognitive resources.

In this sense, there is a strong nonlibertarian dimension to apparently liberty-preserving approaches that ask people to choose between active choosing and a default rule. If these claims do not seem self-evident, or if they appear a bit jarring, it is because the idea of active choosing is so familiar, and so obviously appealing, that it may not be seen for what it is: a form of choice architecture, and one that many choosers may dislike, at least in settings that are unfamiliar or difficult.

Varieties of Choice

Is government untrustworthy? Always? Many of those who embrace active choosing believe that consumers of goods and services, and indeed choosers of all sorts, should be free from government influence. Of course they recognize that in markets, producers will impose influences of multiple kinds, but they contend that when third parties are not affected, and when force and fraud are not involved, the government itself should remain neutral. They reject paternalism on government's part.

Perhaps it is legitimate for public officials to require the provision of accurate information in order to ensure that consumers' choices are adequately informed. Perhaps reminders are justified as well. But some people think that if government seeks to nudge people in its preferred directions in other ways—by imposing default rules or embracing paternalism of any kind—it is exceeding its appropriate bounds. In particular, they prefer active choosing, and they want to encourage it. And even if their focus is on the public sector, they might say the same thing for the private sector as well.

But what does active choosing entail? What does it mean to "require" people to indicate their preferences? The question is more difficult than it might seem. Those who insist on the inevitability of default rules will object that it has no clear answer. Even if choice architects seek to promote active choosing, they have to specify what happens if people *simply refuse to choose*. Isn't the answer some kind of default rule?

The question is a good one, because some kind of default rule is ultimately necessary. Choice architects have to establish what happens if people decline to choose—a point that critics of nudging often miss. Choice architecture itself is inevitable. But this point should not be taken to collapse the distinction between active choosing and default rules. To see why, consider three possibilities.

1. Criminal or civil punishment for those who refuse to make an active choice.

In most contexts, no one contends that if people fail to make a choice, they should be killed, imprisoned, fined, or otherwise punished. The usual sanction for that failure is that they do not receive a good or service. But there are exceptions. In some nations, including Australia, Belgium, and (before 1970) the Netherlands, people have been subject to civil sanctions if they fail to vote, and in that sense they may be punished for refusing to make an active choice. Similarly, a provision of the Affordable Care Act, now repealed, required people to obtain health insurance, subject to punishment (in the form of a tax penalty) if they failed to do so. If people are required to obtain health insurance, they will normally be required to choose which plan to obtain.

With respect to active choosing, both of these cases do have a wrinkle: People are being forced to choose along one dimension (for whom to vote and which health insurance plan to obtain), but are being prohibited from choosing along another dimension (whether to vote or to obtain health insurance). But insofar as one kind of choice is being required, we may fairly speak of *coerced choosing*. In both cases, coerced choosing can be justified as a means of overcoming a collective action problem: the democratic system might be jeopardized unless most or all adults are voting, and perhaps a health insurance system requires very broad participation.

But we could easily imagine an effort to defend both forms of coercion on simple paternalistic grounds—for example, to protect themselves against disaster, people should be required to purchase health insurance, and to ensure that people have the right health insurance plan, people should be required to make a personal choice about what plan they should have. (To be sure, the second form of paternalism reflects a form of respect for individual agency that the first form of paternalism does not display. But on plausible assumptions, both forms make sense, and they do not really contradict each other.)

We could also imagine other contexts in which people would face sanctions if they do not choose, though admittedly some such cases look more like science fiction than the real world. For realistic examples, consider cases in which people must decide whether to become organ donors (or face criminal penalties) or must choose privacy settings on their computers (subject to civil sanctions if they do not). The fact that sanctions are rarely imposed on people who choose not to choose seems to suggest an implicit recognition that in a free society, such choices are generally acceptable and indeed a legitimate part of consumer sovereignty. One reason involves information: People know best what they want, and others should not choose for them, even if the choice is not to choose. I will press this point, which has been insufficiently emphasized by those who claim to prize individual choice.

2. Active choosing with respect to a related or ancillary matter as a condition for obtaining a good or a service (or a job).

Sometimes active choosing is mandatory in a distinctive sense: *Unless people make an active choice on some matter, they cannot obtain a good or service, even though that good or service, narrowly defined, is not the specific topic of the choice that they are being asked to make.* We can imagine a continuum of connections between the matter in question, for which an active choice is being required, and the specific good that has already been chosen. There would be a close connection if, for example, people were told that unless they indicate their preferences with respect to car insurance, they cannot lease a car. So too, there would be a close connection if people were told that unless they create a password, or indicate their preferences with respect to privacy settings, they cannot use their computer. And indeed, both of these cases are standard. In markets, sellers sometimes insist that purchasers must make an active choice on some related matter to obtain or use a product.

By contrast, there would be a somewhat weaker connection if people were informed that they cannot work with a particular employer until they indicate their preferences with respect to their retirement plan. The connection would be weaker still if people were told that they cannot obtain a driver's license unless they indicate their preferences with respect to organ donation. The connection would be even weaker if people were told that they cannot register to vote unless they make a choice about their preferred privacy settings on their computer.

In the final example, there is no connection between the matter on which people are being asked to make a choice and the good that they are specifically seeking. In some cases, the choice architect is requiring an active choice on a matter that is genuinely ancillary. Note that in imaginable cases that fall in this category, the requirement of active choosing has a strongly coercive dimension insofar as the good in question is one that people cannot easily reject (such as a driver's license, a job, or a right to vote). The choice architect is, in effect, leveraging that good to ensure an active choice on some other matter.

From the normative point of view, we might want to distinguish between public and private institutions here. Perhaps private institutions, disciplined as they are by market forces, should freely compete along this dimension as they do along others, and perhaps public institutions should hesitate before requiring people to choose unless there is a close connection between the good or service in question and the object of active choice.

3. Active choosing among goods, services, or jobs as a condition for obtaining a good, a service, or a job.

For most consumption decisions, people are given a wide range of options, and they can choose one or more of them. Unless they make a choice, they will not obtain the relevant good or service. They are not defaulted into purchasing sodas, tablets, cell phones, shoes, or fishing poles. Indeed, this is the standard pattern in free markets. When people visit a website, a restaurant, or a grocery or appliance store, they are generally asked to make an active choice. The default—understood as what happens if they do nothing—is that no product will be purchased. People do not receive goods or services unless they have actively chosen them. The same point holds for the employment market. People are not typically defaulted into particular jobs, at least not in any formal sense. They have a range of options, and unless they take one they will be unemployed. In this respect, free markets generally require active choosing.

There is nothing inevitable about this situation. We could imagine a situation in which sellers assume, or presume, that people want certain products and in which buyers obtain them, and have to pay for them, passively. Imagine, for example, that a bookseller has sufficient information to know, for a fact, that Johnson would want to buy any new book by Harlan Coben, Richard Thaler, or Joyce Carol Oates, or that Smith would like to purchase a new version of a particular tablet, or that LaMotte would want to buy a certain pair of sneakers, or that Ullmann would like to purchase a particular product for his dog, or that when Williams runs out of toothpaste, he would like new toothpaste of exactly the same kind. If the sellers' judgments are unerring, or even nearly so, would it be troublesome and intrusive, or instead a great benefit, for them to arrange the relevant purchases by default? Existing technology is increasingly raising this question.

There is a good argument that the strongest reason to require active choosing is that sufficiently reliable predictive shopping algorithms do not (yet) exist, and hence active choosing is an indispensable safeguard against erroneous purchases. The use of algorithms is not (yet) in the interest of those who might be denominated purchasers (by default). On this view, the argument for active choosing is rooted in the view that affirmative consent protects against mistakes—which leaves open the possibility of "passive purchases" if and when a reliable technology becomes available. We are getting there, and for some things we may already be there, but so long as such technology does not exist, passive purchases will be unacceptable. A hypothesis: Once reliable algorithms are indeed in place, we will see far more support for their use in cases like those of Johnson, Smith, Ullmann, and Williams.

What Choosers Choose

As the examples suggest, both private and public institutions might choose option 2 or 3, though of course only government can choose option 1. It should be clear that active choosing is far from inevitable. Instead of imposing active choosing, an institution might select some kind of default rule, specifying what happens if people do nothing. Of course options 2 and 3 also come with a kind of default rule: unless people make an active choice, they will have no good, no service, and no employment. But other approaches are possible.

For example, those who obtain driver's licenses might be defaulted into being organ donors, or those who start work with a particular employer might be defaulted into a specific retirement or health care plan. These examples are not hypothetical. Alternatively, those who make an active choice to purchase a particular product—say, a book or a subscription to a magazine—might be enrolled into a program by which they continue to receive a similar product on a periodic basis, whether or not they have made an active choice to do so. The Book of the Month Club famously employs a strategy of this sort.

An active choice to purchase a product might also produce a default rule that is unrelated to the product—as, for example, when the purchase of a particular book creates a default enrollment in a health care plan, or when an active choice to enroll in a health care plan creates a default enrollment in a book club. In extreme cases, when disclosure is insufficiently clear, an approach of this kind might be a form of fraud, though we could also imagine cases in which such an approach would track people's preferences.

Suppose, for example, that a private institution knows that people who purchase product X (say, certain kinds of music) also tend to like product Y (say, certain kinds of books). Suggestions of various kinds, default advertisements, default presentations of political views, and perhaps even default purchases could be welcome and in people's interests, unfamiliar though the link might seem. For example, the website Pandora tracks people's music preferences, from which it can make some inferences about likely tastes and judgments about other matters, including politics.[5]

We could also imagine cases in which people are explicitly asked to choose whether they want to choose. Consumers might be asked: Do you want to choose your cell phone settings, or do you want to be defaulted into settings that seem to work best for most people or for people like you? Do you want to choose your own health insurance plan, or do you want to be defaulted into the plan that seems best for people in your demographic category? In such cases, many people may well decide in favor of a default rule and thus decline to choose because of a second-order desire not to do so. They might not trust their own judgment; they might not want to learn. The topic might make them anxious. They might have better things to do.

Simplified active choosing—active choosing with the option of using a default—has considerable promise and appeal, not least because it avoids many of the influences contained in a default rule and might therefore seem highly respectful of autonomy while also giving people the ability to select the default. For cell phone settings or health insurance plans, active choosers can choose actively if they like, while others can (actively) choose the default.

Note, however, that this kind of question is also an intrusion and a kind of tax. For that reason, it is not a perfect solution, at least for those people who genuinely do not want to choose. After all, they are being asked to do exactly that. (One more time: "Do you want to choose your route to the airport?" asked the taxi driver.) At least some of those people likely do not want to have to choose between active choosing and a default rule, and hence they would prefer a default rule to an active choice between active choosing and a default rule. Even that active choice takes time and effort and imposes costs, and some or many people might not want to bother. In this respect, supposedly libertarian paternalism, in the form of an active choice between active choosing and a default, itself has a strong nonlibertarian dimension—a conclusion that brings us directly to the next topic.

Choice-Promoting Paternalism

I now turn to the heart of my argument, which is very simple: Those who favor active choosing and who force people to choose are often acting paternalistically, at least if they are requiring choices in circumstances in which people would prefer not to choose. Because those circumstances are pervasive, those who require choices are, in the relevant sense, acting as paternalists. Paternalism might be justified, here as elsewhere; but choice-promoting paternalism may intrude on autonomy, welfare, or both. It may run into the same objections that are made against paternalism of the more familiar kinds. As we shall see, however, choice-promoting paternalism also has a distinctive defense.

Paternalism

Is active choosing paternalistic when people would prefer not to choose? To answer that question, we should start by defining paternalism. There is an immensely large body of literature on that issue.[6] Let us bracket the hardest questions and note that though diverse definitions have been given, it seems clear that the unifying theme of paternalistic approaches is that *a private or public institution does not believe that people's choices will promote their welfare and is taking steps to influence or alter people's choices for their own good.*

What is wrong with paternalism, thus defined? Those who reject paternalism typically invoke welfare, autonomy, or both. They tend to believe that individuals are the best judges of what is in their interests and of what would promote their welfare and that outsiders should decline to intervene because they lack crucial information.[7] Placing a bright spotlight on welfare, John Stuart Mill himself emphasized that this is the essential problem with outsiders, including government officials. Mill insisted that the individual "is the person most interested in his own well-being" and that the "ordinary man or woman has means of knowledge immeasurably surpassing those that can be possessed by any one else."[8] When society seeks to overrule the individual's judgment, it does so on the basis of "general presumptions," and these "may be altogether wrong, and even if right, are as likely as not to be misapplied to individual cases." Mill's goal was to ensure that people's lives go well, and he contended that the best solution is for public officials to allow people to find their own paths.

Mill offered an argument about welfare, grounded in a claim about the superior information held by individuals. But there is an independent argument from autonomy, which emphasizes that even if people do not know what is best for them and even if they would choose poorly, they are entitled to do as they see fit (at least so long as harm to others, or some kind of collective action problem, is not involved). Freedom of choice has intrinsic and not merely instrumental value. It is an insult to individual dignity, and a form of infantilization, to eliminate people's ability to go their own way.

Paternalists Who Force People to Choose

Whether or not these objections to paternalism are fully convincing, they have considerable force in many situations. But there might seem to be legitimate questions about whether and how they apply to efforts to override the choices of people whose choice is not to choose. Perhaps those who want people to choose are not acting paternalistically at all; perhaps they are seeking to promote self-determination and showing people a high level of respect.

That is probably what they believe they are doing. Recall the case of the taxi driver, who may be doing just that, and who may have passenger rage ("why did you choose that crazy route?") and tips in mind. Doctors and lawyers asking patients and clients to choose might be analogous. If public officials promote or require choices, they might think that their own goal is to avoid any kind of paternalism. Focusing on Mill's concerns, or some variation on them, they might insist that respect for individual agency calls for a two-word proclamation: you choose. What is paternalistic about that?

On reflection, however, the objections to paternalism apply quite well, so choice-promoting paternalism and choice-requiring paternalism are not oxymorons. If an outsider tells people that they must choose, she is rejecting their own conception of what they should be doing and thus endangering their welfare (on Mill's premises) and refusing to respect their autonomy. People might decline to choose for multiple reasons. Their choice not to choose is, in their view, the best way to promote their welfare, and they want that choice to be treated with respect. They might have a kind of intuitive framework: they want to minimize decision costs and error costs. When choosing would impose high decision costs (and in a sense amount to a cognitive or hedonic tax), they might not want to do it, unless incurring those costs is a good way to reduce error costs. And if they think that someone (a cab driver, an employer, a public official) would be more likely to make the right decision, they might think that the best way to reduce error costs is not to choose. They might effectively appoint someone else as their agent; they might see themselves as the principal and delegate a choice to that agent with conviction, contentment, or pleasure.

More particularly, they might believe that in the context at hand, they lack information or expertise. They might fear that they will err. They might not enjoy the act of choosing; they might like it better if someone else decides for them. They might be too busy. They might not want to incur the emotional costs of choosing, especially for situations that are painful or difficult to contemplate (such as organ donation or end-of-life care). They might find it a relief, or even fun, to delegate. They might not want to take responsibility. They might not want to pay the psychic costs associated with regretting their choice. Active choosing saddles the chooser with responsibility for the choice and reduces the chooser's welfare for that reason.

In daily life, people defer to others, including friends and family members, on countless matters, and they are often better off as a result. In ordinary relationships, people benefit from the functional equivalent of default rules, some explicitly articulated, others not. Within a marriage, for example, certain decisions (such as managing finances or planning vacations) might be made by the husband or wife by default, subject to the right to opt out in particular circumstances. That practice has close analogues in many contexts in which people are dealing with private or public institutions and choose not to choose. They might want their rental car company, their health care provider, or their employer to make certain choices for them. Indeed, people often are willing to pay others a great deal to make such choices. But even when there is no explicit payment or grant of the power of agency, people might well prefer a situation in which they are relieved of the obligation to choose because such relief will reduce decision costs, error costs, or both.

Suppose, for example, that Jones believes that he is not likely to make a good choice about his retirement plan, that he does not want to be educated to be able to do so, and that he would therefore prefer a default rule chosen by someone who is a specialist in the subject at hand. In Mill's terms, doesn't Jones know best? Recall Mill's insistence that the "ordinary man or woman has means of knowledge immeasurably surpassing those that can be possessed by any one else."[9]

Or suppose that Smith is exceedingly busy and wants to focus on her most important concerns, not on a question about the right health insurance plan for her or on the right privacy setting for her computer. Doesn't Mill's argument support respect for Smith's choice? Whatever the chooser chooses, the welfarist arguments seem to call for deference to the chooser's choice, even if that choice is not to choose. If we believe in freedom of choice on the ground that people are uniquely situated to know what is best for them, then that very argument should support respect for people when they freely choose not to choose.

Or turn from welfare to considerations of autonomy and dignity. Suppose that Winston, exercising her autonomy, decides to delegate decision-making authority to someone else and thus to relinquish the power to choose, in a context that involves health insurance, energy providers, privacy, or credit card plans. Is it an insult to Winston's dignity, or instead a way of honoring it, if a private or public institution refuses to respect that choice? It is at least plausible to suppose that respect for autonomy requires respect for people's decisions about whether and when to choose. That view is especially reasonable in light of the fact that people are in a position to make countless decisions, and they might well decide that they would like to exercise their autonomy by focusing on their foremost concerns, not on what seems trivial, boring, or difficult.

But are people genuinely bothered by the existence of default rules, or would they be bothered if they were made aware that such rules had been chosen for them? We do not have a full answer to this question; the setting and the level of trust undoubtedly matter. But note in this regard the empirical finding, in the context of end-of-life care, that even when they are explicitly informed that a default rule is in place and that it has been chosen because it affects people's decisions, there is essentially no effect on what people do.[10] This finding suggests that people are not uncomfortable with defaults, even when they are made aware both that choice architects have selected them and that they were selected because of their significant effect. There is increasing evidence that transparency about defaults does not decrease their effects.[11]

Freedom and Its Alienation

To be sure, we could imagine hard cases in which a choice not to choose seems to be an alienation of freedom. In the most extreme cases, people might choose to relinquish their liberty in some fundamental way, as in the aftermath of 9/11. In a less extreme case, people might choose not to vote, not in the sense of failing to show up at the polls, but in the sense of (formally) delegating their vote to others. Such delegations are impermissible, perhaps because they would undo the internal logic of a system of voting (in part by creating a collective action problem that a prohibition on vote selling solves), but perhaps also because individuals would be relinquishing their own freedom.

Or perhaps people might choose not to make choices with respect to their religious convictions, or their future spouse, and they might delegate those choices to others. In cases that involve central features of people's lives, we might conclude that freedom of choice cannot be alienated and that people must make their own decisions.

We cannot easily specify which cases fall in this category. People can have nice debates on that question. But even if the category is fairly large, it cannot easily be taken as a *general* objection to the proposition that on autonomy grounds, people should be allowed not to choose in multiple domains.

Asymmetries

Choice-promoting paternalism is no oxymoron, but it might have a distinctive appeal, and along some dimensions it is quite different from forms of paternalism that (1) do not promote choosing, (2) actively discourage choosing, and (3) forbid choice. As a familiar example of the first category, consider a default rule; as an example of the second, consider a warning or a reminder designed to persuade people to delegate authority and not to choose on their own. Examples of the second type are admittedly rare, but we could certainly imagine them in the domain of financial or medical choices. Examples of the first category are, of course, common. Examples of the third category are also common and are the most standard target of those who reject paternalism.

Those who favor choice-promoting paternalism might acknowledge the plausibility of the phrase but object that we are really dealing here with a debater's point, even a kind of pun. They might contend that their motivations are distinctly attractive and that so long as choices are being promoted, the standard concerns about paternalism are weakened or even eliminated. I have argued that those concerns are very much in play. But those who favor active choosing might argue that they are not, in fact, showing disrespect to choosers or insulting them in any way; on the contrary, they are honoring them.

They might add that their real concern is the welfare of choosers. Alert to the risks of mistakes on the part of choice architects, who may be ignorant or biased or neglectful of the importance of individual circumstances, they might claim to be the most faithful followers of Mill. They might make that claim even as they acknowledge that some people choose not to choose. To be sure, a decision to delegate the route to the airport to the cab driver might not be a mistake—but what about a decision involving one's own medical care or financial situation?

There are some fair points here. No one doubts that those who do not want to choose might object to outsiders (intermeddlers?) who seek to influence or override their desire. But it is true that choice promoters do have distinctive motivations, associated with respect for choosers—which leads us to the question of justification.

Is Paternalism Justified? Welfare

It is important to acknowledge that even if a chooser freely chooses not to choose, that particular choice might turn out not to be in the chooser's interest (as the chooser would define it). For that reason, choice-promoting or even choice-requiring paternalism might have a welfarist justification. Perhaps the chooser chooses not to choose only because he lacks important information, which would reveal that the default rule might be harmful or that the choice architect is ignorant or untrustworthy. Perhaps he suffers from some form of bounded rationality. A behavioral market failure (understood as a nonstandard market failure that comes from human error) might infect a choice not to choose, just as it might infect a choice about what to choose.

A nonchooser might, for example, be unduly affected by availability bias because of an overreaction to a recent situation in which his own choice went wrong. Or perhaps the chooser is myopic and is excessively influenced by the short-term costs of choosing, which might require some learning (and hence some investment), while underestimating the long-term benefits, which might be very large. A form of "present bias" might infect the decision not to choose. People might face a kind of intrapersonal collective action problem, in which such a decision by Jones, at Time 1, turns out to be welfare reducing for Jones at Times 2, 3, 4, and 5.

But for those who reject paternalism on welfarist grounds, these kinds of concerns are usually a justification for providing more and better information—not for blocking people's choices, including their choices not to choose. Perhaps choosers should be nudged to choose. Choice-promoting paternalism, as a form of libertarian paternalism, might be preferred to choice-requiring paternalism.

On welfare grounds, the argument in favor of promoting or requiring choice-making is the same, in broad outline, as the argument for promoting or requiring any kind of behavior. Of course, welfarists might be wrong to object to paternalism; we can easily imagine contexts in which paternalism is amply justified on welfare grounds. But with respect to their objections, the question is whether the choice not to choose is, in general or in particular contexts, likely to go wrong, and in the abstract there is no reason to think that a particular choice would be especially error-prone. In light of people's tendency to fall prey to overconfidence, the choice not to choose might even be peculiarly likely to be right, which would create serious problems for choice-requiring paternalism. At most, concerns about individual error would seem to support choice-promoting paternalism, not a more aggressive variety.

Consider in this regard evidence that people spend too much time trying to make precisely the right choice, in a way that leads to significant welfare losses. In many situations, people underestimate the temporal costs of choosing and exaggerate the benefits, producing "systematic mistakes in predicting the effect of having more, versus less, choice freedom on task performance and task-induced affect."[12] If people make such systematic mistakes, it stands to reason that they might well choose to choose in circumstances in which they ought not to do so on welfare grounds. And if choosing has intrinsic value, then people will choose in circumstances in which they would do better, at least in material terms, to make some kind of delegation.

My aim is not to endorse the welfarist rejection of paternalism; it is only to say that the underlying arguments apply to all forms of paternalism, including those that would interfere with the decision not to choose. To be sure, some welfarists are willing to interfere with people's choices; they may well be libertarian or nonlibertarian paternalists. The simplest points are that the standard welfarist arguments on behalf of freedom of choice apply to those who (freely) choose not to choose and that those who want to interfere with such choices might well be paternalists. Whether their paternalism is justified, on welfare grounds, depends on the context.

Is Paternalism Justified? Autonomy

We have seen that from the standpoint of autonomy, interference with the choice not to choose is presumptively objectionable. When cab drivers ask passengers to choose, they might be intruding on their passengers' autonomy; when a passenger says, "you decide," he is exercising his autonomy. It is respectful of choosers, and a recognition of their dignity, to allow them to devote their attention to those topics to which they *want* to devote their attention.

As we have seen, the most obvious exceptions are those in which the choice counts as some kind of alienation of freedom. But perhaps there are other exceptions, raising the question whether choice-promoting or choice-requiring paternalism might often be justified on autonomy grounds. An employer might believe that employees should choose their own health insurance plan so that their own capacity for agency is exercised and increased—not only with respect to health insurance plans but with respect to a wide range of choices that call for statistical literacy. For medical matters generally, it might be best to try to boost people's capacities—perhaps by providing simple information, perhaps by teaching statistical competence—with the thought that a successful effort on that count will increase people's autonomy in multiple domains. Similar considerations might support active choosing in the context of retirement plans. The examples could easily be multiplied.

These points show that if the goal is to respect or promote autonomy, it is not always clear whether we should embrace or reject choice-promoting paternalism. On the one hand, people do exercise their autonomy by deciding when and whether to choose. In fact, that is a fundamental way that autonomy is exercised. That is a strong reason to reject choice-preserving paternalism. On the other hand, choice making is like a muscle, and it can be strengthened through use. For choice architects, the most general suggestion is that on autonomy grounds, people should be able to choose or not choose as they see fit, but in some circumstances the promotion of autonomy can itself justify influencing or overriding the choice not to choose—with the strength of the argument depending on the value, for autonomy, of promoting choice making in a particular context.

6 Welfare

Some nudges are designed to reduce externalities: consider fuel economy labels that draw attention to environmental consequences or default rules that automatically enroll people in green energy. But many nudges are designed to increase the likelihood that people's choices will improve their own welfare. The central goal of such nudges is to "make choosers better off, *as judged by themselves.*"[1] Social planners—or choice architects—might well have their own ideas about what would make choosers better off— but in our view, the lodestar is people's own judgments. To be a bit more specific, the lodestar is welfare, and people's own judgments are a good (if imperfect) way to test whether nudges are increasing their welfare.

The last sentence raises many questions, and it is certainly reasonable to wonder about potential ambiguities in the "as judged by themselves" (here-inafter AJBT) criterion. Should the focus be on choosers' judgments before the nudge or instead after? What if the nudge alters people's preferences so that they like the outcome produced by the nudge when they would not have sought that outcome in advance? What if preferences are constructed by the relevant choice architecture? What if people's ex ante judgments are wrong, in the sense that a nudge would improve their welfare even though they do not think that it would? Do we want to ask about choosers' actual, potentially uninformed or behaviorally biased judgments, or are we entitled to ask what choosers would think if they had all relevant information and were unaffected by relevant biases?

My goal here is to explore the meaning of the AJBT criterion and to sort out some of the ambiguities. As we shall see, three categories of cases should be distinguished: (1) those in which choosers have clear antecedent preferences, and nudges help them to satisfy those preferences; (2) those in which choosers face a self-control problem, and nudges help them to overcome that problem; and (3) those in which choosers would be content with the outcomes produced by two or more nudges or in which ex post preferences are endogenous to or constructed by nudges, so that the AJBT criterion leaves choice architects with several options without specifying which one to choose. Cases that fall in category 1 plainly satisfy the AJBT criterion, and there are many such cases. From the standpoint of the AJBT criterion, cases that fall in category 2 are also unobjectionable—indeed, they can be seen as a subset of category 1—and they are plentiful. Cases that fall in category 3 create special challenges, which may lead us to make direct inquiries into people's welfare or to explore what informed, active choosers typically select.

In an instructive set of comments, critical of the enterprise of nudging, the economist Robert Sugden presses a simple question:[2] "Do people really want to be nudged towards healthy lifestyles?" That is an empirical question, and we have a great deal of evidence about it. The answer is "yes," at least in the sense that in numerous nations—including the United States, the United Kingdom, Germany, France, Ireland, Italy, and Australia—strong majorities endorse nudges toward healthy lifestyles.[3] One might object that general attitudes toward nudges do not specifically answer Sudgen's question and that it is best not to ask people generally (1) whether they approve of nudges, but instead to ask more specifically (2) whether they themselves would like to be nudged. But general approval of health-related nudges strongly suggests that the answer to (2) is probably yes as well, and, in any case, the existing evidence suggests that the answer to (2), asked specifically, is also yes.[4] To be sure, more remains to be learned on these issues.

These findings cannot speak to conceptual and normative questions. What does it even mean to say that people want to make the choices toward which they are being nudged? What is the relationship between people's preferences and imaginable nudges? In light of behavioral findings, how confidently can we speak of people's "preferences"? If people want to be nudged, why are they not already doing what they would be nudged to do? Those are important questions (and they do have empirical features).

It is not possible to understand the operation of the AJBT criterion without reference to examples. In countless cases, we can fairly say that *given people's antecedent preferences*, a nudge will make choosers better off AJBT. For example:

1. Luke has heart disease and needs to take various medications. He wants to do so, but he is sometimes forgetful. His doctor sends him periodic text messages. As a result, he takes the medications. He is very glad to receive those messages.

2. Meredith has a mild weight problem. She is aware of that fact, and though she does not suffer serious issues of self-control and does not want to stop eating the foods that she enjoys, she does seek to lose weight. Because of a new law, many restaurants in her city have clear calorie labels, informing her of the caloric content of various options. As a result, she sometimes chooses low-calorie offerings—which she would not do if she was not informed. She is losing weight. She is very glad to see those calorie labels.

3. Edna is a professor at a large university, which has long offered its employees the option to sign up for a retirement plan. Edna believes that signing up would be a terrific idea, but she has not gotten around to it. She is somewhat embarrassed about that. Last year, the university switched to an automatic enrollment plan, by which employees are defaulted into the university's plan. They are allowed to opt out, but Edna does not. She is very glad that she has been automatically enrolled in the plan.

There is nothing unfamiliar about these cases. On the contrary, they capture a great deal of the real-world terrain of nudging, both by governments and by the private sector. Choosers have a goal, or an assortment of goals, and the relevant choice architecture can make it easier or harder for them to achieve it or them. Insofar as we understand the AJBT criterion by reference to people's antecedent preferences, that criterion is met. Note that it would be easy to design variations on these cases in which nudges *failed* that criterion because they would make people worse off by their own lights.

We could complicate the cases of Luke, Meredith, and Edna by assuming that they have clear antecedent preferences, that the nudge is inconsistent with those preferences, and that as a result of the nudge their preferences are changed. For example, Jonathan likes talking on his cell phone while driving. He talks to friends on his commute to work, and he does business as well. As a result of a set of vivid warnings, he has stopped. He is glad. He cannot imagine why anyone would talk on a cell phone while driving. In his view, that is too dangerous.

After the nudge, Luke, Meredith, Edna, and Jonathan believe themselves to be better off. Cases of this kind raise the question whether the AJBT criterion requires reference to ex ante or ex post preferences. That is a good question, which might be answered by making direct inquiries into people's welfare; I will turn to that question below. My main point is that as originally given, the cases of Luke, Elizabeth, and Edna are straightforward. Such cases are common.

Some cases can be seen as different because they raise questions about self-control:

1. Ted smokes cigarettes. He wishes that he had not started, but he has been unable to quit. His government has recently imposed a new requirement, which is that cigarette packages must be accompanied with graphic images showing people with serious health problems, including lung cancer. Ted is deeply affected by those images; he cannot bear to see them. He quits, and he is glad.

2. Joan is a student at a large university. She drinks a lot of alcohol. She enjoys it, but not that much, and she is worried that her drinking is impairing her performance and her health. She says that she would like to scale back, but for reasons that she does not entirely understand, she has found it difficult to do so. Her university recently embarked on an educational campaign to reduce drinking on campus, in which it (accurately) notes that four out of five students drink only twice a month or less. Informed of the social norm, Joan finally resolves to cut back her drinking. She does, and she is glad.

In these cases, the chooser suffers from a self-control problem and is fully aware of that fact. Ted and Joan can be seen both as *planners*, with second-order preferences, and *doers*, with first-order preferences. A nudge helps to strengthen the hand of the planner. It is possible to raise interesting philosophical and economic questions about self-control and planner-doer models, but insofar as Ted and Joan welcome the relevant nudges, and do so ex ante as well as ex post, the AJBT criterion is met. In a sense, self-control problems require their own GPS devices and so can be seen to involve navigability; people want to exercise self-control, but they are not sure how to do so. Nudges can help them. But for choosers who face such problems, the underlying challenge is qualitatively distinctive, and they recognize that fact.

In such cases, the AJBT criterion is met. But do people acknowledge that they face a self-control problem? That is an empirical question, of course, and my own preliminary research suggests that the answer is "yes." On Amazon Mechanical Turk, I asked about two hundred people this question:

Many people believe that they have an issue, whether large or small, of self-control. They may eat too much, they may smoke, they may drink too much, they may not save enough money. Do you believe that you have any issue of self-control?

A whopping 70 percent said that they did (55 percent said "somewhat agree," while 15 percent said "strongly agree"). Only 22 percent disagreed. (Eight percent were neutral.)

This is a preliminary test, and admittedly, the question might have contained its own nudge ("Many people believe that they have an issue ..."). Whatever majorities say, the cases of Ted and Joan capture a lot of the territory of human life, as reflected in the immense popularity of programs designed to help people to combat addiction to tobacco and alcohol. We should agree that nudges that do the work of such programs, or that are used in such programs, are likely to satisfy the AJBT criterion.

There are harder cases. In some of them, it is not clear if people have antecedent preferences at all. In others—as in the case of Jonathan, who talked on his cell phone while driving—their ex post preferences are an artifact of, or constructed by, the nudge. Sometimes these two factors are combined (as marketers are well aware). As Amos Tversky and Richard Thaler put it long ago, "values or preferences are commonly constructed in the process of elicitation."[5] If so, how ought the AJBT criterion be understood and applied? For example:

1. George cares about the environment, but he also cares about money. He currently receives his electricity from coal; he knows that coal is not exactly good for the environment, but it is cheap, and he does not bother to switch to wind, which would be slightly more expensive. He is quite content with the current situation. Last month, his government imposed an automatic enrollment rule on electricity providers: people will receive energy from wind, and pay a slight premium, unless they choose to switch. George does not bother to switch. He says that he likes the current situation of automatic enrollment. He approves of the policy and he approves of his own enrollment.

2. Mary is automatically enrolled in a bronze-level health care plan. It is
   less expensive than silver and gold levels, but it is also less comprehensive in its coverage and it has a higher deductible. Mary prefers bronze
   and has no interest in switching. In a parallel world (a lot like ours, but
   not quite identical), Mary is automatically enrolled in a gold-level health
   care plan. It is more expensive than silver and bronze, but it is also more
   comprehensive in its coverage and it has a lower deductible. Mary prefers gold and has no interest in switching.
3. Thomas has a serious illness and questions whether he should have an
   operation, which is accompanied by potential benefits and potential
   risks. Reading about the operation online, Thomas is not sure whether
   he should go ahead with it. Thomas' doctor advises him to have the
   operation, emphasizing how much he has to lose if he does not. He
   decides to follow this advice. In a parallel world (a lot like ours, but not
   quite identical), Thomas's doctor advises him not to have the operation,
   emphasizing how much he has to lose if he does. He decides to follow
   this advice.

In the latter two cases, Mary and Thomas appear to lack an antecedent preference; what they prefer is an artifact of the default rule (in the
case of Mary) or the framing (in the case of Thomas). George's case is less
clear, because he might be taken to have an antecedent preference in favor
of green energy, but we could easily understand the narrative to mean that
his preference, like that of Mary and Thomas, is partly a product of the
default rule.

These are the situations on which I am now focusing: People lack an
antecedent preference, and what they like is a product of the nudge.
Their preference is constructed by it. After being nudged, they will be
happy and possibly grateful. We have also seen that even if people have
an antecedent preference, the nudge might change it so that they will be
happy and possibly grateful even if they did not want to be nudged in
advance.

In all of these cases, application of the AJBT criterion is less simple.
Choice architects cannot contend that they are merely vindicating choosers' ex ante preferences. If we look ex post, people do think that they are
better off, and in that sense the criterion is met. For use of the AJBT criterion, the challenge is that *however Mary and Thomas are nudged, they will
agree that they are better off.* In my view, there is no escaping at least some

kind of welfarist analysis in choosing between the two worlds in the cases of Mary and Thomas. We need to ask what kind of approach makes people's lives better. There is a large question about which nudge to choose in such cases. Nonetheless, the AJBT criterion remains relevant in the sense that it constrains what choice architects can do, even if it does not specify a unique outcome (as it does in cases in which people have clear ex ante preferences and in which the nudge does not alter them).

The AJBT criterion is emphatically not designed to defeat a charge of paternalism. It is psychologically fine (often) to think that choosers have antecedent preferences (whether or not "latent"), but that because of a lack of information or a behavioral bias, their choices will not satisfy them. (Recall the cases of Luke, Meredith, and Edna.) To be sure, it is imaginable that some forms of choice architecture will affect people who have information or lack such biases; a reasonable cafeteria visitor might grab the first item she sees because she is busy and because it is not worth it to her to decide which item to choose. Consider this case:

Regan enjoys her employer's cafeteria. She tends to eat high-calorie meals, but she knows that, and she likes them a lot. Her employer recently redesigned the cafeteria so that salads and fruits are the most visible and accessible. She now chooses salad and fruit, and she likes them a lot.

By stipulation, Regan suffers from no behavioral bias, but she is affected by the nudge. But in many (standard) cases, behaviorally biased or uninformed choosers will be affected by a nudge, and less biased and informed choosers will not; a developing body of literature explores how to proceed in such cases, with careful reference to what seems to me a version of the AJBT criterion.[6]

In Regan's case, and all those like it, the criterion does not leave choice architects at sea: if she did not like the salad, the criterion would be violated. From the normative standpoint, it may not be entirely comforting to say that nudges satisfy the AJBT criterion if choice architects succeed in altering the preferences of those whom they are targeting. (Is that a road to serfdom? Recall the chilling last lines of Orwell's *1984*: "He had won the victory over himself. He loved Big Brother.") But insofar as we are concerned with subjective welfare, it is a highly relevant question whether choosers believe, ex post, that the nudge has produced an outcome of which they approve.

Countless nudges increase navigability, writ large, in the sense that they enable people to get where they want to go and therefore enable them to satisfy their antecedent preferences. Many other nudges, helping to overcome self-control problems, are warmly welcomed by choosers and so are consistent with the AJBT criterion. Numerous people acknowledge that they suffer from such problems. When people lack antecedent preferences or when those preferences are not firm, and when a nudge constructs or alters their preferences, the AJBT criterion is more difficult to operationalize, and it may not lead to a unique solution. But it restricts the universe of candidate solutions, and in that sense helps to orient choice architects.

7 Nudges That Fail

No one should deny that some nudges are ineffective or counterproductive. For example, information disclosure might have little impact—certainly if it is too complicated for people to understand and sometimes even if it is simple and clear. If people are told about the number of calories in candy bars, they might not learn anything they do not already know, and even if they learn something, they might be unaffected. A reminder might fall on deaf ears; a warning might be ignored (or even make the target action more attractive). In some cases, a plausible (and abstractly correct) understanding of what drives human behavior turns out to be wrong in a particular context; once a nudge is tested, it turns out to have little or no impact.

In the terms made famous by Albert Hirschman, nudging might therefore be *futile*,[1] or at least close to it. Alternatively, its effects might also be *perverse*, in the sense that they might be the opposite of what is intended— as, for example, when calorie labels increase caloric intake. To complete Hirschman's trilogy, nudges may also *jeopardize* other important goals, as when a nudge designed to reduce pollution ends up increasing energy costs for the most disadvantaged members of society. Hirschman's main goal was to explore "the rhetoric of reaction"—the rhetorical arguments of those who seek to defend the status quo—not to suggest that futility, perversity, and jeopardy are inevitable or even likely. On the contrary, he saw them as predictable rhetorical moves, sometimes offered in bad faith. But there is no question that public-spirited reforms, including nudges, often run into each of the three objections. Futility, perversity, and jeopardy may reflect reality rather than rhetoric.

Of all of the tools in the choice architect's repertoire, default rules may be the most promising; they are almost certainly the most discussed. But sometimes they do very little, or at least far less than anticipated.[2] My principal goal here is to identify two reasons why this might be so. The first involves *strong contrary preferences on the part of the choosers*, which cause them to opt out. The second involves *counternudges, in the form of compensating behavior on the part of those whose economic interests are at stake.* To make a long story short, institutions may be able to move choosers in their preferred directions (often with the assistance of behavioral insights). As we shall see, these two explanations help account for the potential ineffectiveness of many other nudges as well, not only default rules.

It is a useful simplification to assume that in deciding whether to depart from default rules or to reject nudges of any kind, choosers consider two factors: the costs of decisions and the costs of errors. When it is not especially costly to decide to reject a nudge, and when choosers believe that doing so will reduce significant error costs, a nudge will be ineffective. We shall also see, though more briefly, other reasons that nudges might be ineffective; of these, the most important is the choice architect's use of a plausible (but ultimately mistaken) hypothesis about how choice architecture affects behavior.

If nudges do not work, there is of course the question what to do instead. The answer depends on normative criteria. A nudge might turn out to be ineffective, or far less effective than expected, but that might be a good thing; it might explain why choice architects chose a nudge rather than some other instrument (such as a mandate). Suppose that choice architects care about social welfare and that they want to increase it. If so, promoting welfare provides the right criterion, and effectiveness does not. By itself, the ineffectiveness of nudges—or for that matter their effectiveness—tells us little and perhaps even nothing about what has happened to social welfare. Imagine that 90 percent of a relevant population opts out of a default rule, so that the nudge is largely ineffective. Or imagine that 10 percent opts out or that 50 percent does. In all of these cases, choice architects must consider whether the result suggests that the nudge is, all things considered, a success or a failure. To undertake that consideration, they must ask particular questions about the consequences for social welfare.

One answer is that if a nudge is ineffective, or less effective than expected, it is because it is not a good idea for those who were unaffected by it. Its failure is instructive and on balance should be welcomed, in the sense that if choosers ignore or reject it, it is because they know best. That answer makes sense if ineffectiveness is *diagnostic*, in the sense that it demonstrates that people are acting in accordance with their (accurate) sense of what will promote their welfare. Sometimes that conclusion is correct, but for good behavioral reasons, sometimes it is not.

A second answer is to try a different kind of nudge. It is important to test behaviorally informed interventions and to learn from those tests; what is learned might well point in the direction of other nudges. That answer might be best if the people's choices (e.g., to ignore a warning or to opt out) are based on confusion, bias, or misunderstanding and if a better nudge might dispel one or all of these. Many nudges do not, in fact, raise hard normative questions. They are designed to promote behavior that is almost certainly in the interest of choosers or society as a whole; the failure of the nudge is not diagnostic. In such cases, a better nudge may well be the right response. If, for example, a warning fails, it might be a good idea to add a default rule.

A third answer is to undertake a more aggressive approach, going beyond a nudge, such as an economic incentive (a subsidy or a tax) or coercion. A more aggressive approach might make sense when the choice architect knows that the chooser is making a mistake or when the interests of third parties are involved. Some nudges are designed to protect such interests; consider environmental nudges or nudges that are intended to reduce crime. In such cases, choice-preserving approaches might well prove inadequate or at best complementary to incentives, mandates, and bans. I will return to this issue in chapter 10.

Why Default Rules Stick

Default rules are my principal topic here, and it makes sense to begin by explaining why such rules have such a large effect on outcomes. A great deal of research has explored three reasons.[3] The first involves inertia and procrastination (sometimes described as *effort* or an *effort tax*). To alter the default rule, people must make an active choice to reject that rule. Especially (but not only) if they are busy or if the question is difficult or technical, it is tempting to defer the decision or not to make it at all. In view of the power of inertia and the tendency to procrastinate, they might simply continue with the status quo. Attention is a scarce resource, and it is effortful to engage it; a default rule might stick because that effort does not seem to be worth undertaking.

The second factor involves what people might see as the informational signal that the default rule provides. If choice architects have explicitly chosen that rule, many people will believe that they have been given an implicit recommendation, and by people who know what they are doing (and who are not objectionably self-interested). If so, they might think that they should not depart from it and go their own way, unless they have private information that is reliable and that would justify a change. Going one's own way is risky, and people might not want to do it unless they are quite confident that they should.

The third factor involves loss aversion, one of the most important and robust findings in behavioral science: people dislike losses far more than they like corresponding gains.[4] For present purposes, the key point is that the default rule establishes the status quo; it determines the reference point for counting changes as losses or instead as gains. If, for example, people are not automatically enrolled in a savings plan, a decision to enroll might well seem to be a loss (of salary). If people are automatically enrolled, a decision to opt out might well seem to be a loss (of savings). The reference point is established by the default rule.

Strong Antecedent Preferences

To see why default rules may be ineffective, begin with the case of marital names.[5] When people marry, all states in the United States have the same default rule: both men and women retain their premarriage surnames. In the overwhelming majority of cases, American men do stick with the default. Relatively few men change their names. By contrast, the overwhelming majority of American women do change their name—for college graduates, eighty percent.[6] In that respect, the default rule seems to have relatively little impact on women. To be sure, the percentage of women who change their names might be even higher if they were defaulted into doing so. Nonetheless, it is revealing that most married women in the United States reject the default.

Why doesn't the default rule stick for American women? Four factors seem to be important. First and most important, many women strongly want to change their names, and their desire is not unclear. This is not a complex or unfamiliar area in which the default rule helps to construct people's preferences, in which people have vague or ambiguous preferences, or in which people have to work to ascertain their preferences. True, many women are undoubtedly affected by social norms, which some of them may wish to be otherwise; but with those norms in place, their preference is not unclear. When a social norm is strong, it may overwhelm the effect of the legal default rule; in fact, it might operate as the functional equivalent of such a rule—a point with general implications.[7]

Second, the issue is highly salient to married women. It is not exactly in the background. Because marriage is a defined and defining event, the timing of the required action is relatively clear. Procrastination and inertia are therefore less important; the effort tax is well worth incurring.

Third, the change of name is, for some or many of those who do it, a kind of celebration. It is not the sort of activity that most women seek to defer or see as an obligation or as a way of helping their future selves. If people affirmatively like to choose—if choosing is fun or meaningful—a supposed effort tax from the default rule is nothing of the sort. Its sign changes; it may even be a kind of effort subsidy. Sometimes choosing is a benefit rather than a burden.

Fourth, keeping one's name can impose costs, especially (but not only) if one has children. If a wife has a different name from her husband, or vice versa, it might be necessary to offer explanations and to dispel confusion. With some private and public institutions, offering those explanations might be burdensome and time-consuming. For some women, life is made more difficult if they do not have the same name as their husband. Social practices thus create a strong incentive to overcome the default. (To be sure, those practices are shifting, at least in some nations.) When the relevant conditions are met—strong preferences, clear timing, positive feelings about opt in, and greater ease and simplicity from opt in—the default rule is unlikely to matter much.

For present purposes, the central point is that strong preferences are likely to be sufficient to ensure that the default rule will not stick. In such cases, inertia will be overcome. People will not be much moved by any suggestion that might be reflected in the default rule (and in the particular context of marital names, the default probably offers no such suggestion).

Loss aversion will be far less relevant, in part because the clear preference and accompanying social norms, rather than the default rule, define the reference point from which losses are measured.

Consider four other examples, reflecting the importance of strong antecedent preferences:

1. A study in the United Kingdom found that most people opted out of a savings plan with an unusually high default contribution rate (12 percent of pretax income).[8] Only about 25 percent of employees remained at that rate after a year, whereas about 60 percent of employees shifted to a lower contribution rate. The default contribution rate was not entirely ineffective (25 percent is a large number), but it was far less effective than it would have been if the savings plan had a default contribution rate that fit more closely with people's preferences.

2. Many workers opt out if a significant fraction of their tax refund is defaulted into US savings bonds. In large numbers, they reject the default, apparently because they have definite plans to spend their refunds and do not have much interest in putting their tax refunds into savings bonds.[9] Their preferences are strong, and they predate the default rule.

3. Consistent with the standard finding of the effectiveness of defaults, a change in the default thermostat setting had a major effect on employees at the Organization for Economic Cooperation and Development (OECD).[10] During winter, a 1°C decrease in the default caused a significant reduction in the average setting. But when choice architects reduced the default setting by 2°C, *the reduction in the average setting was actually smaller*, apparently because sufficient numbers of employees thought that it was too cold and returned the setting to the one that they preferred. In the face of clear discomfort, inertia is overcome. From this finding, we might venture the following hypothesis, taken very broadly: People will be inclined to change a default rule if it makes them uncomfortably cold. To be sure, strong social norms or feelings of conscience[11] might counteract that effect—but they will have to be quite strong.

4. A great deal of work shows that the placement of food in cafeterias and grocery stores can have a large effect on what people choose. But there are limits to how much the placement of food can influence choices.[12] Rene A. de Wijk et al. sought to increase consumption of whole-grain bread, which

is generally healthier than other kinds of bread. For several weeks, they placed the whole-grain bread at the entrance to the bread aisle—the most visible location. And for different weeks, they placed it at the aisle's exit (the least visible location).

The behavioral prediction is that when whole-grain bread is more visible, more people will buy it. But there was no such effect. Whole grain accounted for about one-third of the bread sold—and it did not matter whether it was encountered first or last. As the authors suggest, the best explanation for their finding is that people know what bread they like, and they will choose it, whatever the architecture of the supermarket. Strong antecedent preferences trump the effect of the default rule. Note too the finding that while school children could well be nudged (through the functional equivalent of default rules) into healthier choices, researchers were not able to counteract the children's strong preference for (unhealthy) French fries.[13]

In all of these cases, it is a useful oversimplification to hypothesize that choosers are making a rational decision about whether to depart from a default based on the costs of decisions and the costs of errors. When a preference does not exist at all, or when it is weak, choosers will accept the default rule or decline to focus on it; attention is a limited resource, and people ought not to use it when they have no reason to do so. When a preference does not exist at all, or when it is weak, the informational signal contained in the default rule justifiably carries weight. But when choosers have a strong contrary preference, the cost of making the relevant decision is lower (because people already know what they think), and the cost of sticking with the default is higher (because people know that it points them in the wrong direction).

Any such analysis of costs and benefits is often intuitive and automatic rather than deliberative and reflective, and it might well involve heuristics and biases. For many choosers, inertia might well have more force than it should on the basis of a fully rational weighing of costs and benefits. Moreover, recent events in someone's life—involving, for example, a lack of available income in a certain period or a bad experience with a certain food—might trigger the availability heuristic and lead people wrongly to reject a default or any kind of choice architecture. The point is not that the decision to reject a default reflects an accurate calculation but that people may make either an intuitive (and fast) or a deliberative (and slow) judgment about whether to reject nudges.

Counternudges

Suppose that self-interested actors have a strong incentive to convince people (say, their customers) to opt in or out. If so, they might be able to take effective steps to achieve their goals. They might be able to persuade people to choose and thus to overcome the default, rendering it ineffective.[14] They undertake effective counternudges.

Consider the regulatory effort in 2010 by the Federal Reserve Board to protect consumers from high bank overdraft fees.[15] To provide that protection, the board did not impose any mandate but instead regulated the default rule. It said that banks could not automatically enroll people in overdraft "protection" programs; instead, customers had to sign up. More particularly, the board's regulation forbids banks from charging a fee for overdrafts from checking accounts unless the accountholder has explicitly enrolled in the bank's overdraft program.[16] One of the goals of the nonenrollment default rule is to protect customers, and especially low-income customers, from taking the equivalent of extraordinarily high-interest loans—indeed, loans with interest rates of up to 7,000 percent. The central idea is that many people end up paying large fees essentially by inadvertence. If the default rule is switched so that consumers end up in the program only if they really want to be, then they will benefit from a safeguard against excessive charges.

In principle, the regulation should have had a very large effect, and indeed, an understanding of the power of default rules helped to motivate its promulgation. The board explicitly observed that "studies have suggested consumers are likely to adhere to the established default rule, that is, the outcome that would apply if the consumer takes no action." The board also referred to research on the power of automatic enrollment to increase participation in retirement savings plans. It emphasized the phenomenon of unrealistic optimism, suggesting that consumers might well think, unrealistically, that they would not overdraw their accounts. No one argues that a default rule can entirely cure the problem of unrealistic optimism, but it can provide a remedy against its most serious harmful effects, at least if the default is sticky.

As Lauren Willis shows in an important article,[17] the effect of the regulation has not been nearly as large as might have been expected. The reason is that people are opting into the program, and thus rejecting the nonenrollment default, in large numbers. The precise figures remain unclear, but the overall level of opt in seems to be around 15 percent, and at some banks it is as high as 60 percent. Here is the most striking finding: among people who exceed the amount in their checking account more than ten times per month, the level appears to be over 50 percent.

A central reason is that many banks *want* to be able to charge overdraft fees and hence use a number of behaviorally informed strategies to facilitate opt in. For those who believe that opting in is a bad idea for many or most customers, this is a clear case of self-interested exploitation of behavioral findings. As Willis demonstrates, they have taken steps to make opt in as easy as possible—for example, simply by pushing a button on an ATM. They have also engaged in active marketing and created economic incentives to persuade people to opt in. They have cleverly exploited people's belief, which is often inaccurate, that it is costly not to be enrolled in the program. For example, they have sent materials explaining, "You can protect yourself from ... fees normally charged to you by merchants for returned items," and "The Bounce Overdraft Program was designed to protect you from the cost ... of having your transactions denied." They have sent their customers a great deal of material to persuade them that enrollment is in their economic interest.

Consider the following excerpt from one bank's marketing materials, explicitly exploiting loss aversion:

Yes: Keep my account working the same with Shareplus ATM and debit card overdraft coverage.

No: Change my account to remove Shareplus ATM and debit card overdraft coverage.[18]

There is a large contrast here with the retirement context, in which providers enthusiastically endorse automatic enrollment and have no interest in getting people to opt out. Those who run retirement plans are quite happy if more people are participating, and hence they are glad to work with employers, or the government, to promote enrollment. By contrast, the Federal Reserve Board called for a default that banks dislike, and at least to some extent, the banks have had their revenge. In the savings context, the default rule would not be nearly as sticky if providers wanted people to opt out.

From this illuminating tale, we can draw a general lesson, which is that if regulated institutions are strongly opposed to the default rule and have easy access to their customers, they may well be able to use a variety of strategies, including behavioral ones, to encourage people to move in the institution's preferred directions—and thus to abandon the default. In such cases, the default is ineffective not because choosers independently dislike it but because companies and firms convince them to choose to reject it. Here too it is useful to see people as making a slow or fast judgment about costs of decisions and the costs of errors, with the important twist that the targets of the default (for the most part, affected companies) work to decrease the (actual and perceived) costs of decisions and to increase the perceived costs of errors in order to render the nudge ineffective.

Consider the domain of privacy, in which many people also favor a particular default rule, one that will safeguard privacy unless people voluntarily choose to give it up.[19] If companies want people to relinquish privacy, they might well be able to convince them to do so—perhaps by using tactics akin to those of financial institutions in the Federal Reserve case, perhaps by denying people services or website access unless they waive their privacy rights.[20] Willis herself gives the example of the Netherlands, which created a "don't-track-me" default. As she explains, "virtually all firms (and even nonprofits) responded to the law by requiring consumers to opt out as a condition of using the firm's website, not by competing on promises not to track."[21]

The general point is plain: When default rules or other forms of choice architecture are ineffective, it is often because self-interested actors (e.g., cigarette companies) have the incentive and the opportunity to impose some kind of counternudge, leading people to choose in their preferred way.

What Should Be Done?

If a default rule proves ineffective, there are three possible responses. The first is to rest content on the ground that freedom worked. The second is to learn from the failure and to try a different kind of nudge, with continuing testing. The third is to take stronger measures—counter-counter-nudges, or even mandates and bans—on the ground that freedom caused a problem.

As we have seen, evaluation of these responses depends on normative considerations; the fact that a nudge has proved ineffective does not, by itself, tell us what else should be done. If a nudge has failed, we might conclude that on welfare grounds, nothing is amiss; people are going their own way, and perhaps that is fine. But many nudges are not controversial. They might be designed to encourage people to take very low-cost steps to improve their lives, and if they fail, people's lives will be worse. If choice architects have good reason to think that people's choices are not promoting their welfare, it is worth considering alternatives. And if the interests of third parties are at stake, the ineffectiveness of nudging may be a reason to consider mandates and bans (see chapter 10).

One clarification before we begin: It is important to consider the possibility of diverse responses within the affected population, and the aggregate effect may tell us far less than we need to know. Some nudges that seem ineffective overall might turn out to be have large effects on distinct subpopulations, during distinct time periods, or in specific contexts. Suppose, for example, that calorie labels have little or no effect on a large population. Even if this is so, it might be effective, in a relevant sense, if it has a significant impact on people with serious weight problems.

Or suppose that 40 percent of people opt out of a default rule—say, a rule calling for enrollment in pension or wellness plans. Those who opt out may be precisely the group that ought to opt out, given their preferences and situations; for example, young people who need money this month or this year might rationally opt out of a pension plan. Alternatively, the aggregate numbers may disguise a serious problem, as when the population that is unaffected by a nudge (say, by a warning or a reminder) includes those who would most benefit from it.

Freedom Worked

Suppose that default rules fail to stick because people do not like them. In such cases, the fact that they are mere defaults, rather than mandates, might be both good and important. Any default rule might be ill-chosen or might not fit individual circumstances. If so, the fact that people can reject it is a valuable safeguard. In the case of very large default contribution rates, that claim seems quite plausible. Or consider a situation in which an institute adopts a default rule in favor of double-sided printing and many people switch to single-sided: if the latter fits their situations, there is no problem.

Something similar might well be said if and when self-interested institutions that are burdened by a default rule use counternudges to convince people to reject it. The tale of overdraft protection seems to be one of regulatory failure or at least of incomplete success, but things are not so clear.

Recall that many people (perhaps as high as 85 percent) do not opt in to the program. Recall too that the largest proportion of people who do opt in are those who go over their checking limits. For such people, it is not implausible to think that opt in is a good idea. At least some of them, or perhaps the majority, might well be rational to make that choice. If they cannot borrow from their bank—and overdraft protection is a form of borrowing—they might have to borrow from someone else, which would mean a level of inconvenience and at least potentially even higher interest rates. If so, many people might have to resort to payday lenders, whose rates may or may not be lower.

Because inconvenience can be a real problem and because higher rates might hit people especially hard, overdraft protection might well be in the interest of many or most of the people who end up opting in. Note in this regard that state-level regulation of payday lenders has led consumers to have to resort to equally expensive sources of credit.[22] This finding strongly suggests that if people cannot use overdraft protection, they might simply go elsewhere.

With this point in mind, we might even think that the Federal Reserve's policy has been a significant success. People are no longer automatically enrolled in overdraft protection, and the vast majority of customers no longer have such protection, which may well be saving them money. At the same time, those who want such protection, or need it, have signed up for it. That sounds like a success for nudging, all things considered. Is there really a problem? That question can be asked whenever institutions succeed in convincing people to opt out of a default rule. Such institutions might be self-interested, but they might also be producing mutually advantageous deals. To know, we need to investigate the details. Who is getting what? Who might be losing?

The same points might be made if people reject a default rule in favor of protection of privacy in online behavior. Perhaps that form of privacy does not much matter to people. Perhaps those who want them to waive it can offer something to make doing so worth their while. A default rule gives people a kind of entitlement, and entitlements have prices. If people are willing to give up an entitlement for what seems to be a satisfactory price, where is the objection? A counternudge might be quite welcome.

Nudge Better

Choice architects might have started with a hypothesis, which is that a nudge—say, disclosure of information—will change behavior in a desirable direction. Perhaps the hypothesis was plausible, but turns out to be wrong. Once people are given more information, they keep doing exactly what they have been doing.

Again, the failure of the hypothesis does not, by itself, tell us whether something else should be done. Perhaps people are given a warning about the risks associated with some anticancer drug; perhaps they continue to use the drug in spite of the warning. If so, there might be no problem at all. The goal of the warning is to ensure that choices are informed, not that they are different. If people's behavior does not change after they receive information about the risks associated with certain activities (say, football or boxing), nothing might have gone wrong.

Suppose, however, that the underlying problem is significant, and that once people are informed, we have every reason to think at least some of them should do something different. Perhaps people are not applying for benefits for which an application would almost certainly be in their interest. Perhaps they are failing to engage in behavior that would much improve their economic situation or their health (say, taking prescription medicine or seeing a doctor). If so, then other nudges might be tried and tested instead—for example, a clearer warning, uses of social norms, or a default rule. By itself, information might not trigger people's attention, and some other approach might be superior. And if a default rule fails, it might make sense to accompany it with information or with warnings. There may well be no alternative but to experiment and to test—to identify a way to nudge better.

Consider a few possibilities. We have seen that if the goal is to change behavior, choice architects should "make it easy"; in the case of an ineffective nudge, the next step might be to "make it even easier." Information disclosure might be ineffective if it is complex but succeed if it is simple. A reminder might fail if it is long and poorly worded but succeed if it is short and vivid. We have also seen that people's acts often depend on their social meaning, which can work like a subsidy or a tax; if a nudge affects meaning, it can change a subsidy into a tax or vice versa. For example, certain kinds of information disclosure, and certain kinds of warnings, can make risk-taking behavior seem silly, stupid, or uncool. A nudge might be altered so that it affects social meaning in the desired direction. Publicizing social norms might move behavior, but only if they are the norms in a particular community, not in the nation as a whole. If publicizing national norms does not work, it might make sense to focus on those that have sway in the relevant community.

Freedom Failed

In some cases, freedom of choice itself might be an ambiguous good. For behavioral or other reasons, an apparently welcome and highly effective counternudge, leading consumers or employees in certain directions, might turn out to be welfare reducing. In extreme cases, it might ruin their lives. People might suffer from present bias, optimistic bias, or a problem of self-control. The counternudge might exploit a behavioral bias of some kind. What might be necessary is some kind of counter-counternudge—for example, a reminder or a warning to discourage people from opting into a program that generally is not in their interest.

In the case of overdraft protection programs, some of those who opt in and who end up receiving that protection are probably worse off as a result. Perhaps they do not understand the program and its costs; perhaps they were duped by a behaviorally informed messaging campaign. Perhaps they are at risk of overdrawing their accounts not because they need a loan, but because they have not focused on those accounts and on how they are about to go over. Perhaps they are insufficiently informed or attentive. To evaluate the existing situation, we need to know a great deal about the population of people who opt in. In fact this is often the key question, and it is an empirical one. The fact that they have opted in is not decisive.

The example can be taken as illustrative. If a default rule or some other nudge is well-designed to protect people from their own mistakes and it does not stick, then its failure is nothing to celebrate. The fact of its ineffectiveness is a tribute to the success of a self-interested actor seeking to exploit behavioral biases. The counternudge is a form of manipulation or exploitation, something to counteract rather than to celebrate. Perhaps the counternudge encourages people to smoke or to drink excessively; perhaps it undoes the effect of the nudge, causing premature deaths in the process.

The same point applies to strong antecedent preferences, which might be based on mistakes of one or another kind. A GPS device is a defining nudge, and if people reject the indicated route on the ground that they know better, they might end up lost. The general point is that if the decision to opt out is a blunder for many or most, then there is an argument for a more aggressive approach. The overdraft example demonstrates the importance of focusing not only on default rules, but also on two other kinds of rules as well, operating as counter-counternudges: altering rules and framing rules.[23]

Altering rules establish how people can change the default. If choice architects want to simplify people's decisions, and if they lack confidence about whether a default is suitable for everyone, they might say that consumers can opt in or opt out by making an easy phone call (good) or by sending a quick email (even better). Alternatively, choice architects, confident that the default is right for the overwhelming majority of people, might increase the costs of departing from it. For example, they might require people to fill out complex forms or impose a cooling-off period. They might also say that even if people make a change, the outcome will "revert" to the default after a certain period (say, a year), requiring repeated steps. Or they might require some form of education or training, insisting on a measure of learning before people depart from the default.

Framing rules establish and regulate the kinds of "frames" that people can use when they try to convince people to opt in or opt out. We have seen that financial institutions enlisted loss aversion in support of opt in. Behaviorally informed strategies of this kind could turn out to be highly effective. But that is a potential problem. Even if they are not technically deceptive, they might count as manipulative, and they might prove harmful. Those who believe in freedom of choice but seek to avoid manipulation or harm might want to constrain the permissible set of frames—subject, of course, to existing safeguards for freedom of speech. Framing rules might be used to reduce the risk of manipulation.

Consider an analogy. If a company says that its product is "90 percent fat-free," people are likely to be drawn to it, far more so than if the company says that its product is "10 percent fat." The two phrases mean the same thing, and the 90 percent fat-free frame is legitimately seen as a form of manipulation. In 2011, the American government allowed companies to say that their products are 90 percent fat-free—but only if they also say that they are 10 percent fat. We could imagine similar constraints on misleading or manipulative frames that are aimed to get people to opt out of the default. Alternatively, choice architects might use behaviorally informed strategies of their own, supplementing a default rule with, say, uses of loss aversion or social norms to magnify its impact.[24]

To the extent that choice architects are in the business of choosing among altering rules and framing rules, they can take steps to make default rules more likely to stick, even if they do not impose mandates. They might conclude that mandates and prohibitions would be a terrible idea, but that it makes sense to make it harder for people to depart from default rules. Sometimes that is the right conclusion. The problem is that when choice architects move in this direction, they lose some of the advantages of default rules, which have the virtue of easy reversibility, at least in principle. If the altering rules are made sufficiently onerous, the default rule might not be all that different from a mandate.

There is another possibility: Choice architects might venture a more personalized approach. They might learn that one default rule suits one group of people and that another suits a different group; by tailoring default rules to diverse situations, they might have a larger effect than they would with a mass default rule.[25] Or they might learn that an identifiable subgroup is opting out, either for good reasons or for bad ones. (Recall that aggregate effectiveness data might disguise very large effects or very small ones for relevant subgroups.) If the reasons do not seem good, choice architects might adopt altering rules or framing rules as safeguards, or they might enlist, say, information and warnings. If they can be made to work well, more personalized approaches have the promise of preserving freedom of choice while simultaneously increasing effectiveness.

But preserving freedom of choice might not be a good idea. Indeed, we can easily imagine cases in which a mandate or ban might be justified on behavioral or other grounds. Most democratic nations have mandatory social security systems, based in part on a belief that "present bias" is a potent force and a conclusion that some level of compulsory savings is justified on welfare grounds. Food-safety regulations forbid people from buying goods that pose risks that reasonable people would not run. Such regulations might be rooted in a belief that consumers lack relevant information (and it is too difficult or costly to provide it to them), or they might be rooted in a belief that people suffer from limited attention or optimistic bias. Some medicines are not allowed to enter the market, and for many others a prescription is required; people are not permitted to purchase them on their own.

Many occupational safety and health regulations ultimately have a paternalistic justification, and they take the form of mandates and bans, not nudges. Consider, for example, the domains of fuel economy and energy efficiency. To be sure, they reduce externalities in the form of conventional air pollutants, greenhouse gases, and energy insecurity. But if we consider only those externalities, the benefits of those requirements are usually lower than the costs. The vast majority of the monetized benefits accrue to consumers, in the form of reduced costs of gasoline and energy.

On standard economic grounds, those benefits should not count in the analysis of costs and benefits, because consumers can obtain them through their own free choices; if they are not doing so, it must be because the relevant goods (automobiles, refrigerators) are inferior along some dimension. The US government's current response is behavioral; it is that in the domain of fuel economy and energy efficiency, consumers are making some kind of mistake, perhaps because of present bias, perhaps because of a lack of sufficient salience. Some people contest this argument. But if it is correct, the argument for some kind of mandate is secure on welfare grounds. (I return to this issue in chapter 10.)

The same analysis holds, and more simply, if the interests of third parties are involved. Default rules are typically meant to protect choosers, but in some cases, third parties are the real concern. For example, a green default rule, designed to prevent environmental harm, is meant to reduce externalities and to solve a collective action problem, not to protect choosers as such. A nudge, in the form of information disclosure or a default rule, is not the preferred approach to pollution (including carbon emissions). If a nudge is to be used, it is because it is a complement to more aggressive approaches or because such approaches are not feasible (perhaps for political reasons). But if a default rule proves ineffective—for one or another of the reasons sketched here—there will be a strong argument for economic incentives, mandates, and bans.

Further Considerations

Default rules are often thought to be the most effective nudge—but for two reasons, they might not have the expected impact. The first involves strong antecedent preferences. The second involves the use of counternudges by those with an economic or other interest in convincing choosers to opt out.

These two reasons help account for the potential ineffectiveness of nudges in many other contexts. Information, warnings, and reminders will not work if people are determined to engage in the underlying behavior (smoking, drinking, texting while driving, eating unhealthy foods). And if, for example, cigarette companies and sellers of alcoholic beverages have opportunities to engage choosers, they might be able to weaken or undo the effects of information, warnings, and reminders.

It is important to observe that nudges may be ineffective for independent reasons. Consider five.

1. If a nudge is based on a plausible but inaccurate understanding of behavior and of the kinds of things to which people respond, it might have no impact. This is an especially important point, and it suggests the immense importance of testing apparently reasonable behavioral hypotheses. We might believe, for example, that because people are loss averse, a warning about potential losses will change behavior. But if such a warning frightens people or makes them think that they cannot engage in self-help, and essentially freezes them, then we might see little or no change. We might believe that people are not applying for important services because of excessive complexity and that simplification will make a big difference. But perhaps it will not; skepticism, fear, or inertia might be the problem, and simplification might not much help.

Or we might hypothesize that an understanding of social norms will have a large effect on what people do. But if the target audience is indifferent to (general) social norms and is happy to defy them, then use of social norms might have no impact. Some nudges seem promising because of their effects on small or perhaps idiosyncratic populations. Whether their impact will diminish or be eliminated when applied elsewhere is a question that needs to be tested. It is true that the failure of a behavioral hypothesis should pave the way to alternative or more refined hypotheses, including a specification of the circumstances in which the original hypothesis will or will not hold.

2. If information is confusing or complex to process, people might be unaffected by it. There is a lively debate about the general effectiveness of disclosure strategies; some people are quite skeptical. What seems clear is that the design of such strategies is extremely important. Disclosure nudges, or

educative nudges in general, may have far less impact than one might think in the abstract.[26]

3. People might show *reactance* to some nudges, rejecting an official effort to steer *because* it is an official effort to steer. Most work on the subject of reactance explores how people rebel against mandates and bans because they wish to maintain control.[27] Default rules are not mandates, and hence it might be expected that reactance would be a nonissue. But as for mandates, so for defaults: they might prove ineffective if people are angry or resentful that they have been subjected to it. So too, an effort to invoke social norms might not work if people do not care about social norms or if they want to defy them. We are at the early stages of learning about the relationship between reactance and nudges, and thus far it seems safe to say that, for the most part, reactance is not likely to be an issue, simply because autonomy is preserved. But in some cases, it might prove to be important (see chapter 9 for more details).

4. Nudges might have only a short-term effect.[28] If people see a single reminder, they might pay attention to it—but only once. If people receive information about health risks, their behavior might be influenced—but after a time, that information might become something like background noise or furniture. It might cease to be salient or meaningful. Even a graphic warning might lose its resonance after a time. By contrast, a default rule is more likely to have a persistent effect, because people have to work to change it—but after a while, its informational signal might become muted, or inertia might be overcome. We continue to learn about the circumstances in which a nudge is likely to produce long-term effects.[29]

5. Some nudges might have an influence on the desired conduct but also produce compensating behavior, nullifying the overall effect. Suppose, for example, that smart cafeteria design can lead high school students to eat healthy foods. Suppose too that such students eat unhealthy foods at snack time, at dinner, or after school hours. If so, the nudge will not improve public health. There is a general risk of a "rebound effect"—as, for example, when fuel-efficient cars lead people to drive more, reducing and potentially nullifying the effects of interventions designed to increase fuel efficiency. Perhaps a nudge will encourage people to exercise more than they now do, but perhaps they will react by eating more.

The general point is that any form of choice architecture, including the use of default rules, may have little or no effect on net if people are able to find other domains in which to counteract it. The idea of compensating behavior can be seen as a subset of the general category of strong antecedent preferences, but it points to a more specific case, in which the apparent success of the nudge is an illusion in terms of what choice architects actually care about. Recall the risk that a nudge will have unintended side effects, including unwelcome distributional consequences—as, for example, when environmental nudges impose costs on people who are not easily able to afford them. As noted, this is Hirschman's notion of jeopardy.

What matters is welfare, not effectiveness. A largely ineffective nudge may have positive welfare effects; an effective nudge might turn out to reduce welfare. A strong reason for nudges, as distinguished from more aggressive tools, is that they preserve freedom of choice and thus allow people to go their own way. In many contexts, that is indeed a virtue, and the ineffectiveness of nudges, for some or many, is nothing to lament. But when choosers are making clear errors, and when third-party effects are involved, the ineffectiveness of nudges provides a good reason to consider stronger measures on welfare grounds.

8 Ethics

No one should doubt that certain nudges, and certain kinds of choice architecture, can raise serious ethical questions. Consider, for example, a government that used nudges to promote discrimination on the basis of race, sex, or religion. Even truthful information (e.g., about crime rates) might fan the flames of violence and prejudice. Groups or nations that are committed to violence often enlist nudges in their cause. Even when nudges do not have illicit ends, it is possible to wonder whether those who enlist them are treating people with respect.

Possible concerns about nudging and choice architecture point to four foundational commitments: (1) welfare, (2) autonomy, (3) dignity, and (4) self-government. Some nudges could run afoul of one or more of these commitments. It is easy to identify welfare-reducing nudges that lead people to waste time or money; an unhelpful default rule could fall in that category, as could an educational campaign designed to persuade people to purchase excessive insurance or to make foolish investments. Nudges could be, and often are, harmful to the environment. Excessive pollution is, in part, a product of unhelpful choice architecture.

Consider in this light a tale from the novelist David Foster Wallace: "There are these two young fish swimming along and they happen to meet an older fish swimming the other way, who nods at them and says 'Morning, boys. How's the water?' And the two young fish swim on for a bit, and then eventually one of them looks over at the other and goes 'What the hell is water?'"[1] This is a tale about choice architecture. Such architecture is inevitable, whether or not we see it. It is the equivalent of water. Weather is itself a form of choice architecture, because it influences what people decide.[2] Human beings cannot live without some kind of weather. Nature nudges.

We can imagine the following view: Choice architecture is unavoidable, to be sure, but it might be the product of nature or some kind of spontaneous order, rather than of conscious design or of the action of any designer. Invisible-hand mechanisms often produce choice architecture. Alternatively, choice architecture might be the product of a genuinely random process (and a choice architect might intentionally opt for randomness, on the ground that it has a kind of neutrality).

On certain assumptions, self-conscious choice architecture is especially dangerous, because it is explicitly and intentionally directed at achieving certain goals. But what are those assumptions, and are they likely to be true? Why and when would spontaneous order be benign? (Is there some kind of social Darwinism here?) What is so good about randomness? We should agree that a malevolent choice architect, aware of the power of nudges, could produce a great deal of harm. But the most serious harms tend to come from mandates and bans—from coercion—not from nudges, which maintain freedom of choice.

It is true that spontaneous orders, invisible hands, and randomness can avoid some of the serious dangers, and some of the distinctive biases, that come from self-conscious nudging on the part of government. People might be especially averse to intentional nudges. If we are especially fearful of official mistakes—coming from incompetence or bad motivations—we will want to minimize the occasions for nudging. And if we believe that invisible-hand mechanisms promote welfare or freedom, we will not want to disturb their products, even if those products include nudges. But a degree of official nudging cannot be avoided.

In this chapter, I will offer seven principal conclusions:

1. It is pointless to object to choice architecture or nudging as such. The private sector inevitably nudges, as does the government. We can object to particular nudges and particular goals of choice architects and particular forms of choice architecture, but not to nudging and choice architecture in general. For human beings (or for that matter dogs and cats and mice), choice architecture cannot be avoided. It is tempting to defend nudging on the part of government by saying that the private sector already nudges (sometimes selfishly, even in competitive markets). On certain assumptions, this defense might be right, but it is not necessary because the government is nudging even if it does not want to do so.

2. In this context, ethical abstractions (e.g., about autonomy, dignity, and manipulation) can create serious confusion. We need to bring those abstractions into contact with concrete practices. Nudging takes many diverse forms, and the force of an ethical objection depends on specific form.

3. If welfare is our guide, much nudging is required on ethical grounds.

4. If autonomy is our guide, much nudging is also required on ethical grounds.

5. Choice architecture should not, and need not, compromise either dignity or self-government, though imaginable forms could do both.

6. Many nudges are objectionable because the choice architect has illicit ends. If the ends are legitimate, and if nudges are fully transparent and subject to public scrutiny, a convincing ethical objection is far less likely to be available.

7. There is, however, room for such an objection in the case of highly manipulative interventions, certainly if people have not consented to them. The concept of manipulation deserves careful attention, especially because of its relationship to the ideas of autonomy and dignity.

The Dangers of Abstraction

I have noted that in behavioral science, it has become standard to distinguish between two families of cognitive operations: System 1, which is fast, automatic, and intuitive, and System 2, which is slow, calculative, and deliberative.[3] System 2 can and does err, but System 1 is distinctly associated with identifiable behavioral biases. Some nudges attempt to strengthen the hand of System 2 by improving the role of deliberation and people's considered judgments—as, for example, through disclosure strategies and the use of precommitment. Other nudges are designed to appeal to, or to activate, System 1—as in the cases of graphic health warnings. Some nudges work because of the operation of System 1—as, for example, when default rules have large effects because of the power of inertia.

A nudge might be justified on the ground that it helps counteract a behavioral bias, but (and this is an important point) such a bias is *not* a necessary justification for a nudge. Disclosure of information can be helpful even in the absence of any bias. GPS is useful even for people who do not suffer from present bias, probability neglect, or unrealistic optimism. A default rule simplifies life and might therefore be desirable whether or not a behavioral bias is involved.

As the GPS example suggests, many nudges have the goal of *increasing navigability*—of making it easier for people to get to their preferred destination. Such nudges stem from an understanding that life can be simple or hard to navigate, and a goal of helpful choice architecture is desirable as a way of promoting simple navigation. To date, there has been far too little attention to the close relationship between navigability and (good) nudges. Insofar as the goal is to promote navigability, the ethical objections are greatly weakened.

It must be acknowledged that choice architecture can be altered, and new nudges can be introduced, for illicit reasons. Indeed, many of the most powerful objections to nudges, and to changes in choice architecture, are based on a judgment that the underlying motivations are illicit. With these points, there is no objection to nudges as such; the objection is to the grounds for the particular nudges.

For example, an imaginable default rule might skew the democratic process by saying that voters are presumed to vote to support the incumbent politician, unless they specify otherwise. Such a rule would violate principles of neutrality that are implicit in democratic norms; it would be unacceptable for that reason. Alternatively, a warning might try to frighten people about the supposedly nefarious plans of members of a minority group. Social norms might be used to encourage people to buy unhealthy products. In extreme cases, private or public institutions might try to nudge people toward violence.

It must also be acknowledged that the best choice architecture often calls for active choosing. Sometimes the right approach is to *require* people to choose, so as to ensure that their will is actually expressed. Sometimes it is best to *prompt* choice, by asking people what they want, without imposing any requirement that they do so. A prompt is emphatically a nudge, designed to get people to express their will, and it might be unaccompanied by any effort to steer people in a preferred direction—except in the direction of choosing.

Choice architecture should be transparent and subject to public scrutiny, especially if public officials are responsible for it. In general, regulations should be subject to a period of public comment. If officials alter a default rule so as to promote clean energy or conservation, they should not hide what they are doing. Self-government itself requires public scrutiny of nudges—a form of choice architecture for choice architects. Such scrutiny is an important ex ante safeguard against harmful nudges; it is also an important ex post corrective. Transparency and public scrutiny can reduce the likelihood of welfare-reducing choice architecture and of nudges that threaten autonomy or dignity. Nations should also treat their citizens with respect, and public scrutiny shows a measure of respect.

There is a question whether transparency and public scrutiny are sufficient rather than merely necessary. The answer is that they are not sufficient. We could imagine forms of choice architecture that would be unacceptable even if they were fully transparent; consider (transparent) architecture designed to entrench inequality on the basis of sex. Here again, the problem is that the goals of the relevant nudge are illicit. As we shall see, it is also possible to imagine cases of manipulation, in which the goals are not illicit but the fact of transparency might not be sufficient to justify a nudge.

Recall at this point that choice architecture is inevitable. Any website nudges; so does a cell phone or a computer; so do lawyers and doctors. A doctor can try to present options in a neutral way so as to respect patient autonomy, but that is a form of choice architecture, not an alternative to it. Whenever government has websites, offices, or programs, it creates choice architecture, and it will nudge.

It is true that in the face of error, education might be the best response. Some people argue in favor of educational interventions in lieu of nudges. In a way, the opposition is confusing; at least some such interventions fit the definition of a nudge, and they are certainly a form of choice architecture. When education is favored, a natural question arises: Favored over what?

In some cases, a default rule would be preferable to education because it would preserve desirable outcomes (again, from the standpoint of choosers themselves) without requiring people to take the functional equivalent of a course in, say, statistics or finance.[4] For those who purchase cell phones, tablets, and computers, it would be impossibly demanding to insist on the kind of education that would allow active choices about all relevant features. Much of life is feasible because products and activities come with default rules and people are not required to undergo some kind of instruction before selecting them. There is a recurring question whether the costs of education justify the benefits in particular circumstances. Default rules may well be best.

Although choice architecture and nudging are inevitable, some nudges are certainly avoidable. A government might decide not to embark on a campaign to discourage smoking or unhealthy eating. It might refrain from nudging people toward certain investment behavior. To that extent, it is reasonable to wonder whether government should minimize nudging. If we distrust the motives of public officials or believe that their judgments are likely to go wrong, we will favor such minimization. Some of the ethical objections to choice architecture and to nudging are best understood as a plea for minimization, not elimination. In fact the plea might well be more precise than that. At least in some cases, it is a claim that government should avoid particular interventions that are taken to be manipulative and hence to compromise both autonomy and dignity.

Seven Objections

Here is a catalog of potential objections to nudges as such: (1) Nudges are paternalistic. (2) Some nudges intrude on people's autonomy. (3) Some nudges might be seen as coercive, even if they preserve freedom of choice as a technical matter. (4) Some nudges insult people's dignity; they might be infantilizing; they might treat people as children. The idea of the "nanny state" captures this objection. (5) Some nudges could count as forms of manipulation. It is relevant in this regard that nudging is not always transparent. Consider, for example, *negative option marketing*, by which people who purchase certain products find themselves enrolled in programs for which they pay a monthly fee. Nudges of this kind might be said to operate behind people's backs. (6) Some nudges impede or at least do not promote learning. (7) Choice architects may err, especially when they work for government, and for that reason, it is best to avoid nudging (to the extent that this is possible).

It is important not to take these concerns as all-purpose objections to efforts to improve choice architecture. Does any of these objections make sense as applied to initiatives to promote active choosing? To inform consumers of the caloric content of food, to remind people that a bill is due, or to ask people whether they want to enroll in a retirement plan? We might be skeptical about the force of these concerns as applied to the overwhelming majority of real-world nudges. But let us take the objections in sequence.

Paternalism

If paternalism is objectionable, it is because it runs afoul of some kind of foundational commitment or principle. For example, it might undermine autonomy. Although the term is often used as a freestanding objection, the real complaint is that paternalism, in general or in particular circumstances, violates a principle that people rightly value.

Choice architecture may or may not be paternalistic. But it is true that nudges can be seen as a form of "libertarian paternalism" insofar as they attempt to use choice architecture to steer choosers in directions that will promote their welfare (as judged by choosers themselves). A GPS device can be so understood, and the same is true for a reminder, a warning, a use of social norms, and a default rule.

This is a distinctive form of paternalism in the sense that it is (a) soft and (b) means-oriented. It is *soft* insofar as it avoids coercion or material incentives, and thus fully maintains freedom of choice. It is *means-oriented* insofar as it does not attempt to question or alter people's ends. Like a GPS device, it respects those ends. To those who object to paternalism, the most serious concerns arise in the face of coercion (where freedom of choice is blocked) and when social planners, or choice architects, do not respect people's ends. To this extent, nudges aspire to avoid some of the standard ethical objections to paternalism.

Nonetheless, some skeptics object to paternalism as such. Many of those objections point to individual welfare and to the risk that planners or choice architects will compromise it. Perhaps people are the best judges not only of their ends but also of the best means to achieve those ends, given their own tastes and values. People might reject the route suggested by a GPS device on the ground that they prefer the scenic alternative; the GPS device might not easily capture or serve their ends. A coercive GPS device would, in some cases, intrude on people's ends.

Moreover, the distinction between means and ends is not always simple and straightforward. One question is the level of abstraction at which we describe people's ends. If we describe people's ends at a level of great specificity—eating that brownie, having that cigarette, texting while driving—then people's means effectively *are* their ends. The brownie is exactly what they want; it is not a means to anything at all (except the experience of eating it).

If we describe people's ends at a level of high abstraction—"having a good life"—then nearly everything is a means to those ends. But if we do that, then we will not be capturing people's actual concerns; we will be disregarding what really matters to them. These points do raise some problems for those who favor a solely means-oriented form of paternalism. They must be careful to ensure that they are not describing people's ends at a sufficiently high level of abstraction as to misconceive what people care about.

But insofar as a GPS device is a guiding analogy, and insofar as freedom of choice is fully maintained, it is not easy to see nudges as objectionably paternalistic. At least some nudges are entirely focused on means. Consider cases in which people are *mistaken about facts* (with respect to the characteristics of, say, a consumer product or an investment). If a nudge informs them, then it is respecting their ends. Or suppose that people suffer from a behavioral bias—perhaps because they use the availability heuristic, perhaps because of unrealistic optimism. A nudge that corrects their mistake can help them to achieve their ends.

To be sure, some behavioral biases are not easy to analyze in these terms. If people suffer from present bias, is a nudge a form of paternalism about means? Suppose that people eat high-calorie food or drink a great deal or fail to exercise because they value today and tomorrow, and not so much next year or next decade. If a nudge succeeds in getting people to focus on their long-term interests, it might increase aggregate (intrapersonal) welfare over time. But is such a nudge focused solely on means? If a person is seen as a series of selves extending over time, the choice architect is effectively redistributing welfare from earlier selves to later ones (and by hypothesis maximizing welfare as well). But it is not clear that we can speak, in such cases, of means paternalism. And if a person is seen as continuous over time, and not a series of selves, efforts to counteract present bias are, by hypothesis, undermining the ends of the chooser at the time of choice. It is hard to question whether the relevant ends are those that the chooser has at that time or at a later time or whether it is best (as I tend to think) to identify the chooser's ends by focusing on some aggregation or index of selves over a lifetime.

Let us bracket the most difficult issues and acknowledge that some forms of choice architecture count as paternalistic. Is that a problem? As we have seen, one reason to reject paternalism involves welfare: Perhaps people are the best judges of what will promote their interests, and perhaps outsiders will blunder (as Mill believed). Consider Hayek's remarkable suggestion that "the awareness of our irremediable ignorance of most of what is known to somebody [who is a chooser] is *the chief basis of the argument for liberty*."[5] Hayek was speaking of welfare, not autonomy. He was suggesting that the "somebody," acting as chooser, would inevitably know more than "we" know. Consider someone who is choosing what to eat for lunch, where to live, who to date, what job to take. A form of paternalism that maintains liberty and that is focused on means is less likely to be objectionable on welfare grounds. An understanding of behavioral biases suggests that people might err with respect to means; but an appreciation of the special knowledge of choosers suggests that we should respect their judgments about their ends.

A possible response is that even means-oriented nudges will be inadequately informed, at least if they come from government. When public officials produce default rules, they might steer people in bad directions; when they inform people, they might tell them something that is false, or that it is not useful to know. If we are deeply skeptical of the good faith and competence of public officials, we will want to minimize official nudges and we will prefer choice architecture that comes from invisible hands and spontaneous orders.

This view cannot be ruled out in the abstract. It depends on certain assumptions about the risk of government error; whether or not it is right, it is not clear that it should be counted as a distinctly *ethical* objection. Nor it is clear that it should count as an objection to efforts to increase navigability, unless we think that those efforts are themselves likely to be misconceived.

In the face of ignorance of fact and behavioral biases, some welfarists are drawn to coercive paternalism.[6] When paternalism would improve welfare, welfarists should support it. For welfarists, there is a good argument that paternalism, hard or soft, should be evaluated on a case-by-case basis— unless there is some systematic, or rule-welfarist, justification for a principle or presumption against paternalism.

There may be good reason for such a presumption, rooted in a judgment that choosers are likely to have better information than choice architects. But in some cases, that judgment is incorrect, because choosers lack, and choice architects have, accurate knowledge of relevant facts. There are serious risks in using this point as a reason for coercion, at least when the interests of third parties are not involved. The advantage of nudges is that they reduce those risks, because people are allowed to go their own way (see chapter 10 for discussion).

In the face of missing information, information-providing nudges are a natural corrective. But in some cases, a good default rule—say, automatic enrollment in pension programs—is hard to reject on welfarist grounds. To be sure, active choosing might be better, but that conclusion is not obvious; much depends on the costs of decisions and the costs of errors. Welfarists might well be inclined to favor choice-preserving approaches, on the theory that individuals usually know well what best fits their circumstances, but default rules preserve choice; the fact that they have a paternalistic dimension should not be decisive against them.

Another reason to reject paternalism involves autonomy and the idea of respect for persons. Stephen Darwell writes that the "objectionable character of paternalism of this sort is not that those who seek to benefit us against our wishes are likely to be wrong about what really benefits us.... It is, rather, primarily a failure of respect, a failure to recognize the authority that persons have to demand, within certain limits, that they be allowed to make their own choices for themselves."[7] This brings us to the next objection.

Autonomy

Do nudges intrude on autonomy? Recall that nudges are inevitable, so in a sense the question is confusing. It appears to be premised on a judgment that existing nudges do not compromise autonomy and that a new nudge, proposed or actual, would introduce nudging where it did not exist before. That is a mistake. The real question is whether particular nudges intrude on autonomy.

In any case, autonomy requires informed choices, and many nudges are specifically designed to ensure that choices are informed. In the face of a lack of information, a behavioral bias, or some kind of systematic mistake (by the actor's own reflective lights), it is hardly clear that a nudge, taken as such, infringes on autonomy, rightly understood. And when social contexts are not navigable, a nudge that improves navigability increases autonomy rather than undermining it. A GPS device does not create a problem from the standpoint of autonomy, nor does a user-friendly computer, nor does an effort to simplify a mortgage or a credit card agreement.

It is also important to see that autonomy does not require choices everywhere; it does not justify an insistence on active choosing in all contexts. If people have to make choices everywhere, their autonomy is reduced, if only because they cannot devote attention to those activities that seem to them most worthy of their attention. There is a close relationship between time management and autonomy. To the extent that nudges reduce the difficulty of time management, they increase an important form of autonomy.

It is nonetheless true that on grounds of autonomy and welfare, the best choice architecture often calls for active choosing. Default rules might intrude on autonomy, especially if they do not track people's likely (informed) choices. It is important to remember that because of the force of inertia, people might not reject harmful defaults. If so, there is an intrusion on their autonomy because they will end up with outcomes that they did not specifically select and do not or will not like.

Whether the interest in autonomy calls for active choosing, as opposed to reliance on a default rule, depends on the circumstances. Often active choosing is best and should be built into the relevant choice architecture— but along some dimensions, default rules can be superior to active choosing on autonomy grounds. If people choose not to choose, or if they would make that choice if asked, it is an insult to their autonomy to force them to choose. And if people would like to choose, a default rule does not deprive them of that choice; they can reject the default. Even in the face of inertia, many people will do so. Preservation of freedom of choice goes a long way toward respecting autonomy. With respect to autonomy, the real problem lies in the possibility of manipulation; I will turn to that problem later.

Coercion

If choice architects coerce people, they are no longer merely nudging. But skeptics might again emphasize that because of the power of inertia, people might (passively) accept a default rule even though they have no enthusiasm for the outcome that it produces and would reject that outcome if they focused on the issue involved.

We should doubt whether such situations are properly described as involving coercion; no one is being forced to do anything. But there is certainly a risk that a default rule will produce harmful results even though people have not affirmatively consented to the actions that led to them. Choice architects need to account for that risk. But so long as freedom of choice is maintained and is real rather than formal, coercion is not involved.

Dignity

The antonym of coercion is freedom; the antonym of dignity is humiliation. As we shall discuss, this may be the most interesting objection of all, especially when it is combined with a concern about manipulation.

There are large questions about the place of dignity in ethics. On one (less than conventional) view, dignity is properly part of an assessment of welfare. If people feel humiliated or think that they have been treated disrespectfully, they suffer a welfare loss. That loss might be extremely serious. In any assessment of welfare consequences, such a loss must be considered.

A good welfarist should also acknowledge that an offense to dignity is qualitatively distinct; it is a different kind of loss from the loss of (say) money or an opportunity to visit a beach. But on the welfarist view, a dignity loss is just one kind of loss, to be weighed against the other goods that are at stake. Suppose, for purposes of argument, that a graphic and highly emotional appeal, triggering strong emotions (System 1) to discourage people from smoking, is plausibly seen as an offense of dignity—as a way of treating smokers disrespectfully. (Some smokers might so regard such an appeal and object for that reason.) A welfarist might be willing to support the emotional appeal, notwithstanding the relevant loss, if it saves a significant number of lives.

On another view, an insult to dignity is not merely part of a welfarist calculus. Such an insult does not depend on people's subjective feelings and it is a grave act, perhaps especially if it comes from government. It should not be permitted unless (perhaps) it has an overwhelmingly strong justification. If we endorse this view, it is especially important to ask whether nudges offend human dignity.

To return to my general plea: the force of the objection depends on the particular nudge. A GPS device insults no one's dignity. Disclosure of factual information can hardly be seen as an offense to dignity—certainly not if the information is useful and not based on a false and demeaning belief that people need it. Nudges that increase navigability do not offend dignity.

True, it might be an insult to dignity, and a form of infantilization, if the government constantly reminds people of things that they already know. Every child, and everyone who was once a child, can recall this form of infantilization, and it can be found in adult life as well. If people are informed of the same thing every hour or even every day, they might legitimately feel that their dignity is not being respected. If people are constantly reminded that a due date is coming, they might feel as if they are being treated like children.

If choice architects refer to social norms, to let people know what most people do, they are not likely to be humiliating anyone. In some cases, however, repeated invocations of social norms might run into a concern about dignity. Warnings can run into the same concern insofar as they are repetitive or condescending or (are meant to) trigger strong emotions instead of merely giving people a sense of factual realities.

Here as well, there is no objection to the relevant nudges in the abstract, but there is an objection to imaginable nudging. At the same time, it must be emphasized that outside of exotic hypotheticals, the relevant offense to dignity—coming from unwelcome and numerous reminders—is relatively minor, and from the standpoint of the concerns that have produced the focus on dignity in the Western political tradition, it is laughably modest.

What is the relationship between dignity and default rules? If an employer automatically enrolls employees into retirement and health care plans, dignity is hardly at risk. If a cell phone company adopts a series of defaults for the phone and the contractual arrangement, nothing need be amiss in terms of dignity.

But we could imagine harder cases. Suppose that the government insisted on "default meals" in various restaurants so that people would be given certain healthy choices unless they specifically chose otherwise. The reasonable response is: Why shouldn't free people be asked to choose what they want? Why should they be subject to a default rule at all? Or suppose that a government specified a "default exercise plan" for adults so that they would be assumed to engage in certain activities unless they expressly opted out. People might offer the same reasonable response, perhaps with considerable agitation. A more modest and more realistic proposal is that doctors should enroll smokers into some kind of smoking-cessation plan by default (subject to opt out). Might automatic enrollment offend dignity?

Note that default rules of these kinds might be objectionable for both welfarists and nonwelfarists. Welfarists might want to focus on people's subjective feelings. Their belief that they are being treated as children, and their objection to that treatment, would count in the assessment. Nonwelfarists would insist that the offense to dignity is objectionable even if it has some kind of welfarist justification. (There is a question whether and when nonwelfarists would be willing to allow welfarist consideration to override the objection.)

In extreme situations, default rules could indeed be a serious affront to dignity. If so, there should be a strong presumption against them (whatever our foundational commitments). But it would be a mistake to use extreme situations, or imaginable cases, as a reason to challenge default rules in general. People are not treated disrespectfully if an institution adopts a double-sided default for printing or if they are automatically enrolled in health insurance or retirement plans. The objection from dignity has far more force in the abstract than in the context of the vast majority of real-world cases in which default rules are at work. Admittedly, the objection must be taken seriously in some real-world contexts.

Manipulation

To deal with this objection, we need to say something about the complex idea of *manipulation*. An initiative does not count as manipulative merely because it is an effort to alter people's behavior. If you warn a driver that he is about to drive into a ditch or get into a crash, you are not engaging in manipulation. The same is true if you remind someone that a bill is due or that a doctor's appointment is upcoming.

It is not clear that the idea of manipulation can be subject to a simple definition or a statement of necessary and sufficient conditions. It might be an umbrella concept for an assortment of related practices. But we might begin by saying that manipulation exists *when a choice architect fails to respect people's capacity for reflective choice, as, for example, by trying to alter people's behavior in a covert way, or by exploiting their weaknesses*. If someone has persuaded you to buy an expensive new cell phone by focusing you on a pointless but apparently exciting feature of the product, you have been manipulated. Or if someone has persuaded you to buy a useless exercise machine with videos of fit people getting all the fitter, you can claim to have been manipulated.

A lie can be seen an extreme example of manipulation. Deceptive behavior can be counted as an extreme example of manipulation as well, even if no one has actually spoken falsely. If you imply that certain food is unhealthy to eat when it is not, you are engaged in manipulation.

An action might generally be counted as manipulative if it *lacks transparency*—if the role or the motivation of the choice architect is hidden or concealed. In the pivotal scene in The Wizard of Oz, the wizard says, "Pay no attention to the man behind the curtain." The man behind the curtain is of course a mere human being who is masquerading as the great wizard. If choice architects conceal their own role, it seems fair to charge them with being manipulative.

An action also can be counted as manipulative if it attempts to influence people subconsciously or unconsciously in a way that undermines their capacity for conscious choice. Consider the suggestion that "manipulation is intentionally and successfully influencing someone using methods that pervert choice."[8] Of course the term *pervert choice* is not self-defining; it might well be taken to refer to methods that do not appeal to or produce conscious deliberation. If so, the objection to manipulation is that it "infringes upon the autonomy of the victim by subverting and insulting their decision-making powers."[9] The objection applies to lies, which attempt to alter behavior by appealing to falsehoods rather than truth (where falsehoods would enable people to decide for themselves). In harder cases, the challenge is to concretize the ideas of *subverting* and *insulting*.

Subliminal advertising may be deemed manipulative and insulting because it operates behind the back of the person involved, without appealing to his conscious awareness. People's decisions are affected in a way that bypasses their own deliberative capacities. If this is the defining problem with subliminal advertising, we can understand why involuntary hypnosis would also count as manipulative. But most people do not favor subliminal advertising, and, to say the least, the idea of involuntary hypnosis does not have much appeal. The question is whether taboo practices can shed light on interventions that can command broader support.

On one view, nudges generally or frequently count as manipulative. Sarah Conly suggests that when nudges are at work, "rather than regarding people as generally capable of making good choices, we outmaneuver them by appealing to their irrationality, just in more fruitful ways. We concede that people can't generally make good decisions when left to their own devices, and this runs against the basic premise of liberalism, which is that we are basically rational, prudent creatures who may thus, and should thus, direct themselves autonomously."[10] This is a strong charge, and it is not fairly leveled against most kinds of nudges. Recall some examples: disclosure, reminders, warnings, default rules, simplification. Some forms of choice architecture are rooted in an acknowledgment that human beings suffer from bounded rationality, but they do not appeal to "irrationality" or reflect a judgment that "people can't generally make good decisions when left to their own devices."

But consider some testing cases in which Conly's charge is not self-evidently misplaced:

1. Choice architects might choose a graphic health warning on the theory that an emotional, even visceral presentation might have significant effects.
2. Choice architects might be alert to framing effects and present information accordingly. They might enlist loss aversion, suggesting that if people decline to engage in certain action, they will lose money, rather than suggesting that if they engage in certain action, they will gain money. They might be aware that a statement that a product is 90 percent fat-free has a different impact from a statement that a product is 10 percent fat, and they might choose the frame that has the desired effect.
3. They might make a strategic decision about how to present social norms, knowing that the right presentation—for example, emphasizing behavior within the local community—could have a large impact on people's behavior.
4. They might organize options—say, in a cafeteria or on a form—to make it more likely that people will make certain choices.

It is an understatement to say that none of these cases involves the most egregious forms of manipulation. There is no lying and no deceit. But is there any effort to subvert or to insult people's decision-making powers? I have said that government should be transparent about what it is doing. It should not hide its actions or its reasons for those actions. Does transparency eliminate the charge of manipulation? In cases of this kind, the answer is not self-evident.

Perhaps a graphic health warning could be counted as manipulative if it is designed to target people's emotions, rather than to inform them of facts. But what if the warning is explained, in public, on exactly that ground? What if a warning is introduced and justified as effective because it appeals to people's emotions and thus saves lives? What if it is welcomed by the relevant population—say, smokers—for exactly that reason? Similar questions might be asked about strategic uses of framing effects, social norms, and order effects. T. M. Wilkinson contends, plausibly, that it is too crude to say that manipulation infringes upon autonomy, because "manipulation could be consented to. If it were consented to, in the right kind of way, then the manipulation would at least be consistent with autonomy and might count as enhancing it."[11]

If government is targeting System 1—perhaps through framing, perhaps through emotionally evocative appeals—it may be responding to the fact that System 1 has already been targeted, and to people's detriment. In the context of cigarettes, for example, it is plausible to say that a range of past and current manipulations—including advertising and social norms—have influenced people to become smokers.

If this is so, perhaps we can say that public officials are permitted to meet fire with fire. But some people might insist that two wrongs do not make a right—and that if the government seeks to lead people to quit, it must treat them as adults and appeal to their deliberative capacities. There is no obvious answer to the resulting debates. Some people are committed to welfarism—understood, very roughly, as an approach that attempts to maximize social welfare, taken in the aggregate. Other people are committed to some form of deontology—understood, very roughly, as an approach that is committed to certain principles, such as respect for persons, regardless of whether those principles increase social welfare. Welfarists and deontologists might have different answers to the question when and whether it is acceptable to target System 1 or to manipulate people.

It is not implausible to say that even with full transparency, at least some degree of manipulation is involved whenever a choice architect is targeting emotions or seeking a formulation that will be effective because of its interaction with people's intuitive or automatic thinking. But there are degrees of manipulation, and there is a big difference between a lie and an effort to frame an alternative in an appealing light.

In ordinary life, we would not be likely to accuse our friends or loved ones of manipulation if they offered a smile or a frown if we said that we were seriously considering a particular course of action. It would be an expansive understanding of the word *manipulation* if we used it to cover people who characterized one approach as favored by most members of our

peer group or who emphasized the losses that might accompany an alternative that they abhor. Actions that are conceivably characterized as manipulative fall along a continuum, and if a doctor or a lawyer uses body language
to support or undermine one or another alternative, it would be pretty
fussy to raise objections about "subverting" or "perverting" the deliberative
processes of a patient or client.

We should be able to agree that most nudges are not manipulative in
any relevant sense. But to the extent that some of them can be counted as
such, the force of the objection or concern depends on the degree of any
manipulation. We might well insist on an absolute or near-absolute taboo
on lying or deception on government's part, for welfarist or nonwelfarist
reasons. But surely we should be more lenient toward emotional appeals
and framing. One question is whether such approaches produce significant
welfare gains. If a graphic health warning saves many lives, is it unacceptable if and because it can be counted as a (mild) form of manipulation? A
welfarist would want to make an all-things-considered judgment about the
welfare consequences.

It is true that some people, focused on autonomy as an independent
good, would erect a strong and perhaps conclusive presumption against
defining cases of manipulation. But I hope that I have said enough to show
that the modest forms discussed here strain the boundaries of the concept—and that it would be odd to rule them off-limits.

Learning

Choice making is a muscle, and the ability to choose can be strengthened
through exercise. If nudges would make the muscle atrophy, we would
have an argument against them. Here too, it is necessary to investigate the
particulars.

Active choosing and prompted choice hardly impede learning. Nor do
information and reminders. On the contrary, they promote learning. Here
the point is plain and the evidence is compelling: nudges of this kind exercise the choice-making muscle, rather than the opposite.

With respect to learning, the real problem comes from default rules. It
is possible to say that active choosing is far better than defaults simply
because choosing promotes learning. Consider, for example, the question
whether employers should ask employees to make active choices about
their retirement plans or should instead default people into plans that fit

their situations. The potential for learning might well count in favor of active choosing. If people are defaulted into certain outcomes, they do not add to their stock of knowledge, and that may be a significant lost opportunity.

The argument for learning depends on the setting. For most people, it is not important to become expert in the numerous decisions that lead to default settings on computers and cell phones, and hence the use of such settings is not objectionable. The same point holds in many other contexts in which institutions rely on defaults rather than active choosing. To know whether choice architects should opt for active choosing, it is necessary to explore whether the context is one in which it is valuable, all things considered, for choosers to acquire a stock of knowledge.

Biased Officials

Choice architects are emphatically human as well, and potentially subject to behavioral biases; to say the least, they are often unreliable. It is reasonable to object to some nudges and to some efforts to intervene in existing choice architecture on the ground that the choice architects might blunder. They might lack important information; followers of F. A. Hayek emphasize what they call the *knowledge problem*, which means that public officials often lack important information held by the public as a whole. Choice architects might be biased, perhaps because their own parochial interests are at stake; many skeptics emphasize the *public choice problem*, pointing to the role of self-interested private groups. Choice architects might themselves be subject to important biases—suffering, for example, from present bias, optimistic bias, or probability neglect. In a democratic society, public officials are responsive to public opinion, and if the public is mistaken, officials might be mistaken as well.

It is unclear whether and to what extent this objection is a distinctly ethical one, but it does identify an important cautionary note. One reason for nudges, as opposed to mandates and bans, is that choice architects may err. No one should deny that proposition, which argues in favor of choice-preserving approaches. If choice architects blunder, at least it can be said that people can go their own way.

The initial response to this objection should be familiar: choice architecture is inevitable. When choice architects act, they alter the architecture; they do not create an architecture where it did not exist before. A certain degree of nudging from the public sector cannot be avoided, and there is no use in wishing it away. Nonetheless, choice architects who work for government might decide that it is usually best to rely on free markets and to trust in invisible-hand mechanisms. If so, they would select (or accept) choice architecture that reflects those mechanisms.

This idea raises many conceptual and empirical questions, which I will not engage here. The question is whether it is so abstract, and so rooted in dogmas, that it ought not to command support. To be sure, free markets have many virtues. But in some cases, disclosure, warnings, and reminders can do far more good than harm. As we have seen, active choosing is sometimes inferior to default rules. Someone has to decide in favor of one or another, and in some cases that someone is inevitably the government. It is true that distrust of public officials will argue against nudging, at least where it is avoidable, but if it is dogmatic and generalized, such distrust will likely produce serious losses in terms of both welfare and freedom.

Contexts

Nudges and choice architecture cannot be avoided, but intentional changes in choice architecture, deliberately made by choice architects, can indeed run into ethical concerns—most obviously where the underlying goals are illicit. Indeed, a concern about illicit goals underlies many of the most plausible objections to (some) nudges.

Where the goals are legitimate, an evaluation of ethical concerns needs to be made with close reference to the context. Disclosure of accurate information, reminders, and (factual) warnings are generally unobjectionable. If nothing is hidden or covert, nudges are less likely to run afoul of ethical constraints, not least because and when they promote informed choices.

Default rules frequently make life more manageable, and it does not make much sense to reject such rules as such. At the same time, it must be acknowledged that active choosing might turn out to be preferable to default rules, at least when learning is important and one size does not fit all.

It is also true that some imaginable nudges can be counted as forms of manipulation, raising objections from the standpoint of both autonomy and dignity. That is a point against them. But the idea of manipulation contains a core and a periphery, and some interventions go beyond the periphery. Even when nudges target System 1, it might well strain the concept of manipulation to categorize them as such (consider a graphic warning or a use of loss aversion in an educational message). If they are fully transparent and effective, if their rationale is not hidden, and if they do not limit freedom of choice, they should not be ruled out-of-bounds on ethical grounds, whatever the foundations of our ethical commitments.

9   Control

In the late, great television show *Lost*, one of the central characters, with the telling name of John Locke, exclaimed at crucial moments, "Don't tell me what I can't do!"[1] Locke liked doing things, but perhaps even more, he disliked being told that he could not do things. At every turn, he insisted on his own capacity for agency.

The Lockean Exclamation, as I shall call it, is related to the psychological idea of *reactance*,[2] which refers to people's tendency to do something precisely because they have been told not to do it. It attests to a general phenomenon of which reactance is an example: much of the time, control, understood as liberty of action, has intrinsic and not merely instrumental value. When people feel that their control is being taken away, they will often rebel, even if exercising control would not result in material benefits or might produce material harms.

Tocqueville offered a memorable account: "What has always kindled such a powerful love of liberty in the hearts of certain men is its intrinsic attractiveness, its inherent charm, independent of its benefits. It is the pleasure of being able to speak, act, and breathe without constraint under the sole government of God and the law. Whoever seeks in liberty anything other than liberty itself is born for servitude."[3] As a matter of political science, Tocqueville may or may not be right. But he is certainly capturing an important aspect of political psychology: an insistence on personal agency, or the value of control, for its own sake, "independent of its benefits." As he immediately added, what many people "love about" liberty "is not the material goods it gives them. They consider liberty itself a good."

Both psychologists and economists have investigated the intrinsic value of control, but we need to learn much more, not least because of its immense importance to both politics and law. Whenever a private or public institution blocks choices or interferes with agency, or is perceived as doing so, some people will rebel. In extreme cases, violence is possible. Consider the highly publicized example in 2012 when New York Mayor Michael Bloomberg tried to ban the sale of containers of sodas and other sugary beverages larger than 16 ounces. This was a modest initiative, but the effort created a significant backlash, in part because of what appeared to be a loud, collective Lockean Exclamation from New Yorkers. Any form of paternalism—with respect to food, health care, and cigarettes—risks running into a similar backlash. Of course some nations are quite different from others. The United States is especially prone to such backlashes. But we are one species: in every human heart, you can find the Lockean Exclamation.

Because nudges preserve freedom of choice, they do much better than mandates and bans; we have seen that in diverse nations, they turn out to be approved by strong majorities. But even when majorities embrace nudging, minorities reject them. To the extent that some nudges create concerns, it is because they too trigger a version of the Lockean Exclamation, at least in some circles. For example, default rules (such as automatic enrollment in pension plans or green energy) allow people to opt out and to go their own way. But some people see them as putting a weight on the scales, and to that extent as diminishing agency and control. More broadly, it is even plausible to think that political movements—not only the movement for sex equality and for same-sex marriage but also for Brexit and Donald Trump—have been animated, in significant part, by the Lockean Exclamation. In the United States, the Lockean Exclamation played a large role in Trump's presidency, not least in his attitudes toward immigration, NATO, and the Paris agreement on climate change.

The intrinsic value of control matters for business as well as politics and law. To what extent should companies preserve freedom of choice—and emphasize to consumers and employees that they ultimately have the freedom to go their own way? Banks, grocery stores, soft drink companies, cell phone companies, and automobile manufacturers face that question every day; so do employers of every kind. The answer is greatly complicated by the fact that the intrinsic value of control is countered, in many cases, by *a preference for preserving scarce cognitive and emotional bandwidth*—and hence by an explicit or implicit choice not to choose. Inside everyone's mind, there is an occasionally desperate plea: "You figure it out!"

The plea might be heard when people purchase a home in a new city or enter a store with countless options, or when a government website asks them to register their preferences on lengthy forms as they (try to) apply for benefits, permits, or licenses. You might even want government to ban certain foods and drugs, not because you do not prize your own agency, but on the ground that it knows what is healthy and what is dangerous. Citizens might well be willing to say to their government: "We want you to decide which medicines are safe and effective for their intended use." In view of the informational advantages of public officials, that could easily be a rational delegation.

We can call the underlying plea ("You figure it out!") the Madisonian Exclamation, after James Madison, who emphasized the many advantages of a republic over a democracy—in part because in the former, people delegate authority to relative specialists, who could make better decisions.[4] In the history of political and economic thought, many people have emphasized that point, including (in very different ways) Max Weber and Walter Lippmann. As for the Lockean Exclamation, so too for the Madisonian Exclamation: We know all too little about when we will hear it, and when it is justified.

Principals, Agents, and Rational Choice

The most objectionable denials of control occur when someone deprives you of freedom to act or to choose—say, when you are forbidden to use your money as you see fit or to take the job that you want. But it is important to emphasize that any principal can voluntarily choose to relinquish some of that freedom. Indeed, that is an exercise of control, and it can be exceptionally important to both freedom and well-being. You might rely on or appoint an agent, who might have superior knowledge, might be immune from various biases, and might relieve you of the obligation to devote scarce time and limited cognitive resources to making choices that impose some kind of cognitive or hedonic tax. For these reasons, the Madisonian Exclamation has its appeal. Consider the areas of pension law and health care, in which many people are often willing to delegate a little or a lot of authority.

At the same time, appointing an agent might be a big mistake. Any agent might have inferior knowledge, be ignorant of the principal's real concerns, have her own biases, or be influenced by her own self-interest. Aware of those problems, even a Madisonian principal might decide not to appoint an agent or to appoint an agent with limited powers. Such a principal might think: I want to maintain control over my own pension and my own health care. Those with Lockean dispositions will be suspicious of the relinquishment of control that any such appointment might involve. As a matter of psychology, they tend to have faith in their own judgment and to distrust those who seek to make decisions on their behalf (hence the terms *micromanagers* and *control freaks*).

With respect to the public sphere, it is often useful to think of the citizen as the principal and the agent as the government. Consider the questions of food safety, environmental protection, worker safety, and national security. I have suggested that regulation might be an implicit or even explicit delegation; citizens can decide to delegate the power to choose or even to nudge.[5] In any society, citizens will differ intensely on whether such a delegation is advisable.

Many debates about what public officials should do involve an opposition between the Lockean Exclamation and the Madisonian Exclamation. I speculate that those who are suspicious of relinquishing control often have an immediate, intuitive, even automatic response to anyone who asks them to do so—and that response is intensely negative. In the terms of current psychological work, their automatic system (System 1) insists on maintaining control even if their deliberative system (System 2) counsels in favor of a delegation.

In theory, the decision whether to choose, or instead to delegate the power to choose, should be a fully deliberative one, based on some form of cost-benefit analysis. Choosers might begin by thinking in terms of expected value: Would the payoff be higher with or without a delegation? Choosers might also ask about the value of saving limited time and attention. If the savings would be substantial, choosers might be willing to sacrifice something in terms of expected value. It also matters whether choosing itself has benefits or costs, in the sense that choosers enjoy, or instead dislike, the time that they devote to choosing.

For some people, it may be interesting or fun to think about the best investments or the right health care plan. For other people, those choices are unpleasant and tiring, a kind of hedonic tax, and it is a great relief if someone else can be persuaded (or paid) to make the choice for them. Compare experiences in restaurants, where some people like to linger over the possibilities and to engage with the waiter, whereas others dislike the process and would just like the waiter to decide.[6] There is a great deal of heterogeneity on this count with respect to relatively trivial and far more important decisions. Some people greatly enjoy thinking about their pension and the best investments; other people abhor that process. Some people like the idea of investigating potential mortgages; others really do not.

Choosers might also consider whether the pleasure of a reward, and the pain of a loss, are amplified or instead reduced if they are personally responsible for the outcomes. Studies have shown that people value items they have selected themselves more than identical items that were selected for them.[7] It is not hard to imagine a situation in which choosers would prefer (1) gaining $100 if that gain came from their own efforts to (2) gaining $110 if that gain came from someone else's efforts: the subjective value of the self-attained $100 may be greater than that of the $110 that was attained as a result of an agent's choice. On the other hand, personal responsibility might amplify the adverse effect of a bad result, because people might blame themselves more acutely than they would if the result came from the decisions of a delegate (even if the choice of the delegate was made personally).

Debates over the legislative grants of authority to executive officials often turn on issues of this kind, as legislators might seek to avoid responsibility by giving discretion to administrative agencies (but might be held responsible for the grant). In areas that range from occupational safety to climate change to immigration, legislators might benefit if they can delegate authority to others—and blame them. They are making their own version of the Madison Exclamation.

The Control Premium

Consistent with the Lockean Exclamation, it has been found that people prefer options that permit further choice to those that do not.[8] Similarly, people are willing to pay to control their own payoffs, rather than delegate, when faced with potential rewards: the *control premium*.[9] A sense of control has also been shown to reduce stress and anxiety in the face of unwanted

outcomes.[10] For that reason, making a choice may reduce the aversive utility of a loss, leading people to prefer agency over delegation.

Tali Sharot, Sebastian Bobadilla-Suarez, and I tested whether people
will pay, or demand payment, to be choosers.[11] We conducted an experiment with several trials. On each trial, we asked participants to make a
simple choice between two shapes to maximize reward and minimize loss.
The task took skill, and participants could see how they were performing.
On "gain trials," a correct choice would result in a monetary gain and an
incorrect choice in no gain. On "loss trials," a correct choice would result
in no loss and an incorrect choice in a monetary loss. After performing
the task for an extended period of time on their own, participants were
given an opportunity to delegate the decision-making to an advisor. They
could also see how the adviser performed; hence the expected value of the
advisor was disclosed on each trial and participants' perception of their
own expected value was also elicited. This allowed us to examine whether
participants made "rational" delegation choices given their beliefs when
faced with potential gains and with potential losses. In other words, participants could compare their own performance with that of their advisers,
and they could choose whether or not to delegate, seeing who was likely to
do better.

Our central finding was simple: *Participants are willing to forgo rewards
for the opportunity to control their own payoffs.* In their own way, they were
making, and acting on, the Lockean Exclamation. This preference was
observed not only when participants were faced with potential gains but
also when they were faced with potential losses. In one of our experiments,
for example, a value maximizer would delegate 50 percent of the time, but
participants' average delegation rate was significantly lower. As proof of the
control premium, participants were also much more likely to retain agency
when this was not the optimal decision (i.e., *failure to delegate*) than to delegate when this was not the optimal decision (i.e., *failure to retain agency*).
As a result of these failures, participants earned a lot less than they could
have if they selected optimally.

Importantly, we asked participants to make assessments of the (sub)opti-
mality of their delegation choices. Their assessments were quite accurate,
suggesting that they were entirely aware of the premium they were paying
to maintain control. Our finding of a control premium is consistent with
those in several other studies.[12]

Why Control? When Control?

The existing literature is instructive, but it remains sparse, and it raises many puzzles. One of the most important involves the *sources* of the control premium. In our own study, it is reasonable to think that people were making some kind of mistake. The task was not exactly fun, and so there was no hedonic value in making choices on one's own. On one interpretation, people were using a kind of Lockean Heuristic, in the form of a mental shortcut, or presumption, that generally works well but that creates severe blunders: *Do not delegate consequential choices to other people.* Undoubtedly people do not use the Lockean Heuristic in all domains—but they certainly do in some important ones.

Probably the most important reason for the Lockean Heuristic, associated with John Stuart Mill's great argument on behalf of liberty, is that outcomes that we select ourselves often suit our preferences and values better than those that have been selected for us. Recall Mill's insistence that the individual "is the person most interested in his own well-being" and that the "ordinary man or woman has means of knowledge immeasurably surpassing those that can be possessed by any one else."[13] Behavioral economics raises some serious questions about Mill's argument to this effect. But to the extent that it retains (enough) validity, it argues on behalf of a heuristic that would lead to a control premium. Note that in our experiment, the Lockean Heuristic went wrong—but on plausible assumptions, it usually goes right, at least in many domains in which people find themselves.

We might also speculate that a biologic system that provides higher intrinsic reward for things we have obtained ourselves could be adaptive. (Recall that people who win $100 through their own efforts might well enjoy higher subjective welfare than people who win $110 from the efforts of an agent.) If we learn that an action results in a reward, we can repeat that action in the future to gain more of the same. But if we do not execute an action to obtain reward (or avoid harm), we lose the opportunity to acquire a "blueprint" of how to gain rewards (or avoid harm) again in the future. Like most evolutionary arguments, this one is highly speculative—but it is plausible. The increased value of outcomes we have obtained ourselves emerges both from their immediate utility *and* from the information they offer us for later choices.

But we have also seen that for some decisions, people do not much care about control, and for others, they actually abhor it. In a restaurant in a foreign country, you might tell the waiter, "You choose." When you are making a difficult medical decision, you might ask your doctor to figure it out for you. Control can be a cost, not a benefit.

For rational actors, the relevant considerations can be organized into a simple framework, involving the costs of decisions and the costs of errors. Suppose that a website constantly asks you, "Would you like to change your privacy settings?" Many people do not welcome that question; it is a kind of cognitive tax (it imposes a decision cost), and it is not likely to reduce the number and magnitude of errors (because you are fine with your settings). But if you are deciding what place to buy or rent in a new city, you might welcome a question of that kind, and you might not do a lot of delegating: you have privileged access to your preferences and your values, and any agent might well make costly errors. You will welcome information and advice, but the ultimate decision will be yours. If someone intrudes, you might well offer the Lockean Exclamation.

For boundedly rational agents, heuristics and biases, and supposedly irrelevant factors, will introduce complications. Take the case of the non-chooser offering the Madisonian Exclamation. Perhaps she is refusing to make a worthwhile investment—say, in the acquisition of knowledge. Perhaps she is myopic and is excessively influenced by the short-term costs of choosing, which might require some learning, while underestimating the long-term benefits, which might be very large. A form of present bias might infect the decision not to choose. Perhaps the nonchooser suffers from a kind of self-control problem. She is unable to slow down and to take the time to focus on something that is not especially interesting, at least not in the short-run, but from which she can ultimately benefit a great deal. Perhaps she does not realize that her own tastes are malleable. Or a non-chooser might be unduly affected by availability bias because of an over-reaction to a recent situation in which her own choice went wrong.

For their part, those who choose, or who show a significant control premium, might be making quite similar errors (as, perhaps, in our experiment). Present bias, for example, might lead people to make a decision on their own when it would make far more sense to do the hard work of finding a reliable delegate. A decision to economize on bandwidth and to allow someone else to make choices might take a large measure of self-control.

The Madisonian Exclamation matters, but in my view, the intrinsic value of control and the Lockean Exclamation are far more important to business, politics, and daily life. They help to explain behavior in multiple domains—consumption, education, employment, environmental protection, savings, sports, voting, politics, and more. They show that it is often smart, as well as kind, for those in positions of authority to announce, very clearly, "The ultimate decision is yours."

10   Coercion

In light of behavioral findings demonstrating the occasional human propensity to blunder, some people have been asking whether mandates and bans have a fresh justification.[1] The motivation for that question is clear: If we know that people's choices lead them in the wrong direction, why should we insist on freedom of choice? In the face of human errors, isn't it odd, or even perverse, to insist on that form of freedom? Isn't especially odd to do so if we know that in many contexts, people choose not to choose?

It should be agreed that if a mandate would clearly increase social welfare, there is a strong argument on its behalf. To be sure, we would have to specify what *social welfare* means,[2] but if we could agree on a rough definition, we would find many cases in which mandates make sense. Where people are inflicting harms on others, a nudge is unlikely to be enough. No one believes that defaults are a sufficient approach to the problem of violent crime. No one thinks that people get to choose whether to steal or to assault. In the face of a standard market failure, a mandate has a familiar justification; consider the problem of air pollution. It is true that even in such contexts, defaults may have an important role; recall the possibility of default rules in favor of clean energy. But the effects of defaults, taken by themselves, might well prove too modest for the problem at hand, and they hardly exhaust the repertoire of appropriate responses.

We have seen that there are behavioral market failures as well. If people are suffering from unrealistic optimism, limited attention, or a problem of self-control, and if the result is a serious welfare loss for those people, there is an argument for some kind of public response. When people are running high risks of mortality or otherwise ruining their lives, it might make sense to coerce them. After all, people have to get prescriptions for certain kinds of medicines, and even in freedom-loving societies, people are forbidden from buying certain foods or taking certain risks in the workplace because the dangers are too high. We could certainly identify cases in which the best approach is a mandate or a ban because that response is preferable, from the standpoint of social welfare, to any alternative, including defaults.

Five Objections to Mandates

Nonetheless, there are good reasons to think that if improving social welfare is the goal, nudges have significant advantages and are often the best approach.

First, freedom-preserving approaches tend to be best in the face of heterogeneity. By allowing people to go their own way, defaults reduce the costs associated with one-size-fits-all solutions, which mandates usually impose. In the context of credit markets, some people benefit from overdraft protection programs even if the interest rates are high. Forbidding such enrollment, or sharply limiting people's access to the programs, could turn out to be harmful. For credit cards and mortgages, people have different tastes and needs, and default rules have large advantages over prohibitions. Personalized defaults can reduce the problems posed by heterogeneity, but we have also seen that it can be challenging to devise them.

Second, those who favor nudges are alert to the important fact that public officials have limited information and may themselves err (the knowledge problem). If nudges are based on mistakes, the damage is likely to be significantly less severe than in the case of mandates, because people are free to ignore them. True, some nudges can be sticky, but we have seen that many people opt out when they really do not like them. Return to the instructive example of default thermometer settings in winter: if they are set 1°C colder, people stick with them, but if the default is 2°C colder, it is a lot less sticky. We are taking this example as a metaphor, and a revealing one, for how people will reject the default if it makes them uncomfortable—an important safeguard against inadequately informed choice architects. Here again, the rise of large datasets and of personalized default rules can reduce the problem, but we would have to be optimistic to think that they can eliminate it.

Third, nudges respond to the fact that public officials may be affected by the influence of well-organized private groups (the public choice problem). Even if such officials have a great deal of knowledge, they might not have the right incentives, even in well-functioning democracies. Powerful private groups might want particular nudges, and sometimes they can convince officials to endorse what they want. If so, the fact that people can go their own way provides real protection, at least when compared with mandates.

Fourth, nudges have the advantage of avoiding the welfare loss that people experience when they are deprived of the ability to choose. In some cases, that loss is severe. As we have seen, people sometimes want to choose, and when they are forbidden to do so, they might be frustrated, angered, or worse. A nudge avoids that kind of loss.

Fifth, nudges recognize that freedom of choice can be seen, and often is seen, as an intrinsic good, which government should respect if it is to treat people with dignity. Some people believe that autonomy has independent value and is not merely part of a large category of goods that people enjoy. If people are deprived of freedom, they are infantilized. Nudges allow people to go their own way if they like.

People sometimes object that nudges are more covert and less transparent than mandates and therefore more insidious and difficult to monitor. But nudges need not be, and ought not be, covert. There is nothing covert about automatic enrollment in savings and health insurance plans. It is true that many people may not pay attention to default rules or understand their effects. But recall the evidence that people's behavior, in the face of a default, would not be changed even if they were informed that a particular default, and not another imaginable one, has been chosen for them.

Illustrations

The five arguments on behalf of choice-preserving approaches will have different degrees of force in different contexts. They suggest reasons to favor nudges over mandates, but those reasons may not be decisive. In some settings, for example, the interest in freedom of choice has overwhelming importance. In others, people do not much care about it, and its intrinsic value is only modest. Consider some illustrative problems:

1. Suppose that a large university has long had a single-sided default for its printers, and it is deciding whether to change to double-sided. On the basis of careful investigation, suppose that it has learned that at least 80 percent

of its students, faculty, and other employees would prefer a double-sided default, on the ground that they would like to save paper. Armed with this information, and aware of the economic and environmental savings that a double-sided default could bring, the university switches to that default.

Now suppose that some university administrators, enthusiastic about the idea of majority rule, ask whether double-sided printing should be mandatory. The answer to that question is plain. About one-fifth of users prefer a single-sided default, and there is little doubt that single-sided printing is often best—for example, for PowerPoint presentations and for lecture notes.

The assessment might be different if the use of single-sided printing imposes significant costs on nonusers (e.g., paper costs on the university or environmental costs). If so, there is some weighing to be done. But if the welfare of those who use printers is the only or primary variable, a default is clearly preferable to a mandate. From the standpoint of users, a mandate would impose unnecessary costs in the face of heterogeneity across persons and projects. Here, then, is a clear case in which a default is preferable to a mandate.

2. As we have seen, a great deal of work explores the effects of automatic enrollment in retirement plans. We have also seen that automatic enrollment increases participation rates, and thus people's savings, while also preserving freedom of choice: so far, so good. The problem is that if the default contribution rate is lower than what employees would choose (say, 3 percent, as it has been under many automatic enrollment plans), then the result of automatic enrollment might be to *decrease* average savings because the default rate turns out to be sticky. This is an ironic result for those who want to use defaults to increase people's welfare during retirement.

The natural response, however, is not to abandon default rules in favor of mandates, but to choose a better default. One possibility is *automatic escalation*, which increases savings rates each year until the employee hits a predetermined maximum. And in fact, there has been a significant increase in the use of this approach; automatic escalation is increasingly popular. Another possibility is to select a higher default contribution. No one denies that defaults can go wrong. If they do, the challenge is to get them right.

But there is a more fundamental objection, which questions freedom of choice altogether. Suppose that people opt out of pension plans for bad reasons, in the sense that the decision to opt out makes their lives worse (by their own lights). Perhaps the relevant people have a general (and unjustified) distrust of the financial system or of their employer, and so they elect to save little or not to save at all. Perhaps they suffer from an acute form of present bias. Perhaps those who opt out are most likely to suffer as a result of doing so.

These are empirical questions, but if those who opt out would be hurt, the argument for a mandate gains force on welfare grounds. If public officials know, from practice, that a behavioral market failure or some kind of error is leading people to make self-destructive blunders, it is tempting to contend that government should mandate savings and eliminate the right to opt out. After all, most democratic nations have mandatory pension plans of one kind or another; perhaps they should expand those plans, rather than working to allow or encourage voluntary supplementation. Indeed, some critics might argue for some kind of comprehensive welfare assessment by public officials of optimal savings rates and ask those officials to build mandates on the basis of that assessment.

This approach cannot be ruled out in principle, but there are good reasons for caution. In assessing the rationality of those who opt out, public officials might be wrong (recall the knowledge problem). As compared to a default, a mandate might get people into the system who would benefit from inclusion, but it might also get people into the system who would be seriously harmed. It is important, and it may be difficult, to know the size of the two groups. Those who opt out might do so not for bad reasons, or because they are ignoring their future selves, but because they need the money now and they are making a sensible trade-off between their current and future welfare.

To say the least, a comprehensive welfare assessment of optimal savings rates is exceedingly difficult, especially in view of diversity of the population and changes over time. What is the right savings rate for those who are twenty-five or thirty or forty or sixty? How does it change when people have to pay school loans or mortgages, or pay for their children, young or old? How does it change for people who earn $30,000 per year or $60,000 or $100,000? What is the impact of changing macroeconomic conditions?

Any such assessment would have to acknowledge that different approaches make sense for different people and over time. In a recession, for example, a lower contribution rate might make more sense, at least for relatively low-income people, than in a time of growth. So too, those who have to pay off their college loans might not want to save while they are struggling to make those payments, and people who are reasonably spending a great deal on current consumption (perhaps they have young children or children in college) might not want to save much in that period. These points suggest the need for personalized rather than one-size-fits-all mandates, which would not be easy to design and which would amount to a risky form of social engineering.

Moreover, any form of coercion will impose a welfare loss on at least some choosers, who would want to exercise their autonomy and who would undoubtedly be frustrated to find that they cannot. And if freedom of choice has intrinsic value or can promote learning, then there are further reasons to avoid mandates.

Although these various points raise cautionary notes, they might not be decisive. As I have noted, many nations compel savings through some kind of social security program, and for perfectly legitimate reasons. Perhaps existing programs should be expanded to increase the level of mandatory savings. If it could be demonstrated that those who opt out, under automatic enrollment, are making genuinely bad decisions, there would be a strong argument for mandates (or at least for altering rules that reduce the risk of harm). But even if so, private retirement plans play an important role for savers; the question is whether the current voluntary system should become more coercive. The fact of heterogeneity and the risk of government error argue strongly in the direction of defaults.

3. Most motor vehicles emit pollution, and the use of gasoline increases national dependence on foreign oil. On standard economic grounds, there is a market failure here, and some kind of corrective tax seems the best response, designed to ensure that drivers internalize the social costs of their activity. Behaviorally informed regulators would be inclined to think that at the time of purchase, many consumers do not give sufficient attention to the costs of driving a car. Even if they try, they might not have a sufficient understanding of those costs because it is not simple to translate differences in miles per gallon (MPG) into economic and environmental consequences. An obvious approach that preserves freedom of choice would be disclosure, in the form of a fuel-economy label that would correct that kind of behavioral market failure.

But it is possible to wonder whether such a label will be sufficiently effective; this is an empirical question. Perhaps many consumers will pay little attention to it and hence will not purchase cars that would save them a significant amount of money. True, a corrective tax might help solve that problem, but if consumers really do neglect fuel costs at the time of purchase, it might be best to combine the tax with some kind of subsidy for fuel-efficient cars to overcome consumer myopia. And if consumers are genuinely inattentive to the costs of operating a vehicle (at the time of purchase), then it is possible that fuel-economy standards, which are not favored on standard economic grounds, might themselves turn out to be justified.

In support of that argument, it would be useful to focus directly on two kinds of consumer savings from fuel-economy standards, not involving externalities at all: money and time. In fact, the vast majority of the quantified benefits from recent fuel-economy standards come not from environmental improvements but from money saved at the pump; turned into monetary equivalents, the time savings are also significant. For the most recent and ambitious of those standards, the Department of Transportation found consumer economic savings of about $529 billion, time savings of $15 billion, energy security benefits of $25 billion, carbon dioxide emissions reductions benefits of $49 billion, other air pollution benefits of about $14 billion, and less than $1 billion in benefits from reduced fatalities.[3] The total projected benefits are $633 billion over fifteen years, of which a remarkable 84 percent comes from savings at the pump and no less than 86 percent from those savings along with time savings.

I have noted that on standard economic grounds, it is not at all clear that these consumer benefits are entitled to count in the analysis, because they are purely private savings and do not involve externalities in any way. In deciding which cars to buy, consumers can certainly take account of the private savings from fuel-efficient cars; if they choose not to buy such cars, it might be because they do not value fuel efficiency as compared to other vehicle attributes (such as safety, aesthetics, and performance). Where is the market failure? If the problem lies in a lack of information, the standard economic prescription overlaps with the behaviorally informed one: *provide that information so that consumers can easily understand it.*

In this context, however, there is a risk that any kind of choice-preserving approach will be inadequate. Even with the best fuel-economy label in the world, consumers might well be insufficiently attentive to those benefits at the time of purchase—not because consumers have made a rational judgment that such benefits are outweighed by other factors, but simply because consumers focus on other variables.[4] How many consumers think about time savings when they are deciding whether to buy a fuel-efficient vehicle?

This question raises a host of empirical questions to which we lack full answers. But if consumers are not paying enough attention to savings in terms of money and time, a suitably designed fuel-economy mandate—hard paternalism, and no mere default—might well be justified because it would produce an outcome akin to what would be produced by consumers who are at once informed and attentive. If the benefits of the mandate greatly exceed the costs, and if there is no significant consumer welfare loss (e.g., in the form of reductions in safety, performance, or aesthetics), then the mandate does serve to correct a behavioral market failure. And indeed, the US government has so argued:

The central conundrum has been referred to as the Energy Paradox in this setting (and in several others). In short, the problem is that consumers appear not to purchase products that are in their economic self-interest. There are strong theoretical reasons why this might be so:

- Consumers might be myopic and hence undervalue the long term.
- Consumers might lack information or a full appreciation of information even when it is presented.
- Consumers might be especially averse to the short-term losses associated with the higher prices of energy-efficient products relative to the uncertain future fuel savings, even if the expected present value of those fuel savings exceeds the cost (the behavioral phenomenon of "loss aversion").
- Even if consumers have relevant knowledge, the benefits of energy-efficient vehicles might not be sufficiently salient to them at the time of purchase, and the lack of salience might lead consumers to neglect an attribute that it would be in their economic interest to consider.
- In the case of vehicle fuel efficiency, and perhaps as a result of one or more of the foregoing factors, consumers may have relatively few choices to purchase vehicles with greater fuel economy once other characteristics, such as vehicle class, are chosen.[5]

To be sure, we should be cautious about accepting a behavioral argument on behalf of mandates or bans. Behavioral biases have to be demonstrated, not simply asserted; perhaps most consumers do pay a lot of attention to the benefits of fuel-efficient vehicles.[6] The government's numbers, projecting costs and benefits, might be wrong; recall the knowledge problem. Consumers have highly diverse preferences with respect to vehicles, and even though they are not mere defaults, fuel-economy standards should be designed to preserve a wide space for freedom of choice. The use of fleet-wide averages helps to ensure that such space is maintained.

With these qualifications, the argument for fuel-economy standards, made by reference to behavioral market failures, is at least plausible. In this context, nudges (in the form of improved fuel-economy labels) and mandates (in the form of standards) might march hand in hand. With an understanding of behavioral findings, a command-and-control approach, promoting consumer welfare, might turn out to be far better than the standard economic remedy of corrective taxes.

Less Risky

The fuel-economy example is important, but it should not be read for more than it is worth. It certainly does not establish that in the face of human error, mandates are *generally* preferable to choice-preserving alternatives. As we have seen, such alternatives, above all defaults, reduce the costs of imposing solutions on heterogeneous populations, reduce the risks associated with government error, and avoid the many costs associated with eliminating freedom of choice. In light of the frequently unanticipated and sometimes harmful effects of mandates, default rules are generally less risky.

No one should deny that in the end, mandates might turn out to be justified. But in a free society, it makes sense to give careful consideration to less intrusive, choice-preserving alternatives and, at least when standard market failures are not involved, to adopt a rebuttable presumption in their favor—with the rebuttal available only if it can be shown that a mandate will clearly improve social welfare.

11 On Preferring A to B, While Also Preferring B to A

In the last quarter century, one of the most intriguing findings in behavioral science goes under the unlovely name of "preference reversals between joint and separate evaluations of options."[1] The basic idea is that when people evaluate options A and B separately, they prefer A to B; but when they evaluate the two jointly, they prefer B to A. Preference reversals of this kind have received far too little attention; they bear on many questions in law and policy. They also raise fundamental questions about choice, rationality, choice architecture, and the relationship between choice and welfare. In subtler ways, they tell us something important about when change will occur.

In many circumstances, people are making choices in separate evaluation. They are assessing an option: an appliance, a book, a movie, a policy option, a political candidate, or a potential romance. They focus intently on the option *in isolation*. In other circumstances, people are making choices in joint evaluation. They are assessing two options, and they compare them along one or another dimension. They focus intently on the two options and the particular dimensions along which they differ.

Of course they might also assess three options or four or five hundred. The distinction between separate and joint evaluation might be unrealistic in situations in which the alternative to *separate* is better described as *multiple*. I will return to that point, but let us bracket it for now. The central idea is that in assessing an option, people may not be comparing it with other options in the same general vicinity.

My principal goal here is to show that both separate and joint evaluation often lead to bad outcomes, though for intriguingly different reasons. To simplify the story, a characteristic problem with separate evaluation is a lack of relevant information. Some features of an option are hard to assess in isolation; their meaning, for life or actual experience, is unclear. For that reason, those characteristics may be ignored. By contrast, a characteristic problem with joint evaluation is the undue salience of a single factor (or a subset of factors). People focus on what distinguishes the two options, whether or not they mean much for either life or experience.

I devote considerable space to elaborating these problems, which show why individual choices often go wrong in both markets and politics. Contrary to a widespread view, I argue that there is no justification for preferring separate evaluation to joint evaluation or vice versa. For purposes of producing good decisions and good outcomes, both modes of evaluation run into serious problems. We should seek structures that avoid the problems and pathologies associated with each. At first glance, *global* evaluation seems better than separate or joint evaluation, but that conclusion is too simple. Such structures must be based on an assessment of the goal of the relevant task: Is it to increase consumer welfare? To promote social welfare more broadly? To ensure optimal deterrence? An understanding of the relevant problems and pathologies paves the way toward identification of the appropriate structures.

Consumer Goods

For consumers, here is an example of the kind of preference reversal on which I will be focusing:[2]

Dictionary A: twenty thousand entries, torn cover, but otherwise like new

Dictionary B: ten thousand entries, like new

When the two options are assessed separately, people are willing to pay more for B; when they are assessed jointly, they are willing to pay more for A. A prominent explanation for such preference reversals points to evaluability.[3] In separate evaluation, it is difficult for most people to know how many words a dictionary should have or whether ten thousand is a lot or a little.[4] For that reason, ten thousand and twenty thousand might be taken to be indistinguishable in separate evaluation and hence produce essentially the same willingness to pay. The numbers do not and indeed cannot matter, to the extent that it is difficult to know what they mean. By contrast, *torn cover* is clearly a negative, and *like new* is clearly a positive, even in separate evaluation. That characteristic looms large. Who wants a dictionary with a torn cover?

The problem of evaluability, used in the psychology literature, is best understood in more conventional economic terms. It points to *a lack of adequate information*, which can be costly to obtain, and which people might not seek out even if obtaining it is not costly. In separate evaluation, insufficient information is a pervasive problem. (Whether it is rational to try to obtain it is a separate question, which depends on the costs and benefits of the effort.) Many characteristics of options—dictionaries, appliances, cell phones, jobs, people, cities—are essentially meaningless in the abstract. Consistent with standard practice, I shall use the term *evaluability* throughout, understanding it to refer to a lack of adequate information.

Some characteristics that are hard or impossible to evaluate are numbers, whose meanings depend on context and background. For Geekbench 3 SC 32, a laptop might show a number of 3680, but it might be hard or impossible for consumers to know the consequences of that number for what they care about. With respect to some numbers (such as battery life), many or most consumers might have a good understanding even in separate evaluation. But even for such numbers, separate evaluation might not make it easy for people to make appropriate distinctions between impressive numbers (nine hours, ten hours) or less impressive ones (six hours, five hours). To overcome a problem of evaluability (understood as lack of adequate information), consumers must do some work, and they will often decline to do it.

The problem of evaluability, in this sense, belongs in the same family as *opportunity cost neglect*: people might be willing to pay $X for a certain good, but not if they are focused on other things for which they might pay $X.[5] Drawing people's attention to opportunity costs is analytically similar to joint evaluation; it broadens the viewscreen to focus attention on a comparison to which they would otherwise be oblivious.

For consumer goods, and indeed for countless options, evaluability presents a serious challenge—and at the time of choice, characteristics that can be readily evaluated will dominate people's decisions. We can understand the behavioral phenomenon of present bias in similar terms.[6] The present is often easy to evaluate; the future is often surrounded in some kind of cloud. A challenge of evaluability, with respect to future states of affairs, may well contribute to present bias. For choices in politics and law, evaluability of certain characteristics of options may be especially difficult—a point to which I will return.

In joint evaluation, by contrast, it is easy to see that ten thousand words is less good than twenty thousand words. To consumers, those numbers greatly matter, and they become more meaningful in a comparative setting. Because the point of a dictionary is to define words, a dictionary with twenty thousand words seems much better than one with half that amount. If one dictionary has twice as many words as the other, who cares whether its cover is torn?

Or consider this example[7] (involving an admittedly outdated technology):

CD changer A: can hold five CDs; total harmonic distortion = .003 percent

CD changer B: can hold twenty CDs; total harmonic distortion = .01 percent

Subjects were informed that the smaller the total harmonic distortion, the better the sound quality. In separate evaluation, they were willing to pay more for CD changer B. In joint evaluation, they were willing to pay more for CD changer A.[8] Here too evaluability is the most plausible explanation. Even if an individual knows that a lower figure is preferable for total harmonic distortion, 0.01 percent sounds very low in the abstract, and it is not particularly meaningful. In separate evaluation, 0.01 percent and 0.003 percent might seem the same (low). But in joint evaluation, 0.003 percent is obviously much better. Apparently, people think that for a CD changer, what most matters is the sound quality, and hence they would willingly sacrifice on a relatively unimportant dimension (the number of CDs held) in return for better sound quality.

Here is one more example, involving data from an actual marketplace:[9]

Baseball card package A: ten valuable baseball cards, three not-so-valuable baseball cards

Baseball card package B: ten valuable baseball cards

In separate evaluation, inexperienced baseball card traders would pay more for package B. In joint evaluation, they would pay more for package A. Intriguingly, experienced traders also show a reversal, though it is less stark. They too would pay more for package A in joint evaluation. In separate evaluation, they would pay more for package B (though the difference is not statistically significant). For experienced traders, it is fair to say that in a relatively small population, the preference is for package A in joint evaluation, but there is no preference in separate evaluation.

The explanation is similar to what we have seen before, and it is straightforward for inexperienced traders. In joint evaluation, it is easy to see that package A is better. People get something of value that they do not get with package B. In separate evaluation, it is hard to assess the two packages or to know which one is better. Some people might use a version of the representativeness heuristic to downgrade package A; because it contains cards that are not so valuable, the entire package looks worse. As John List explains, this particular reversal, "examining real choices in actual markets," produces a nice test of "the stability of preferences in riskless decisionmaking."[10] The central finding is that preferences are not stable.

Politics

Here is one more example, from a different domain:[11]

Congressional candidate A: would create five thousand jobs; has been convicted of a misdemeanor

Congressional candidate B: would create one thousand jobs; has no criminal convictions

In separate evaluation, people rated candidate B more favorably, but in joint evaluation, they preferred candidate A. The best explanation should now be familiar. In the abstract, it is hard to know whether one thousand or five thousand jobs is a large number, and a great deal of work would be necessary to make sense of the difference. But a misdemeanor conviction is obviously a strong negative—which explains the relatively greater appeal of candidate B in separate evaluation. But in joint evaluation, most people think that the benefit of four thousand additional jobs outweighs the cost of having a member of Congress with a misdemeanor conviction, and hence candidate A prevails.

This example is highly stylized, and the outcome depends on predispositions within the relevant population. We could easily imagine a group for which a misdemeanor conviction would be decisive in joint or separate evaluation; we could even imagine a group for which such a conviction would be especially weighty in joint evaluation.[12] Shrewd political consultants should be alert to the possibility that one or another mode of evaluation is in their candidate's interest. I will return to this point, because it raises the specter of manipulation (and poses a challenge for some accounts of rationality). The only point is that in choosing among candidates, as among products, people's preferences may shift as between the two modes.

Global Evaluation and Real Life

It should be emphasized that joint evaluation is not global evaluation, understood as evaluation of all relevant options with all relevant characteristics. In the cases just given, joint evaluation has two distinctive features: First, the two options vary along only two dimensions. Second, there are only two options. In real life, any option has a large assortment of characteristics, some of which will be evaluable in separate evaluation and some of which will not. And in real life, there are usually numerous options, not merely two.

For these reasons, experiments involving joint and separate evaluation should be seen as mere approximations of actual decisions, illuminating their characteristics. In well-functioning markets, we might be inclined to assume that something like global evaluation is involved. But that inclination should be resisted. Recall the baseball card study, involving an actual market, in which experienced traders show a kind of reversal. Some options are, in fact, evaluated separately, or close to it; people focus on purchasing a product or not doing so. It may take effort, and exposure to a kind of friction, to focus as well on alternatives; people may avoid "comparison friction."

The point helps explain why global evaluation is usually a mere thought experiment. People cannot easily hold in their minds an entire option set, even if we could agree on how to define it (microwave ovens, books about time travel, hybrid cars). To be sure, many choices involve multiple evaluation rather than joint evaluation, especially when multiple options are squarely faced in front of people (e.g., at supermarkets or drug stores).

It is also important to see that in the cases given, the selection of one other option in joint evaluation is hardly random. It is specifically designed to make one important characteristic more evaluable than it was before or evaluable when it was not evaluable before. For dictionaries, CD changers, politicians, and baseball cards, we could imagine, in joint evaluation, a wide range of options that would accentuate, and make evaluable, one or another characteristic. As we shall see, there are ample opportunities for manipulation here. We could easily imagine tests not of joint evaluation, but of evaluation of three, four, or forty options.[13] The fact that joint evaluation is not global evaluation, or close to it, also has normative implications, to which I will return.

Note as well that in actual life, there is a continuum between joint and separate evaluation, rather than a sharp dichotomy.[14] In some cases, people explore an option entirely on its own, but in other cases, another option, or two or more, are in some sense in the background. People might go to a store to purchase a cell phone with a clear understanding that other cell phones are available. In some cases of joint evaluation, two or more options are simultaneously visible, but in others, the chooser has to do some work to make a comparison; they are not quite side by side. Efforts to reduce comparison friction can be helpful insofar as they eliminate the need for that work. The general point is that the line between joint and separate evaluation might not be so crisp.

Is Less More?

Preference reversals between joint and separate evaluations can be found in multiple domains.[15] It is possible to predict when they will occur and when they will not. As a first approximation: if an option has some characteristic X that is (1) difficult to evaluate in separate evaluation, (2) much easier to evaluate in joint evaluation, (3) dominated by characteristic Y in separate evaluation (solely because of the problem of evaluability), and (4) deemed to be more important than characteristic Y in joint evaluation, then we will see a preference reversal. Sometimes conditions 1 through 4 arise without any conscious efforts by sellers. But sometimes they are deliberately engineered by those whose economic, political, or legal interests are at stake.

There is a relationship here to extremeness aversion, which also produces a kind of preference reversal and which also can be manipulated.[16] For example, suppose that I prefer option A, a small piece of chocolate cake, to option B, a medium-sized piece of chocolate cake, in a pairwise comparison. But if I am offered three options—those two sizes and also a large piece—I switch to the medium-sized piece and thus prefer option B to option A. The reason is a kind of heuristic, sometimes understood as a compromise effect: choose the middle option. Extremeness aversion also makes people susceptible to manipulation. A seller might deliberately add to options A and B some not-so-attractive option C, so as to shift people from option A to option B. They might exploit the compromise effect so as to encourage choosers to select the more expensive option. Politicians might do the same thing.

With respect to joint and separate evaluation, the normative questions— my central focus here—remain insufficiently understood. When is joint evaluation preferable to separate evaluation and vice versa? By what criteria? Might both modes of evaluation be subject to characteristic problems?

Resisting Temptation

Let us stipulate that for consumption choices, the question is what will improve consumer welfare—and let us bracket the hardest questions about what, exactly, that means. Even with that bracketing, it is tempting to conclude that joint evaluation is better simply because it makes one or more relevant considerations easier to evaluate. That is indeed an advantage. Consider the cases given previously: in all of them, an important variable was discounted or ignored simply because people did not know how to evaluate it. Joint evaluation supplied relevant information, and the variable received the attention that people thought that it deserved. The baseball card example is the most straightforward. In joint evaluation, people could see that it is better to have more than less.

But this conclusion is much too simple. First, joint evaluation *might make salient a difference that does not much matter in an actual experience.*[17] For dictionaries, more words are better than fewer (within limits), but how much better? It is possible that for most users a ten-thousand-word dictionary is as good as a twenty-thousand-word dictionary. It is also possible that a torn cover is a constant annoyance. Second, life generally is lived in separate evaluation. (I will raise complications about this point in due course.) It might greatly matter whether a CD changer holds five or twenty CDs. And in terms of listening experience, the difference between 0.003 percent and 0.1 percent might not matter at all. The bare numbers do not tell us. To be sure, a gain of four thousand jobs is significant, and in the case of congressional candidates, joint evaluation does seem better. But if a misdemeanor conviction is predictive of corruption or of misconduct that would cause real harm, then joint evaluation might lead to some kind of mistake.

We can therefore see some choices in joint evaluation as reflecting a disparity between "decision utility" and "experience utility"[18] or (more simply) a "hedonic forecasting error,"[19] in which people make inaccurate predictions about the effects of their choices on their subjective welfare. There is a specific reason: joint evaluation often places a bright spotlight on a characteristic that does not much matter.[20] Here is an intuitive example. Jones is deciding between two houses:

House A: very large, with a long commute to work

House B: large, with a short commute to work

In separate evaluation, Jones might well be willing to pay more for house B. After all, it is large, and the commute is short. In joint evaluation, Jones might well favor house A. A very large house seems a lot better than a large house, and perhaps the commute will not loom particularly large in his decision. This is a hedonic forecasting error in the sense that Jones is undervaluing the day-to-day inconvenience of a long commute. He is inattentive to that inconvenience because he is focused on something more immediate: the concrete difference in size.

Do these points apply outside of the context of consumer choices? Suppose that the goal is to make good personnel decisions. It is reasonable to suppose that joint evaluation is better: if an employer is presented with two or more options, it might focus on attributes that greatly matter, and so the quality of the decision would be higher in joint evaluation. Consider the following:

Potential employee A: strong record, good experience, recommended by a friend, attended the same college as the CEO

Potential employee B: exceptional record, exceptional experience, recommended by a stranger, attended a superb college with no alumni at the company

We could easily imagine a preference for potential employee A in separate evaluation. But in joint evaluation, potential employee B looks better—and might well be chosen. Here too, however, it is important to be careful. On certain assumptions about what matters to employers, separate evaluation could produce better outcomes. Perhaps the chooser cares greatly about a recommendation from a friend, and in joint evaluation that turns out to be decisive. Or perhaps the chooser cares greatly about cultivating the CEO, and hiring someone who went to the same college would seem to do the trick. If we stipulate that potential employee B is better, then joint evaluation might produce mistakes.

In this light, we can raise a question about the view that in separate evaluation, people make emotional judgments, and that in joint evaluation, their judgments are more deliberative.[21] To be sure, it is possible to devise situations in which that is true, leading to the reasonable suggestion, supported by data, that "emotions play too strong a role in separate decision making."[22] But the opposite may also be true. Consider the following, understood as options for dating:

Person A: great personality, fun, always kind, attractive

Person B: good personality, incredibly fun, usually but not always kind, devastatingly attractive

I have not collected data, but we can imagine people who would prefer person A in separate evaluation but person B in joint evaluation. Is separate evaluation more emotional and less deliberative? The same question raises a concern about the closely related view that in separate evaluation, people focus on what they "want," whereas in joint evaluation, people focus on what they "should" want (or do).[23] The view fits with some of the data. Consider this example:

Option A: improve air quality in your city

Option B: get a new cell phone

It is possible that in separate evaluation, people would be willing to pay more for a new cell phone, but that in joint evaluation, they would be willing to pay more for air quality.[24] We could easily devise situations in which separate evaluation triggers a desire, while joint evaluation focuses people in a way that produces a response connected with their normative judgments. But we could devise situations that yield exactly the opposite outcomes. Here is a candidate:

Option A: contribute to pay down the national debt

Option B: take your romantic partner to a romantic dinner

Among some populations, option A would produce a higher figure in separate evaluation, and option B would do so in joint evaluation. Everything depends on the antecedent distribution of preferences and on what becomes the focus in joint evaluation—a point to which I now turn.

How to Win Friends and Influence People

In either separate evaluation or joint evaluation, sellers (and others) have identifiable routes by which to influence or to manipulate choosers. The appropriate design should be clear.

Using Separate Evaluation

In separate evaluation, sellers should show choosers a characteristic that they can easily evaluate (if it is good) and show them a characteristic that they cannot easily evaluate (if it is not so good). In these circumstances, the option will seem attractive even if it has a serious problem. In fact, sellers should choose separate evaluation if they can whenever this presentation of options is feasible.

I have emphasized that in real markets, options do not simply have two characteristics; they have an assortment of them. Recall that much of the experimental evidence is a radical simplification. But the essential point remains. In fact, it is fortified. Sellers (and others) can choose among a range of easily evaluable options (appealing ones) and display a range of others that are difficult or impossible to assess (not-so-appealing ones). It is well known that some product attributes are *shrouded*, in the sense that they are hidden from view, either because of selective attention on the part of choosers or because of deliberative action on the part of sellers.[25] A problem with evaluability belongs in the same category; it is a close cousin. Nothing is literally shrouded, but choosers cannot make much sense of the information they are given. In real markets, they might be able to find out. In fact, that might be easy. But because of comparison friction—defined as people's unwillingness to obtain comparative information, even when it is available—a problem of evaluability in separate evaluation might persist.

Using Joint Evaluation

In joint evaluation, by contrast, sellers should allow an easy comparison along a dimension that is self-evidently important to choosers, even if the difference along that dimension matters little or not at all to experience or to what actually matters. The trick is to highlight a characteristic on which the product in question looks good, or better, or great. It is best, of course, if in reality, that characteristic does matter a great deal. But even if it does not, use of joint evaluation, putting a spotlight on the characteristic whose appeal is heightened by way of comparison, is a good strategy. The point holds for consumer products and political candidates, but it should work for options of all kinds.

An imaginable example: A new computer is introduced with a reduction in size and a superb screen; it is far lighter and it has a far better screen than that of existing models. When the existing models are compared with the new one, the difference in weight and between the screens is easy to see. They stand out. Assume, however, that consumers have no problem with the existing weights and screens; they find them inferior only in joint evaluation. Assume finally that the new computer has to sacrifice along an important dimension to have the spectacular screen—say, its battery time is much reduced or its keyboard is much less comfortable to use. It is easy to imagine that in joint evaluation, people will choose (and purchase) the new computer, but in separate evaluation, they will have a much better experience with the old one.[26] A more general way to put this point is to suggest that in joint evaluation, people might overweight attributes that are simple to evaluate or that trigger a strong response, including a visceral one.[27]

Net Welfare Gains

These points should be sufficient to show that there is no abstract answer to the question whether joint evaluation or separate evaluation produces better decisions on the part of consumers. Neither is ideal, and both might lead to mistakes. Both modes of evaluation have characteristic problems and pathologies. With separate evaluation, the most important of these is incomplete information, producing a failure of evaluability. With joint evaluation, the most important is a focus on one characteristic, producing excessive salience.

In the baseball card case, joint evaluation is obviously better; more is better than less. But in the dictionary and CD cases, we need more information to know whether joint evaluation is better. The same is probably true for the case of the congressional candidates. In the context of consumption choices, the question is whether the ability to evaluate a characteristic of an option and the salience of that characteristic produces decisions with net welfare gains for choosers in joint evaluation. If the factor that is evaluable in joint evaluation does not matter much, and if the factor that is downplayed or ignored in joint evaluation is actually important, then separate evaluation is likely to be better.

There is a psychological wrinkle here. It is tempting to think that life is lived in separate evaluation, which helps explain why and when joint evaluation leads to mistakes.[28] But is life really lived in separate evaluation? The answer depends on the context and on the person. Suppose that a consumer buys a dictionary with ten thousand words or a computer with a terrific keyboard but a less-than-ideal screen. If that consumer does not think about dictionaries with more words or computers with ideal screens, her purchasing decision will be shown to be correct. If her attention is not spent on issues of comparison, she will live in separate evaluation. But suppose that she does think about those products, at least some of the time, and focuses on her dictionary with limited words or her computer with a screen that, while excellent, pales by comparison with a screen that she rejected. If so, she is living, to a greater or lesser extent, in joint evaluation.

People vary in their propensity to engage in product comparisons. The universe of comparison products defines the frame of reference by which many of us define our experiences—which helps explain why product improvements may impose serious welfare losses on people who had been enjoying their goods a great deal.

Law and Policy

I have emphasized that preference reversals between joint and separate evaluation have been found in the domains of law and politics as well. The domain for analysis here is very large, and research remains in an early state. One of my goals here is to vindicate the suggestion with which I began: the choice between joint and separate evaluation depends on the relevant task and the underlying goals of the enterprise. For that reason, we might well end up rejecting both modes of evaluation. We might simply block some grounds for action (such as racial prejudice). We might seek to rely on global evaluation. We might want to use some kind of algorithm.

If, for example, optimal deterrence is the goal, neither joint nor separate evaluation is likely to do a great deal of good.

Consider some examples.

Discrimination

Let us stipulate that in many domains, some people discriminate on legally impermissible grounds: race, sex, religion, disability, age. Discrimination might be a product of conscious bias, in the form of a desire to benefit or burden people of specific social groups. Alternatively, it might be a product of unconscious bias, in the form of automatic devaluation of which people are not aware and which they might reject, or be embarrassed by, if they were made aware of it. Whether conscious or unconscious, discrimination raises puzzles for preference reversals. Does joint or separate evaluation matter? If so, is one better? As we shall see, no simple answer makes sense. But there is a fortunate qualification, which is that if the goal is to stop discrimination, we can specify the circumstances in which joint or separate evaluation will be more likely to achieve that goal.

Iris Bohnet and her coauthors have found that in joint evaluation, people decide on the merits, but in separate evaluation, gender matters, so men have an advantage over women.[29] To simplify the story: Suppose that people are evaluating two candidates, Jack and Jill. In separate evaluation, Jack has an advantage because he is male; people automatically value men more highly than women, and in separate evaluation that automatic assessment matters. But in joint evaluation, the advantage dissipates. People compare the two candidates, and if Jill's qualifications are better, then she will be hired. Merit becomes decisive. That is the central finding by Bohnet et al.: discrimination occurs in separate evaluation; merit dominates in joint evaluation.[30]

The mechanism here seems straightforward. It does not involve evaluability. In the relevant population, there is a bias in favor of men, which means that in separate evaluation they will do better. But people know, in some sense, that they should not discriminate, and in joint evaluation the fact that they are discriminating will stare them in the face. If they see that they are discriminating, they will be embarrassed—and stop. It follows that when women have stronger qualifications than men, women will be chosen. We could easily imagine similar findings in the context of discrimination on the basis of race, religion, age, or disability.

From this finding, however, it would be a mistake to conclude that joint evaluation is *generally* a safeguard against discrimination. It works that way only under specified conditions; under different conditions, it might actually aggravate discrimination. Suppose, for example, that people have a self-conscious bias of some kind and that they are not at all ashamed of it. In joint evaluation, those who have such a bias might discriminate more, not less, than in separate evaluation. In separate evaluation, sex or race might not loom so large; discriminators might focus mainly on qualifications. But if people are biased against women or African Americans, they might discriminate more in joint evaluation simply because sex or race might crowd out other considerations; it might operate like total harmonic distortion in the case of the CD changers.

Imagine, for example, these cases:

Potential employee A: very strong record, excellent experience

Potential employee B: strong record, good experience, from a prominent family, not Jewish

In separate evaluation, potential employee A might well be preferred. (Let us suppose that potential employee A is not from a prominent family and is Jewish, but neither of those characteristics is salient in separate evaluation.) But if social attitudes take a particular form, potential employee B might well be preferred in joint evaluation. With respect to discrimination, everything depends on the relevant constellation of attitudes.

Punitive Damages

In the US legal system (and many others), juries are allowed to award punitive damages to punish wrongdoing. There is a pervasive question, to which the Supreme Court has occasionally been attentive, whether such awards are arbitrary or excessive.[31] In deciding whether to give punitive damages and choosing what amount to award, juries are not permitted to consider comparison cases. They are making decisions in separate evaluation. Does that matter? If so, how? Here are some answers.

1. Normalization   Consider this pair of cases:

Case A: childproof safety cap fails and child needs hospital stay

Case B: repainted cars sold as new to a leasing agency

When people see two cases of this kind in isolation, they tend to receive similar punishment ratings (on a bounded scale of 1 to 8) and similar monetary awards.[32] But when they see them jointly, case A receives much higher punishment ratings and much higher punitive awards.[33] There is a clear reversal, but the mechanism is different from what we have seen previously. There is no problem of evaluability—at least not in the same sense. Nor is there anything like a characteristic that people might find relevant only or mostly in separate evaluation (such as gender). When people see a case of physical harm in separate evaluation, *they spontaneously normalize it by comparing it to other cases of physical harm.*[34] A failed childproof safety cap is, in the category of physical harms, not good—but it is not all that bad. When people see a case of financial harm in separate evaluation, they engage in a similar act of normalization. Repainted cars are, in that category, not good—but not all that bad. Hence the two receive similar ratings and similar awards.

At the same time, people agree that a case of physical harm is generally worse than one of financial harm. It follows that in joint evaluation, the failed safety caps look significantly worse, in the sense that they deserve more severe punishment. The effect of joint evaluation is to dislodge people from their spontaneous use of category-bound judgments. They will think more broadly. In experiments of this kind, joint evaluation has a significant effect because it enlarges the universe of cases about which participants will think. The mechanism is related to that in the context of sex discrimination, for which joint evaluation forces a different and better form of deliberation.

There is a broad point about outrage here. Outrage is category-bound, in the sense that the level of felt outrage will be a function of category in which the offending behavior falls. If someone cuts ahead in an airport security line or makes a rude comment on social media, people might feel high levels of outrage. But if they compare such behavior to, say, child abuse or assault, they might be a bit embarrassed (and feel far less outrage). Punitive damage judgments are a product of outrage.[35] Because outrage is category-bound, preference reversals are essentially inevitable.

2. Manipulation Again Here again, joint evaluation affords ample opportunity for manipulation in the selection of the comparison cases. Suppose that people are thinking about cases involving financial harm. If they are exposed to cases involving rape, financial harm might seem trivial and receive significantly lower ratings. But if they are exposed to cases involving minor acts of trespass on private property, financial harm might seem serious and receive significantly higher ratings. To see the point, compare these cases:

Case A: Jones, an editor at a national news magazine, sexually harassed a female employee; he tried, on several occasions, to kiss her against her will, and he made her extremely uncomfortable at work

Case B: Smith, who has had several tickets for reckless driving, recently hit a pedestrian at night; the pedestrian suffered five broken bones (including a severe concussion)

It is easily imaginable that in separate evaluation, Jones and Smith would receive equally severe punishment, or even that Jones' punishment would be more severe—but that in joint evaluation, Smith's punishment would be more severe. Now imagine a different case B:

Case B: Smith, a high school student in a rock band, has repeatedly played very loud music late at night, keeping his neighbor, Wilson, wide awake

It is easily imaginable that in joint evaluation, case B would produce a higher punishment for Jones than Jones would receive in separate evaluation.

3. Normative Considerations   Notwithstanding these points, it is true that for problems of this kind joint evaluation has an important advantage over separate evaluation: the latter will produce a pattern of results that people will themselves reject on reflection.[36] In other words, separate evaluation will yield what separate evaluators will consider to be an incoherent set of results. As noted, punitive damage awards must be assessed in isolation; the legal system now forbids juries from considering comparison cases, and if jury awards are challenged, judicial consideration of such cases may occur—but in practice, it is severely restricted.

That does seem to be a mistake. If we want coherent patterns, joint evaluation is better. But there are two problems with joint evaluation: The first is that it is not global evaluation. If the goal is to produce reasoned outcomes, and to prevent what decisionmakers would themselves consider unfairness, they should look at a universe of cases, not two, and not a handful. The second problem is that in these kinds of cases, we might not want to celebrate what comes from either mode of evaluation. In the context of punitive damage awards, we cannot offer a normative judgment without some kind of theory about what punitive damages are *for*.

Suppose that we adopt an economic perspective focused on optimal deterrence and see punitive damage awards as justified to make up for the fact that the probability of detection and compensation is less than 100 percent. If so, the question is whether separate or joint evaluation focuses people on how to achieve optimal deterrence. Unfortunately, neither does so. People are intuitive retributivists.[37] They do not naturally think in terms of optimal deterrence, and they will be reluctant to do so even if they are asked (see chapter 14).[38] From the standpoint of optimal deterrence, the conclusion about joint and separate evaluation is simple: a pox on both your houses.

If we embrace a retributive theory of punishment, joint evaluation seems better. On one view, the question is how best to capture the moral outrage of the community, and in separate evaluation category-bound thinking ensures that the question will not be answered properly (by the community's own lights). But one more time: the major problem with joint evaluation is that it is not global evaluation. That point argues in favor of some effort to broaden the jury's viewscreen to consider cases in light of a range of other cases, to allow reviewing judges to do the same, or to create a damage schedule of some kind.

These conclusions bear on some philosophical questions on which preference reversals have been observed.[39] To summarize a complex story,[40] most people say that they would not push a person off a bridge and in front of a train, even if that is the only way to divert the train and thus to save five people who are in the train's path. But most people say that they would be willing to flip a switch that would divert the train away from the five people and kill a bystander. Typically the two problems (usually called the *footbridge* and the *trolley problems*) are tested separately, and moral intuitions in the two cases diverge.

But what if people assess the problems jointly? The simple answer is that they endeavor to give the same answer to the two questions—either to say that they would save the five or that they would refuse to kill the one. (Perhaps surprisingly, there is no strong movement in the direction of the utilitarian direction, which counsels in favor of saving the five.) But it is not clear how to evaluate this shift. Nor is it even clear that in joint evaluation, people are showing moral consistency. Whether they are doing so depends *on whether, on normative grounds, the footbridge and trolley problems are the same.* The answer depends on whether we accept a utilitarian or nonutilitarian account, and whether we should be utilitarians cannot be dictated by how people respond in joint or separate evaluation.

Contingent Valuation

When regulators engage in cost-benefit analysis, they sometimes have to value goods that are not traded on markets or for which market evidence is unavailable or unreliable. In such circumstances, they engage in surveys, sometimes described as involving "stated preference" or "contingent valuation."[41] Let us bracket the serious controversies over the usefulness and reliability of these methods[42] and ask a simple question: Do people's valuations differ depending on whether they see cases separately or jointly?

Consider these cases, in which, on a bounded scale, people were asked about their satisfaction from providing help and their willingness to pay:

Cause A: program to improve detection of skin cancer in farm workers

Cause B: fund to clean up and protect dolphin breeding locations

When people see the two in isolation, they show a higher satisfaction rating from giving to cause B and they are willing to pay about the same.[43] But when they evaluate them jointly, they show a much higher satisfaction rating from A and they want to pay far more for it.[44] Here, the best explanation involves category-bound thinking.[45] Detection of skin cancer among farm workers is important, but in terms of human health it may not be the most pressing priority. Protection of dolphins plucks at the heartstrings. But most people would want to pay more for the former than the latter if they are choosing among them.

For contingent valuation, is joint evaluation better than separate evaluation or vice versa? Is either approach reliable? For those who embrace contingent valuation methods, the goal is to discern how much informed people value various goods, replicating the idealized use of the willingness to pay criterion in well-functioning markets. If that is the goal, separate evaluation faces a serious problem, which is that people make judgments with a narrow viewscreen. On that count, joint evaluation seems better to the extent that it broadens the viewscreen—which means that joint evaluation cannot involve cases from the same category. But even with that proviso, from what category do we find cause B? There is a risk of manipulation here, driving judgments about cause A up or down.

Global evaluation or something like it seems better than joint evaluation, but it is challenging to design anything like it in practice. If the theory of contingent valuation is generally plausible—a big if—then preference reversals give us new reason to emphasize the importance of broad viewscreens for participants.

Evaluating Nudges

Do people approve of nudges? Which ones? In recent years, that question has produced a growing literature.[46] A central finding is that in the domains of safety, health, and the environment, people generally approve of nudges of the kind that have been adopted or seriously considered in various democracies in recent years.[47] At the same time, majorities generally seem to favor educative nudges, such as mandatory information disclosure, over noneducative nudges, such as default rules.[48]

But do they really? Shai Davidai and Eldar Shafir have shown that in joint evaluation, they do—but in separate evaluation, they do not.[49] Consider this stylized example:

Policy A: promote savings by automatically enrolling employees into pension plans, subject to opt out

Policy B: promote savings by giving employees clear, simple information about the benefits of enrolling into pension plans

In joint evaluation, most people will prefer an educative nudge and also rank it higher on a bounded scale. But in separate evaluation, the rankings are identical or at least similar.[50] The best explanation, which should now be familiar, involves salience. In separate evaluation, people do not specifically focus on whether a nudge is or is not educative. In joint evaluation, the distinction along that dimension (educative or not?) becomes highly salient, and it drives people's judgments.

Is joint or separate evaluation better? Note that in this context, the question is whether we have reason to trust one or another evaluative judgment. At first glance, the answer seems straightforward. Joint evaluation would be better if, on normative grounds, it is appropriate to make a sharp distinction between System 1 and System 2 nudges. If it is indeed appropriate, joint evaluation is best because it places a bright spotlight on that distinction. But if, on normative grounds, that distinction is entitled to little or no weight, its salience in joint evaluation leads people in the wrong direction. One more time: the problem with joint evaluation is that it draws people's attention very directly to a factor that might deserve little normative weight.

With respect to evaluation of policies, there is a much broader point here, connected with what we have seen in the context of consumer goods. Policy A might look good or bad in the abstract; it might be difficult to evaluate it unless its features are placed in some kind of context. The opportunity to see policy B can provide helpful information, but it might focus people on what distinguishes policy A from policy B and give it undue prominence. Here again, experimenters or politicians can engage in manipulation on this count. Global evaluation would be better, but, as before, it is challenging to implement. In cases like those presented by Davidai and Shafir, there is no escaping a normative question: Does the distinction made salient in joint evaluation matter or not? The normative question must be engaged on its merits, not by asking what people prefer and how the answer differs depending on joint or separate evaluation. It is tempting, and not wrong, to emphasize that in separate evaluation, people will not pay attention to a factor that might turn out to be critical in joint evaluation. But that is not an answer to the normative question.

What if we are trying to discover what people actually think or what they think on reflection? In this context, it is reasonable to wonder whether there is an answer to that question, at least for purposes of choosing between joint and separate evaluation. Because people's answers are a product of which kind of evaluation is being asked of them, all that can be said is that to that extent, their preferences are labile.

Welfare and Experience

For consumer goods, the central question (putting externalities to one side) is which choice will improve the welfare of choosers. In cases subject to preference reversals, the problem is that in separate evaluation, some characteristic of an option is difficult or impossible to evaluate—which means that it will not receive the attention that it may deserve. A characteristic that is important to welfare or actual experience might be ignored. In joint evaluation, the problem is that the characteristic that is evaluable may receive undue attention. A characteristic that is unimportant to welfare or to actual experience might be given great weight.

Sellers can manipulate choosers in either separate evaluation or joint evaluation, and the design of the manipulation should now be clear. In separate evaluation, the challenge is to show choosers a characteristic that they can evaluate, if it is good (intact cover), and to show them a characteristic that they cannot evaluate, if it is not so good (0.01 total harmonic distortion). In joint evaluation, the challenge is to allow an easy comparison along a dimension that is self-evidently important, even if the difference along that dimension matters little or not at all to experience or to what matters.

If external observers had perfect information, they could of course decide what the chooser should do. The problem is that external observers usually have imperfect information. Among other things, they tend to lack a full sense of the chooser's preferences and values. Nonetheless, we can find easy cases in which separate evaluation is best and easy cases in which joint evaluation is best, and we are now in a position to understand why some cases are hard. The larger lesson is that separate evaluation and joint evaluation have serious and characteristic defects.

The problem of discrimination can be analyzed in broadly similar terms. The general idea is that a bias may have more weight in separate evaluation than in joint evaluation if (1) people are made explicitly aware, in joint evaluation, that the only way to make a certain decision is to show bias and (2) they are ashamed or otherwise troubled about doing that. On different assumptions, joint evaluation could increase discrimination. Everything depends on people's reflective judgments about their own propensity to discriminate.

In the context of punitive damages, the problem is that people generate their own frame of reference, typically limited to the category that the case spontaneously brings to mind. Joint evaluation solves that problem. It does not follow, however, that joint evaluation produces sensible awards. From the standpoint of optimal deterrence, it will not do that. From the retributive point of view, joint evaluation does seem better because it better reflects people's moral judgments. The problem is that joint evaluation is not global evaluation. If a single case from a single category is added to another, there is a risk of manipulation.

Contingent valuation studies and evaluations of nudges can be analyzed similarly. Separate evaluation creates serious risks because people's judgments might be category-bound or because they might neglect important characteristics of options. Joint evaluation also creates serious risks because it is inevitably selective or because it accentuates a characteristic of options that does not deserve much weight. If it is feasible, something in the direction of global evaluation is best. If it is not feasible, a choice between separate and joint evaluation must depend on an independent judgment about whether a characteristic, ignored in the former but potentially decisive in the latter, really deserves weight.

We can find cases in which joint evaluation solves some kind of problem; discrimination, under the stated assumptions, is an example. But the largest points lie elsewhere. Separate evaluation can create serious trouble because of the challenge of evaluability or its cousin, category-bound thinking. Joint evaluation can create serious trouble because it focuses people on a characteristic of a product, a person, or a context that does not deserve the attention that they give it. Sellers, doctors, lawyers, and politicians can easily enlist these points to achieve their goals. But both forms of trouble should be avoided. For purposes of producing good decisions and good outcomes, we need to look beyond both separate and joint evaluation and instead design structures that avoid the problems and pathologies associated with each.

III Excursions

12 Transparency

There is a distinction between two kinds of transparency: output transparency and input transparency. Suppose that the Department of Transportation has completed a detailed study of what kinds of policies help to reduce deaths on the highways or that the Department of Labor has produced an analysis of the health risks associated with exposure to silica in the workplace. Or suppose that the Environmental Protection Agency produces a regulation to curtail greenhouse gas emissions from motor vehicles or adopts a policy about when it will bring enforcement actions against those who violate its water-quality regulations. All these are *outputs*.

The government might also become aware of certain *facts*—for example, the level of inflation in European nations, the number of people who have died in federal prisons, the apparent plans of terrorist organizations, or levels of crime and air pollution in Los Angeles and Chicago. For the most part, facts also should be seen as outputs, at least if they are a product of some kind of process of information acquisition.

In all of these cases, transparency about outputs can be a nudge. It might be designed to influence the private sector—for example, by promoting companies to do better to increase safety or by helping consumers and workers to avoid risks. Transparency can also nudge government, by showing officials, and those whom they serve, that they are not doing as well as they might.

Now suppose that officials within the Department of Energy and the Environmental Protection Agency staffs have exchanged views about what form a greenhouse regulation should take or that political appointees within the Department of Labor have had heated debates about the risks associated with silica in the workplace and about how those risks are best handled. The various views are *inputs*.

To be sure, there are intermediate cases. The EPA might conclude that a substance is carcinogenic, and in a sense that conclusion is an output—but it might also be an input into a subsequent regulatory judgment. The Department of Transportation might reach certain conclusions about the environmental effects of allowing a highway to be built, which seem to be an output, but those conclusions might be an input into the decision whether to allow the highway to be built. The National Environmental Policy Act can be seen as a requirement that agencies disclose outputs in the form of judgments about environmental effects—but those outputs are, by law, mere inputs into ultimate decisions about what to do. Some outputs are inputs, and in the abstract it would be possible to characterize them as one or the other or as both. As we shall see, the appropriate characterization depends in part on whether and how the public would benefit from disclosure.

Acknowledging the existence of hard intermediate cases, I offer two claims here. The first is that for outputs, the argument on behalf of transparency is often exceptionally strong. If the government has information about levels of crime in Boise; about water quality in Flint, Michigan; about security lines at LaGuardia Airport; about the hazards associated with certain toys; or about the effects of driverless cars, it should usually disclose that information—certainly on request and, if people stand to gain from it, even without request. (The latter point is especially important.) In all of these cases, the benefits of transparency are significant. Sometimes members of the public can use the information in their daily lives, and output transparency can promote accountability and therefore increase transparency. Most of the time, the costs of output transparency are trivial. All over the world, governments should offer much more in the way of output transparency. In particular, they should make outputs freely available to the public as a matter of course—at least if the public could or would benefit from them and unless there is a particular reason why they need to remain confidential.

But input transparency is a much more complicated matter. The costs of disclosure are often high and the benefits may be low, and in any case they are qualitatively different from those that justify output transparency. There are strong reasons to protect processes of internal deliberation, above all to ensure openness, candor, and trust. In addition, it is often unclear that the public would gain much from seeing inputs, not least because of their massive volume (and usual irrelevance to anything that matters). Outside of unusual circumstances, the public would usually gain little or nothing (except perhaps something like gossip). Another way to put the point is that while those who seek to attract eyeballs or to embarrass their political opponents often like input transparency, the public usually does not much benefit from it.

To be sure, transparency about inputs can be informative, and inputs may have keen historical interest. If the public learns that the deputy secretary of transportation had a different view from that of the secretary on the content of a fuel-economy regulation, it knows something; internal disagreement paints a different picture from internal unanimity. But how much, exactly, does the public learn, and why is it important for the public to learn it? It should be acknowledged that in some cases input transparency is a good idea, especially under circumstances of corruption (or anything close to it) and when relevant inputs have genuine historic importance (and when their disclosure can reduce mistakes). Nations need catalogs. But the argument for input transparency is much different from the argument for output transparency, and it often stands on weaker ground.

It should be clear from these remarks that my approach to this topic is insistently and unabashedly *welfarist*: What are the benefits of transparency and what are the costs? It is true that the benefits and the costs may not be easy to quantify, but some kind of assessment of both is, I suggest, indispensable to an evaluation of when transparency is most and least necessary. For those who are not comfortable with talk of costs and benefits in this context, it might be useful to understand those terms as an effort not to create some kind of arithmetic straightjacket, but to signal the importance of asking concrete questions about the human consequences of competing approaches. At least for difficult problems, those questions are (I suggest) far more productive than abstractions about "legitimacy" and "the right to know."

Sunlight

Begin with the remarkable finding, by the economist Amartya Sen, that in the history of the world, there has *never* been a famine in a system with a free press and democratic elections.[1] Sen's starting point here, which he demonstrates empirically, is that famines are a social product, not an inevitable product of scarcity of food. Whether there will be a famine, as opposed to a mere shortage, depends on people's *entitlements*—that is, what they are able to obtain. Even when food is limited, entitlements can be allocated in such a way as to ensure that no one will starve.

But when will a government take the necessary steps to prevent starvation? The answer depends on that government's own incentives. When there is a democratic system with free speech and a free press, the government faces a great deal of pressure to ensure that people generally have access to food. And when officials are thus pressured, they respond. But a system without a free press or democratic elections is likely to enable government to escape public accountability and hence not to respond to famines. Government officials will not be exposed, nor will they be at risk of losing their jobs.

Here, then, is a large lesson about the relationships among a well-functioning system of free expression, disclosure of relevant information (outputs), and citizens' well-being. Free speech and freedom of information are not mere luxuries, catering to the tastes of members of the most educated classes. On the contrary, they increase the likelihood that government will actually serve people's interests. This lesson suggests some of the virtues not only for liberty but also for economic goals of having freedom of speech and freedom of information.[2]

In recent years, most of the most prominent transparency initiatives have involved outputs. A revealing example involves GPS devices. In 1993, President Clinton chose to unlock (by making public and useable) the data that was ultimately adapted to make the GPS device a familiar part of everyday life. Its availability has helped countless people, often in profound ways; it has even saved lives. A GPS device makes life more *navigable* (literally). If we think about navigability as a more general idea, we can see the value of disclosure of many outputs. Information about safety seats in cars, crime, air and water quality, and much more can be seen as akin to GPS devices, writ large: they tell people how to go in the directions they want.

For all of its years, the Obama administration made transparency a major priority. (I am insisting on that point while acknowledging the many controversies during the Obama presidency over potential trade-offs between transparency and other values.) The priority was signaled by an early and defining presidential memorandum, dedicated specifically to the Freedom of Information Act. The memorandum establishes "a clear presumption:

In the face of doubt, openness prevails." Importantly, it adds that "agencies should take affirmative steps to make information public. They should not wait for specific requests from the public." It directs both the attorney general and the director of the Office of Management and Budget (OMB) to issue new guidance designed to implement the governing principles.

Both resulting documents deserve close attention, but for my purposes here, the OMB's guidance is especially noteworthy.[3] The memorandum directs agencies to publish information online. It adds that "agencies should proactively use modern technology to disseminate useful information, rather than waiting for specific requests under FOIA." Perhaps most significantly, it requires each agency to create an open government plan and an open government webpage, designed to "create and institutionalize a culture of open government." The open government plans are required to have "online in an open format at least three high-value data sets," which are in turn defined as "information that can be used to increase agency accountability and responsiveness; improve public knowledge of the agency and its operations; further the core mission of the agency; create economic opportunity; or respond to need and demand as identified through public consultation."

In the abstract, it is not clear whether this initiative involves output transparency or input transparency, but in practice the former was and remains primary by far.[4] The high-value datasets typically involve outputs. Since 2009, data.gov has become a principal location for posting such datasets, which amount to output transparency in action. The site now offers many datasets, with information on agriculture, finance, health, education, energy, and much more. With a click, you can find "Airline On-Time Performance and Causes of Flight Delays: On-Time Data," "Expenditures on Children by Families" (with estimates of the cost of raising children from birth through age 17 for major budgetary components), or detailed information about product recalls. There is much more in the same vein, focusing on outputs of policymaking or information-gathering activity.

As a result, people in the private sector have produced numerous apps that provide people with information that they can actually use. One example is AirNow, which has up-to-the-moment information about air quality. Another is the College Affordability and Transparency Center, which provides information about college costs. Yet another is eRecall, which gives people information about recall information at the time of purchase.

The outputs released on data.gov serve two independent purposes. First, people can take advantage of them in their daily lives. Like a GPS device, most of this information makes life simpler and more navigable. The availability of such information on cell phones makes the point far from fanciful. This point is no mere abstraction. If we take the idea of navigability in the large, we can see disclosure as a way of helping people to get to their preferred destinations in countless domains, saving money and reducing risks in the process. To my knowledge, the benefits of data.gov have yet to be quantified, but there is little doubt that people are gaining from the disclosures in concrete ways. They are excellent nudges. (Compare the benefits of GPS devices.)

Second, release of the outputs can promote accountability for both private and public sectors. Recall Justice Louis Brandeis's suggestion that "sunlight is ... the best of disinfectants."[5] If the air quality is terrible in Los Angeles, if a particular university is unusually expensive, if students at a for-profit college do not end up with jobs, if drinking water is unsafe in San Diego, or if a company has a lot of recalled toys, transparency can serve as a spur to change. Transparency increases accountability, and when people are accountable their performance is likely to improve.[6] The point bears on both public and private institutions. Transparency can tell citizens about the actions of public officials—for example, how long it takes for them to work on a permit application or the levels of air pollution in San Antonio (for which officials bear some responsibility). It can also inform citizens about the actions of private actors—for example, by disclosing product recalls or ratings of safety seats. In either event, it can spur improved performance.

Missions

One of the most interesting aspects of the OMB memorandum is that it asks agencies to consider whether disclosure might further their "core missions." That is an exceedingly important idea, which deserves far more agency use in the future, and it involves disclosure of outputs.

In environmental policy, one of the most well-known examples is the Toxic Release Inventory (TRI), which was created largely as a bookkeeping measure, designed to ensure that the federal government would have information about toxic releases. To the surprise of many people, the TRI has been a successful *regulatory* approach, because companies did not want to be listed as one of the "dirty dozen" in their states.[7] Accountability served as a spur toward emissions reductions. For a period, the Occupational Safety and Health Administration (OSHA) followed this lead by posting, very visibly on osha.gov, information about recent deaths in American workplaces, with names of the companies whose employees died. The EPA did something quite similar with its Greenhouse Gas Inventory, one of whose goals was to spur emissions reductions. Here again, we are speaking of nudges, which can be used to influence corporate behavior.

In all of these cases, the government is disclosing information that public officials have. We can imagine, of course, a requirement of output transparency imposed by the public sector on the private sector. Requirements of that kind are not always organized under the idea of freedom of information, but they involve transparency, and they can also promote important agency missions. Under the authority of the Affordable Care Act, for example, the Food and Drug Administration has required chain restaurants to disclose the calories associated with their offerings. Some of the early results are quite promising, with significant reductions in body mass index (BMI) among people who really do need to lose weight.[8] It is also hoped that disclosure requirements will affect the behavior of producers and sellers, and there is evidence that calorie disclosure requirements are leading restaurants to offer healthier meals.

I have offered just a few illustrations of disclosures whose goal is to promote agency missions through output transparency. An excellent collection, generally including outputs, can be found in the numerous action plans from dozens of nations of the Open Government Partnership (see opengovernmentpartnership.org). It is, of course, an empirical question whether transparency will promote agency missions. But in many cases, it can.[9] (It is said that China's interest in air pollution and greenhouse gas emissions has been greatly spurred by the ready availability of the air quality index on cell phones.) Because the costs of output transparency are typically low, there is every reason to adopt a presumption in its favor.

I have been painting with a very broad brush—in principle, an unduly broad one. My suggestion has been that disclosure of outputs is justified, or presumptively justified, on welfare grounds, but that is not always the case. We can easily imagine outputs whose disclosure would produce low benefits or high costs. With respect to costs, consider the words of the OMB memorandum: "Nothing in this Directive shall be construed to supersede existing requirements for review and clearance of pre-decisional information by the Director of the Office of Management and Budget relating to legislative, budgetary, administrative, and regulatory materials. Moreover, nothing in this Directive shall be construed to suggest that the presumption of openness precludes the legitimate protection of information whose release would threaten national security, invade personal privacy, breach confidentiality, or damage other genuinely compelling interests." That is jargon, but it points to important qualifications.

In various ways, the Freedom of Information Act recognizes all of these qualifications and more. No one doubts that the government has a great deal of information whose disclosure would endanger national security, and even if that information can be counted as an output, it should be kept confidential. The government also has "personally identifiable information," which receives protection under privacy laws. Although a balance must be struck between transparency and privacy, some forms of disclosure intrude on privacy in an intolerable way. Some kinds of disclosure could compromise trade secrets or otherwise privileged information. And if disclosure is not automatic or automated, the very act of providing transparency can impose costs in terms of both money and time.

On the benefit side, distinctions are also important. In principle, and if the costs of making the assessment were zero, it would make sense not to insist that each and every output should be disclosed, but instead to ask, on a case-by-case basis, whether disclosing specified outputs would or could be beneficial—for example, to consumers and workers. Of the numerous data sets on data.gov, surely some have modest benefits or no benefits; people are not paying the slightest attention to them (and they will not in the future). A welfarist analysis would call for particularized inquiries into that question. The problem, of course, is that those inquiries may not be manageable. When disclosure is being discussed, projection of benefits may be quite difficult. What people will *do* with information (if anything) may not be self-evident. The private sector is ingenious and full of alchemists. What it will find useful or turn into gold cannot be predicted in advance.

In view of that fact, it makes sense for agencies to make reasonable judgments about what count as high-value datasets, broadly understood, and to get them online *as soon as possible*—and announce a general presumption in favor of disclosure of outputs, armed with an intuitive understanding of the domains to which the presumption will be applied. It should be underlined that a degree of automaticity, putting relevant material online as a matter of routine, could be extremely helpful.

With respect to high-value datasets, intuitions should be disciplined by asking two questions: (1) Could people possibly benefit from this information in their daily lives? (2) Could disclosure promote accountability in a way that would improve public or private performance? In the words of the 2009 presidential memorandum: "The Government should not keep information confidential merely because public officials might be embarrassed by disclosure, because errors and failures might be revealed, or because of speculative or abstract fears. Nondisclosure should never be based on an effort to protect the personal interests of Government officials at the expense of those they are supposed to serve." Those words are important and correct—but they have one important qualification, to which I now turn.

Input Transparency

When I was clerking for Justice Thurgood Marshall in 1980, Bob Woodward and Scott Armstrong published a book on the Supreme Court, called The Brethren. I did not speak with Woodward or Armstrong, and I am also confident that none of my three coclerks did so. But numerous clerks (largely or perhaps entirely from previous terms) decided to open up to the authors. The portrait of Justice Marshall was highly unflattering (and, by the way, wildly inaccurate). Marshall was clearly disappointed, much less (I think) because of the unfavorable, unfair, inaccurate portrait than because of what he saw as a breach of loyalty. I do not think it is disloyal to disclose what he said to us, which was roughly this: "I am not going to change how I interact with my clerks, but if you violate my confidence, it's on your conscience."

After I left the White House in 2012, many reporters, and some people outside of the world of journalism, asked me questions about internal dynamics. Who said what to the president? Who disagreed with whom? If something happened or did not happen, who wanted it not to happen or to happen? Who won and who lost? Of course I did not answer any of these questions, but there was no mistaking the (astounding) persistence with which they were asked. How well I recall a conversation with a superb journalist, working for the Washington Post, who was much focused on the who-disagreed-with-whom questions. I finally suggested to her that she should write something on the substance of the issues that most interested her (environmental policy). She did not seem enthusiastic about the suggestion.

As I understand them here (and consistent with the standard parlance), inputs count as both predecisional and deliberative. These are independent requirements. They are predecisional in the sense that they are not themselves official decisions in any respect. They antedate those decisions and are meant to inform them. If an assistant administrator in the Environmental Protection Agency advises the administrator that a new ozone regulation should set a standard of sixty rather than sixty-five parts per billion, the communication is predecisional. Inputs are deliberative in the sense that they are part of a process of ongoing discussion about what to do.

I have acknowledged that even with these clarifications, we can imagine difficult cases, as when a report is compiled on (say) the risks associated with silica and that report will be an input into a regulation. But the core should not be obscure. If law clerks are exchanging memoranda on how to handle a dispute over affirmative action, inputs are involved. If people in the White House are discussing the contents of an open government memorandum, we are dealing with inputs. If White House officials are speaking with the Food and Drug Administration about how to handle the risks associated with certain asthma medicines, inputs are involved.

With respect to inputs, the argument for disclosure is significantly altered, and it is also weakened in two critical respects. First, the benefits of disclosure are usually much lower (not always, but usually). Second, the costs of disclosure are much higher. These are categorical statements with major qualifications, to which I will turn in due course.

Who Said What to Whom?

From the standpoint of the public, it is often not particularly desirable to obtain inputs. To those who believe in transparency, that claim might seem controversial, implausible, or even shocking. But the sheer number and range of inputs is daunting, and it defies belief to think that the public would benefit from seeing all of them. An assistant secretary will have countless conversations in the course of a week, and in many of them she will be receiving suggestions, venturing possible ideas, requesting more information, joking, offering doubts, and seeking out possible inclinations. Some of the inputs that she receives or offers will not be very interesting. If they are interesting, it might be for a reason that does not exactly argue for disclosure: Someone might have been ventured an idea, for purposes of discussion, that was or is on reflection a really bad one. The idea was (let us suppose) rejected, so it never became an output. Is it important, or on balance desirable, for the world to see it?

Or consider the general area of federal regulations, the most significant of which must go through the Office of Information and Regulatory Affairs (in most administrations, about five hundred per year). Many of those regulations will never be discussed seriously in newspapers or online. Their issuance is preceded by a great deal of internal discussion, involving paper documents, electronic documents, and email, often raising questions and doubts. This is the quintessence of a deliberative process. A number of people say a number of things. Much of the time, the benefits of disclosing the content of that process are not much higher than zero.

Within the federal government, what is true for the regulatory process is true for many discussions—but even more so. The volume of emails is extraordinarily high. As in the case of the hypothetical assistant secretary, they might float ideas, offer tentative reactions, report on what some people appear to think. In general, disclosure would serve no purpose at all, except perhaps to those interested in genuine minutiae or those seeking to embarrass, injure, or ruin someone, to create a political uproar, or to uncover some kind of scandal.

Two Qualifications

There are two principal qualifications, and they help explain the appeal of input transparency for many observers. It must be acknowledged that in some administrations, these qualifications will have, or will be perceived to have, a great deal of power. In corrupt or incompetent administrations, their power increases significantly.

Illegitimate or Illicit Arguments

Public disclosure might provide an ex ante deterrent to arguably illegitimate arguments, and it might also provide an ex post corrective. At the very least, it lets the public know how it is being governed. In the worst cases, inputs include corruption or criminality, and We the People are certainly entitled to learn about that.

Suppose, for example, that someone opposes a decision not because it is a bad idea but because it would offend a donor or a powerful interest group, or because a prominent senator might object (with unfortunate consequences for the administration). That sort of thing is not exactly unusual, and it is hardly the worst imaginable input. Let's stipulate that such an argument is objectionable, or at least that the public has a right to know about it, because it might compromise the pursuit of the public interest. Disclosure could make it less likely that such opposition will be voiced, which could be a good thing, and in any case it will create accountability. In this particular respect, an appealing argument about the beneficial effects of sunlight applies to input transparency as well as output transparency. That argument is all the stronger in cases of more egregious inputs. (Readers are invited to use their imaginations, or to consult history.)

To be sure, disclosure could have the principal effect of shifting the locus of the opposition—from email and paper to telephones. Within the federal government, that already happens a great deal. If people do not want their communications to be disclosed to the public or to Congress, they will say, "Call me." (In my own experience, this was always innocent; it did not involve anything illicit, but it did involve issues that were somewhat sensitive, such as strong disagreements that are not best placed in email.) Actually there is a substantial risk here. If internal discussions are potentially subject to disclosure, the shift from written to oral exchanges may impose losses, in the form of diminished reliance on careful economic, legal, and other analyses. Nonetheless, it is true that disclosure of inputs can have the beneficial effect of "laundering" them, or making everything cleaner.

There is no question that a concern about illegitimate or illicit inputs animates the argument in favor of input transparency. Suppose that you believe that some process is corrupt, ugly, or "rigged"—that regularly or as a matter of course, powerful private interests are dominating federal processes or that officials, beholden to certain interests and groups, are pushing outcomes in the directions favored by those groups. Of course you want that to stop. But if you cannot stop it directly, you might insist on input transparency as a way of opening it up to public view. Sunlight might be a disinfectant here as well.[10]

True, there is a risk that you will simply drive the relevant influences underground. But in principle, that is a secondary concern. You want to open up internal processes to public scrutiny. To say the least, that is an honorable goal. For those for whom the Watergate scandal is salient, the transgressions of President Richard Nixon are a defining example, and a degree of input transparency was necessary to ferret out those transgressions.

Learning from Mistakes

The second qualification is that journalists and historians can benefit from seeing the give-and-take, if only because they could give a narrative account of what happened. That might appear to be an abstract, academic benefit, but people (including public officials) do learn from the past, and that learning can provide a valuable corrective. The historical record can be absolutely indispensable for finding out what went wrong, and to understand that record, inputs are necessary. Why did the government make some colossal error, in the form of an action or an omission? To answer that question, input transparency might be essential. It can create warning signs about group interactions that work poorly, about institutional blindnesses, about the need for institutional reform.

Suppose, for example, that the United States government has done (too) little to prevent genocide.[11] It may be difficult or even impossible to document failures without access to inputs. Once the failures are documented, people might take steps to reduce their likelihood in the future. In that sense, the benefits of input disclosure can be high, at least in certain domains.

But there are countervailing points. In many cases, disclosure of inputs has no benefits; it does not reduce the risk of future errors. Disclosure also imposes a risk of distortion. Suppose that people have access to an official's emails—say, the emails of an assistant administrator at the Environmental Protection Agency or of the assistant attorney general for civil rights. Suppose that the email has some complaint about the EPA administrator or about the attorney general or about White House officials. The email might reflect a particular day or mood. It might be based on the author's incomplete understanding. It might be a matter of venting. It might reflect a badly distorted perspective.

Because journalists often enjoy and benefit from accusations and scandal mongering, it might be appealing to give a great deal of publicity to this revelation of internal disagreement. Recall that it is a form of gossip. Readers might enjoy the gossip, and in that sense benefit from it, but accusations and scandal mongering are not necessarily genuine benefits for the public. A genuine scandal is another matter.

The Costs of Input Transparency

For input transparency, the most obvious problem is that disclosure could reduce open-mindedness and discourage candor. In a short space, James Madison captured some of the essential points. His views were reported in this way:

> It was ... best for the convention for forming the Constitution to sit with closed doors, because opinions were so various and at first so crude that it was necessary they should be long debated before any uniform system of opinion could be formed. Meantime the minds of the members were changing, and much was to be gained by a yielding and accommodating spirit. Had the members committed themselves publicly at first, they would have afterwards supposed consistency required them to maintain their ground, whereas by secret discussion no man felt himself obliged to retain his opinions any longer than he was satisfied of their propriety and truth, and was open to the force of argument. ... [No] Constitution would ever have been adopted by the convention if the debates had been public.[12]

In any deliberative process, people's opinions are various and crude, and much is "to be gained by a yielding and accommodating spirit." Once people commit themselves publicly, they might not be willing to shift. Secrecy can promote openness to the force of the argument. And so Madison's knockout punch: "No Constitution would ever have been adopted by the convention if the debates had been public."

What Madison did not emphasize is that input transparency can lead people not to say what they think. It can reduce candor and the free play of ideas. In that sense, it can ensure that groups will have less information than they need. In well-functioning deliberative processes, there is often a sharp separation between an idea-generating phase and a solution-finding phase. In the former phase, many things are on the table, even if they turn out on reflection to be absurd or intolerable. People say "yes" to getting ideas out there regardless of whether there is any chance that they will be adopted. If inputs are transparent, the idea-generating phase may be far more constrained than it ought to be.

Ensuring candor is the central idea behind the notion of executive privilege.[13] At best, input transparency will lead people to communicate orally rather than in writing. And in fact, one of the consequences of FOIA is to reduce reliance on email and written documents. In both Republican and Democratic administrations, it is well-known that whatever is put in writing might find its way into the New York Times—which leads people not to put things in writing. At worst, input transparency can lead certain things not to be said at all.

But reduced candor is not the only problem. In view of the incentives of the media and political opponents, disclosure of inputs can produce extremely unfortunate distractions, destructive to self-government. Instead of focusing on outputs—on how, for example, to reduce premature deaths—a spotlight is placed on comments that seem to make some people into villains or wrongdoers or that put any resulting decisions in the least favorable light. Skeptics might respond, with some passion, that it is paternalistic or worse to deprive members of the public of information on the ground that they will misunderstand it or give it undue salience. On one view, receipt of true information should be subject to the marketplace of ideas. But insofar as the problem lies not in public misunderstanding but in the incentives of those who seek to fuel fires, there is definitely a downside risk.

An Accounting

With respect to input transparency, we seem to have incommensurable values on both sides of the ledger, not easily placed along a single metric. The benefits are often low—but not always, especially when illicit motivations, corruption, and criminality are involved and when the historical record can help to avoid massive or catastrophic mistakes. The costs can be high. But are they always?

It must be acknowledged that the costs of input transparency diminish over time, and they are certainly lower once the relevant people no longer hold public office. It is one thing to tell the director of the Office of Management and Budget that whatever she says will end up in the newspaper that night or the next day. It is quite another to say that at a future date (say, after an administration has ended), there will be a public record of internal communications, subject to safeguards for national security, personal privacy, and other values. And indeed, the Presidential Records Act[14] ventures an approach of this sort (with a five-year gap). With such an approach, the costs of disclosure are significantly reduced. They are not zero, because candor will be chilled and because people's reputation will be wrongly maligned. But in view of the value of obtaining some kind of historical record, that approach is hardly unreasonable. My aim has not been to reach a definitive conclusion about concrete practices and proposals but to outline general concerns to help identify the appropriate trade-offs.

There is a large difference between output transparency and input transparency. For outputs, transparency can be exceedingly important. A central reason is that the government often has information that people can actually use, perhaps to make life more navigable, perhaps to avoid serious risks. It should not keep that information to itself. Another reason is that sunlight can operate as a disinfectant. And whether the information involves the government's own performance or the performance of the private sector, disclosure can spur better performance.

One implication is the immense importance of continuing with, and amplifying, the work of data.gov. It also follows that in numerous contexts, government should not be waiting for FOIA requests; it should be disclosing information on its own. This does not mean that every output should be made available online. But it does mean that whenever an output could or would be valuable to members of the public, it deserves to be made public. For the future, we should expect significant developments in this direction, with a significant increase in automaticity.

Inputs belong in a different category. Outside of unusual circumstances, what most matters is what government actually does, not who said what to whom. For the most part, the public is unlikely to benefit if it learns that the assistant secretary of state disagreed with the chief of staff or the secretary of state on some trade agreement, or that there was an internal division over how aggressively to regulate greenhouse gases. Disclosure can also have significant costs. Most obviously, it can lead people to silence themselves or to communicate in ways that cannot be recorded. More subtly, it can divert attention from the important question, which involves policy and substance, to less important ones, which involve palace intrigue. At the same time, input transparency can put a spotlight on questionable, illicit, or corrupt practices and also can provide an indispensable historical record. People learn from the past, and for current administrations it can be essential to have a concrete sense of where past administrations went wrong.

My framework throughout has been welfarist; it asks about the costs and benefits of disclosure. It should be acknowledged that the very idea of welfarism needs to be specified and that many people would start with different foundations—involving, for example, the idea of political legitimacy. It should also be acknowledged that under a welfarist framework, some output transparency does not make much sense, and some input transparency is amply justified, even indispensable. We are speaking of categories, not individual cases. But categories provide orientation. Output transparency should be the central focus of efforts for freedom of information. We need much more of it. Input transparency can be important, especially after an administration has ended; but it should be treated far more cautiously.

13 Precautions

All over the world, there is keen interest in a simple idea for regulation of risk: In cases of doubt, follow the precautionary principle.[1] Avoid steps that will create a risk of harm. Until safety is established, be cautious; do not require unambiguous evidence. In a catchphrase: better safe than sorry.

In ordinary life, pleas of this kind seem quite sensible—indeed, a part of ordinary human rationality. It can be hazardous to interfere with natural processes, and we often refuse to alter the status quo because of a salutary fear of adverse side effects. Shouldn't the same approach be followed by rational regulators as well? Many people think that it should. For that reason, the precautionary principle has been an organizing principle for social change. In Europe, the United States, and elsewhere, the principle is often invoked by people who seek to strengthen protection of the environment, to safeguard nature, and to diminish risks to health and safety. At many times and in many places, the principle has been a beneficiary of social cascades. It has spread rapidly. Enclave deliberators often invoke it—and attempt to convince others that it provides a good framework.

My central claim here is conceptual. The real problem with the precautionary principle in its strongest form is that it is incoherent; it purports to give guidance, but it fails to do so, because it condemns the very steps that it requires. The regulation that the principle requires always gives rise to risks of its own—and hence the principle bans what it simultaneously mandates. I therefore aim to challenge the precautionary principle not because it leads in bad directions, but because, read for all that it is worth, it leads in no direction at all. The principle threatens to be paralyzing, forbidding regulation, inaction, and every step in between. It provides help only if we blind ourselves to many aspects of risk-related situations and focus on a narrow subset of what is at stake. Protection of nature often makes sense, but the precautionary principle is not a helpful way of identifying when, and how much, protection of nature makes sense.

If all this is right, how can we account for its extraordinary influence—and indeed for the widespread belief that it can and should guide regulatory judgments? We should acknowledge its possible pragmatic value, countering insufficient concern with some kinds of risks. Sometimes it spurs needed efforts to save lives and improve health. Undoubtedly the principle is invoked strategically by self-interested political actors, with European farmers, for example, invoking the idea of precaution to stifle American competitors, who are far more likely to rely on genetically modified crops. But apart from these points, I suggest that an understanding of human rationality and cognition provides useful clues. An appreciation of behavioral findings simultaneously sheds light on the operation of the principle, explains its otherwise puzzling appeal, and suggests why it should be abandoned or at least substantially recast. Indeed, such an understanding provides a better understanding of the uses and pitfalls of the old adage "better safe than sorry," which is subject to many of the same objections as the precautionary principle.

Above all, I urge that such regulators should use a wide rather than narrow viewscreen—and that, as applied, the precautionary principle is defective precisely because it runs afoul of this idea. To be sure, many of those who endorse the principle seek to protect against neglect of the future, disregard of the interests of those suffering from the greatest deprivation, indifference to catastrophic or worst-case scenarios, and impossible demands for unambiguous evidence from regulators. But as we shall see, the precautionary principle is a crude and sometimes perverse way of promoting those goals, which can be obtained through other, better routes.

Definitions

For those interested in precautions, the initial question is this: what exactly does the precautionary principle mean or require? We can imagine a continuum of understandings. At one extreme are weak versions to which no reasonable person could object. At the other extreme are strong versions that would require a fundamental rethinking of regulatory policy.

The most cautious and weak versions suggest, quite sensibly, that a lack of decisive evidence of harm should not be a ground for refusing to protect against risks. Controls might be justified even if we cannot establish a definite connection between, for example, low-level exposures to carcinogens and adverse effects on human health. Thus the 1992 Rio Declaration states, "Where there are threats of serious or irreversible damage, lack of full scientific certainty shall not be used as a reason for postponing cost-effective measures to prevent environmental degradation."

The Ministerial Declaration of the Second International Conference on the Protection of the North Sea, held in London in 1987, is in the same vein: "Accepting that in order to protect the North Sea from possibly damaging effects of the most dangerous substances, a Precautionary Principle is necessary which may require action to control inputs of such substances even before a causal link has been established by absolutely clear scientific evidence." Similarly, the United Nations Framework Convention on Climate Change offers cautious language: "Where there are threats of serious or irreversible damage, lack of full scientific certainty should not be used as a reason for postponing [regulatory] measures, taking into account that policies and measures to deal with climate change should be cost-effective so as to ensure global benefits at the lowest possible cost."

The widely publicized Wingspread Declaration, from a meeting of environmentalists in 1998, goes further: "When an activity raises threats of harm to human health or the environment, precautionary measures should be taken even if some cause and effect relationships are not established scientifically. In this context the proponent of the activity, rather than the public, should bear the burden of proof." The first sentence just quoted is a mildly more aggressive version of the statement from the Rio Declaration. It is more aggressive because it is not limited to threats of serious or irreversible damage. But in reversing the burden of proof, the second sentence goes further still. (Everything depends, of course, on what those with the burden of proof are required to show.)

In Europe, the precautionary principle has sometimes been understood in a still stronger way, asking for a significant margin of safety for all decisions. According to one definition, the precautionary principle means "that action should be taken to correct a problem as soon as there is evidence that harm may occur, not after the harm has already occurred."[2] The word *may* is the crucial one; almost all of the time, there will be "evidence that harm may occur," if *may* is not understood to require some threshold of probability. In a comparably strong version, the Final Declaration of the First

European "Seas at Risk" conference says that if "the 'worst case scenario' for a certain activity is serious enough then even a small amount of doubt as to the safety of that activity is sufficient to stop it taking place."[3]

The weak versions of the precautionary principle state a truism—uncontroversial in principle and necessary in practice only to combat public confusion or the self-interested claims of private groups demanding unambiguous evidence of harm (which no rational society requires). The weakest versions may be important in practice, but in principle they are unobjectionable, even banal; for that reason, I will not discuss them here. To make analytic progress, let us understand the principle in a strong way, to suggest that regulation is required whenever there is a potential risk to health, safety, or nature, even if the supporting evidence remains speculative and even if the economic costs of regulation are high. To avoid palpable absurdity, the idea of *potential risk* will be understood to require a certain threshold of scientific plausibility. To support regulation, no one thinks that it is enough if someone, somewhere, urges that a risk is worth taking seriously. But under the precautionary principle as I shall understand it, the threshold burden is minimal—and once it is met, there is something like a presumption in favor of regulatory controls.

I believe that this understanding of the precautionary principle fits with the understandings of some of its most enthusiastic proponents, and that with relatively modest variations, it fits with many of the legal formulations as well.

Self-Contradiction and Paralysis

It is tempting to object that the precautionary principle, thus understood, is hopelessly vague. How much precaution is the right amount of precaution? By itself, the principle does not tell us. It is also tempting to object that the principle is, but should not be, cost blind. Some precautions simply are not worthwhile, because they cost so much and help so little. But the most serious problem lies elsewhere. The real problem is that the principle offers no guidance—not that it is wrong, but that it forbids all courses of action, including regulation. It bans the very steps that it requires.

To understand the objection, it will be useful to anchor the discussion in some concrete problems:

• Genetic modification of food has become a widespread practice.[4] The risks of that practice are not known with precision. Some people fear that genetic modification will result in serious ecological harm; others believe that the risks are vanishingly low, and that genetic modification will result in more nutritious food and significant improvements in human health.

• Many people fear nuclear power on the ground that nuclear power plants create various health and safety risks, including some possibility of catastrophe. But if a nation does not rely on nuclear power, it might well rely instead on fossil fuels and in particular on coal-fired power plants. Such plants create risks of their own, including risks associated with climate change. At some points in recent history, China has relied on nuclear energy in a way that reduces greenhouse gases and a range of air pollution problems.[5]

• There is a possible conflict between the protection of marine mammals and military exercises. The United States Navy engages in many such exercises, and it is possible that marine mammals will be threatened as a result. Military activities in the oceans might well cause significant harm, but a decision to suspend those activities might also endanger military preparedness (or so the government contends).[6]

In these cases, what kind of guidance is provided by the precautionary principle? It is tempting to say that the principle calls for strong regulatory controls. In all of these cases, there is a possibility of serious harm, and no authoritative scientific evidence demonstrates that the possibility is zero. Put to one side the question of whether the precautionary principle, understood to compel stringent regulation in these cases, is sensible. Let us ask a more fundamental question: Is more stringent regulation therefore compelled by the precautionary principle?

The answer is that it is not. In some of these cases, it should be easy to see that in its own way, stringent regulation would actually run afoul of the precautionary principle. The simplest reason is that such regulation might well deprive society of significant benefits and hence produce many deaths that would otherwise not occur. In some cases, regulation eliminates the opportunity benefits of a process or activity and thus causes preventable deaths. If this is so, regulation is hardly precautionary.

Consider the case of genetic modification of food. Many people object to genetic modification, with the thought that "tampering with nature" can produce a range of adverse consequences for the environment (and also for human health). But many other people believe not only that these fears are baseless but also that a failure to allow genetic modification might well result in numerous deaths and a small probability of many more. The reason is that genetic modification holds the promise of producing food that is both cheaper and healthier—resulting, for example, in golden rice, which might have large benefits in developing countries. The point is not that genetic modification will definitely have those benefits or that the benefits of genetic modification outweigh the risks. The claim is only that if the precautionary principle is taken literally, it is offended by regulation as well as by nonregulation.

Regulation sometimes violates the precautionary principle because it would give rise to *substitute risks*, in the form of hazards that materialize or are increased as a result of regulation. Consider the case of DDT, often banned or regulated in the interest of reducing risks to birds and human beings. The risk with such bans is that in poor nations, they may eliminate what appears to be the most effective way of combating malaria—and thus significantly undermine public health.

Or consider the so-called drug lag, produced whenever the government takes a highly precautionary approach to the introduction of new medicines and drugs into the market. If a government insists on such an approach, it will protect people against harms from inadequately tested drugs—but it will also prevent people from receiving potential benefits from those very drugs. Is it precautionary to require extensive premarketing testing or to do the opposite? In the context of medicines to prevent AIDS, those who favor precautions have asked governments to reduce premarketing testing, precisely in the interest of health. The United States, by the way, is more precautionary about new medicines than are most European nations—but by failing to allow such medicines on the market, the United States fails to take precautions against the illnesses that could be reduced by speedier procedures. More generally, a sensible government might want to ignore the small risks associated with low levels of radiation on the ground that precautionary responses are likely to cause fear that outweighs any health benefits from those responses.

We should now be able to see the sense in which the precautionary principle, taken for all that it is worth, is paralyzing: it stands as an obstacle to regulation and nonregulation and everything in between. But these points simply raise an additional question: Why is the precautionary principle so influential? Why does it speak to so many people? I suggest that the principle becomes operational if and only if those who apply it wear blinders— only, that is, if they focus on some aspects of the regulatory situation but downplay or disregard others. But that suggestion raises further questions. What accounts for the particular blinders that underlie applications of the precautionary principle? When people's attention is selective, why is it selective in the way that it is?

The Mythical Benevolence of Nature

Sometimes the precautionary principle operates by incorporating the belief that nature is essentially benign and that human intervention is likely to carry risks—as in the suggestion that the precautionary principle calls for stringent regulation of pesticides or genetically modified organisms. Many people fear that any human intervention will create losses from the status quo and that these losses should carry great weight, whereas the gains should be regarded with some skepticism or at least be taken as less weighty. For example, "human intervention seems to be an amplifier in judgments on food riskiness and contamination," even though "more lives are lost to natural than to man-made disasters in the world."[7] Studies show that people overestimate the carcinogenic risk from pesticides and underestimate the risks of natural carcinogens. People also believe that nature implies safety, so much so that they will prefer natural water to processed water even if the two are chemically identical.[8]

A belief in the benevolence of nature plays a major role in the operation of the precautionary principle, especially among those who see nature as harmonious or in balance. In fact, many of those who endorse the principle seem to be especially concerned about new technologies. Most people believe that natural chemicals are safer than man-made chemicals.[9] (Most toxicologists disagree.) On this view, the principle calls for caution when people are intervening in the natural world. Here we can find some sense: nature often consists of systems, and interventions into systems can cause serious problems. But there is a large problem with this understanding of the precautionary principle: what is natural may not be safe at all.[10]

Consider in this light the familiar idea that there is a "balance of nature." According to a fairly standard account, this idea is "not true."[11] Nature "is characterized by change, not constancy," and "natural ecological systems are dynamic," with desirable changes often being "those induced through human action."[12] In any case, nature is often a realm of destruction, illness, killing, and death. Hence the claim cannot be that human activity is necessarily or systematically more destructive than nature. Nor is it clear that natural products are comparatively safe.[13] Organic foods, favored by many people on grounds of safety and health and creating annual revenues of $4.5 billion in the United States alone, have many virtues, but it is not clear that they are healthier to eat. According to an admittedly controversial account, they are "actually riskier to consume than food grown with synthetic chemicals."[14] If the precautionary principle is seen to raise serious doubts about pesticides but never about organic foods, it may be because the health risks that come with departures from nature register as especially troublesome.

Some of the most serious risks we face are a product of nature. Nothing is more natural than exposure to sunlight, which many people do not fear. But such exposure is associated with skin cancer and other serious harms. Tobacco smoking kills more than four hundred thousand Americans each year, even though tobacco is a product of nature. To say all this is not to resolve specific issues, which depend on complex questions of value and fact. But a false belief in the benevolence of nature helps to explain why the precautionary principle is thought, quite incorrectly, to provide a great deal of analytical help.

Loss Aversion

People tend to be loss averse, which means that a loss from the status quo is seen as more undesirable than a gain is seen as desirable.[15] When we anticipate a loss of what we now have, we can become genuinely afraid, in a way that greatly exceeds our feelings of pleasure when we anticipate some supplement to what we now have. So far, perhaps, so good. The problem comes when individual and social decisions downplay potential gains from the status quo and fixate on potential losses, in such a way as to produce overall increases in risks and overall decreases in well-being.

In the context of risk regulation, there is a clear implication: people will be closely attuned to the losses produced by any newly introduced risk, or by any aggravation of existing risks, but far less concerned with the foregone benefits that result from regulation. Loss aversion often helps to explain what makes the precautionary principle operational. The opportunity costs of regulation often register little or not at all, whereas the out-of-pocket costs of the activity or substance in question are entirely visible. In fact this is a form of status quo bias. The status quo marks the baseline against which gains and losses are measured, and a loss from the status quo seems much worse than a gain from the status quo seems good.

If loss aversion is at work, we would predict that the precautionary principle would place a spotlight on the losses introduced by some risk and downplay the foregone benefits resulting from controls on that risk. Recall the emphasis, in the United States, on the risks of insufficient testing of medicines as compared with the risks of delaying the availability of those medicines. If the opportunity benefits are offscreen, the precautionary principle will appear to give guidance, notwithstanding the objections I have made. At the same time, the neglected opportunity benefits sometimes present a devastating problem with the use of the precautionary principle. In the context of potential life-saving drugs, this is very much the situation.

Loss aversion is closely associated with another cognitive finding: people are far more willing to tolerate familiar risks than unfamiliar ones, even if they are statistically equivalent.[16] For example, the risks associated with driving often do not occasion a great deal of concern, even though in the United States alone, tens of thousands of people die from motor vehicle accidents each year. The relevant risks are seen as part of life. By contrast, many people are quite concerned about risks that appear newer, such as the risks associated with genetically modified foods, recently introduced chemicals, and terrorism. Part of the reason for the difference may be a belief that with new risks, we are in the domain of uncertainty (meaning that we cannot assign probabilities to bad outcomes) rather than risk (where probabilities can be assigned), and perhaps it makes sense to be cautious when we are not able to measure probabilities. But the individual and social propensity to focus on new risks outruns that sensible propensity. It makes the precautionary principle operational by emphasizing, for no good reason, a mere subset of the hazards involved.

Availability

The availability heuristic is particularly important for purposes of understanding people's fear and their interest in precautions.[17] When people use the availability heuristic, they assess the magnitude of risks by asking whether examples can readily come to mind. If people can easily think of such examples, they are far more likely to be frightened than if they cannot. In fact, a belief in the benevolence of nature often stems from the availability heuristic, as people recall cases in which "tampering" resulted in serious social harm.

Furthermore, "a class whose instances are easily retrieved will appear more numerous than a class of equal frequency whose instances are less retrievable."[18] Consider a simple study showing participants a list of well-known people of both sexes and asking whether the list contains more names of women or more names of men. In lists in which the men were especially famous, people thought that there were more names of men; in lists in which the women were more famous, people thought that there were more names of women.[19]

This is a point about how *familiarity* can affect the availability of instances. A risk that is familiar, like that associated with smoking, will be seen as more serious than a risk that is less familiar, like that associated with sunbathing. But *salience* is important as well. "For example, the impact of seeing a house burning on the subjective probability of such accidents is probably greater than the impact of reading about a fire in the local paper."[20] So too, recent events will have a greater impact than earlier ones. The point helps explain much risk-related behavior, including decisions to take precautions. Whether people will buy insurance for natural disasters is greatly affected by recent experiences.[21] If floods have not occurred in the immediate past, people who live on flood plains are far less likely to purchase insurance. In the aftermath of an earthquake, insurance for earthquakes rises sharply—but it declines steadily from that point as vivid memories recede. Note that the use of the availability heuristic, in these contexts, is hardly irrational. Both insurance and precautionary measures can be expensive, and what has happened before seems, much of the time, to be the best available guide to what will happen again. The problem is that the availability heuristic can lead to serious errors, in terms of both excessive fear and neglect.

The availability heuristic helps to explain the operation of the precautionary principle for a simple reason: sometimes a certain risk, said to call for precautions, is cognitively available, whereas other risks, including the risks associated with regulation itself, are not. For example, it is easy to see that arsenic is potentially dangerous; arsenic is well-known as a poison, forming the first word of a well-known movie about poisoning, *Arsenic and Old Lace*. By contrast, there is a relatively complex mental operation in the judgment that arsenic regulation might lead people to use less safe alternatives. In many cases in which the precautionary principle seems to offer guidance, the reason is that some of the relevant risks are available while others are barely visible. And when people seek to protect nature against human intervention, it is often because the dangers of intervention are visible and familiar while the dangers of nonintervention are not.

Precautions, Uncertainty, and Irreversibility

Some of the central claims on behalf of the precautionary principle involve four legitimate points: (1) uncertainty, (2) learning over time, (3) irreversibility, and (4) the need for epistemic humility on the part of scientists. With the help of these points, we might make our way toward more refined and defensible understandings of the principle. A central question involves the appropriate approach to "worst-case" thinking. This is not the place for a full analysis, which would require investigation of some complex issues in decision theory,[22] but three points should be uncontroversial (bracketing hard questions about quantification).

First, if a product or activity has modest or no benefits, the argument for taking precautions is far stronger than if the benefits are significant. Second, if a product or activity imposes a trivially small risk (taking into account both the probability and the magnitude of a bad outcome), then the product or activity should not be banned or regulated (including through labels) if it also promises significant benefits. Third, if a product creates a small (but not trivial) risk of catastrophe, there is a strong argument for banning or regulating it (including through labels) if the benefits are very modest and thus do not justify running that risk.

Some of the most difficult cases arise when (1) a product or activity has significant benefits and (2) (a) the probability of a bad outcome is difficult or impossible to specify (creating a situation of uncertainty rather than risk)[23], and (b) the bad outcome is catastrophic or (c) the harms associated with the bad outcome cannot be identified (creating a situation of ignorance). In such difficult cases, it is not simple to balance the two sides of the ledger, and there is a real argument for eliminating the worst-case scenario.[24] And if a risk is irreversible (a concept that requires independent analysis), the argument for addressing it is fortified. A more refined precautionary principle, or several such principles, might be justified in this light; consider the irreversible harm precautionary principle, or the catastrophic harm precautionary principle.[25]

Wider Viewscreens

I have not suggested any particular substitute for the precautionary principle. But none of the arguments here supports the views of Aaron Wildavsky, an acute and influential political scientist with a special interest in risk regulation, who also rejects the precautionary principle.[26] In Wildavsky's view, the notion of precaution should be abandoned and replaced with a principle of *resilience*, based on an understanding that nature and society are quite able to adjust to even strong shocks and that the ultimate dangers are therefore smaller than we are likely to fear. It would follow from Wildavsky's resilience principle that people should be less concerned than many now are with the risks associated with, for example, climate change, foodborne illness, and the destruction of the ozone layer.

Unfortunately, the principle of resilience is no better than that of precaution. Some systems, natural and social, are resilient, but some are not. Whether an ecosystem or a society is resilient cannot be decided in the abstract. In any case, resilience is a matter of degree. Everything depends on the facts. The resilience principle should be understood as a heuristic, or mental shortcut, one that favors inaction in the face of possibly damaging technological change. Like most heuristics, the resilience principle will work well in many circumstances, but it can also lead to systematic and even deadly errors.

A better approach would be to acknowledge that a wide variety of adverse effects may come from inaction, regulation, and everything between. Such an approach would attempt to consider all of those adverse effects, not simply a subset. When existing knowledge does not allow clear assessments of the full range of adverse effects, such an approach would develop rules of thumb, helping to show the appropriate course of action in the face of uncertainty. When societies face risks of catastrophe, it is appropriate to act, not to stand by and merely to hope. A sensible approach would attempt to counteract, rather than to embody, the various cognitive limitations that people face in thinking about risks. An effort to produce a fair accounting of the universe of dangers on all sides should also help to diminish the danger of interest-group manipulation.

To be sure, public alarm, even if ill-informed, is itself a harm, and it is likely to lead to additional harms, perhaps in the form of large-scale ripple effects. A sensible approach to risk will attempt to reduce public fear even if it is baseless. My goal here has been not to deny that point, but to explain the otherwise puzzling appeal of the precautionary principle and to isolate the strategies that help make it operational.

At the individual level, these strategies are hardly senseless, especially for people who lack much information or who do the best they can by focusing on only one aspect of the situation at hand. But for governments, the precautionary principle is not sensible, for the simple reason that once the viewscreen is widened, it becomes clear that the principle provides no guidance at all. Rational nations should certainly take precautions, but they should not adopt the precautionary principle.

14 Moral Heuristics

Pioneering the modern literature on heuristics in cognition, Amos Tversky and Daniel Kahneman contended that "people rely on a limited number of heuristic principles which reduce the complex tasks of assessing probabilities and predicting values to simpler judgmental operations."[1] But the relevant literature has only started to investigate the possibility that in the moral and political domain, people also rely on simple rules of thumb that often work well but that sometimes misfire.[2] The central point seems obvious. Much of everyday morality consists of simple, highly intuitive rules that generally make sense but that fail in certain cases. It is wrong to lie or steal, but if a lie or a theft would save a human life, lying or stealing is probably obligatory. Not all promises should be kept. It is wrong to try to get out of a longstanding professional commitment at the last minute, but if your child is in the hospital, you may be morally required to do exactly that.

One of my major goals here is to show that heuristics play a pervasive role in moral, political, and legal judgments and that they sometimes produce significant mistakes. I also attempt to identify a set of heuristics that now influence both law and policy and try to make plausible the claim that some widely held practices and beliefs are a product of those heuristics. Often moral heuristics represent generalizations from a range of problems for which they are indeed well-suited,[3] and most of the time, such heuristics work well. The problem comes when the generalizations are wrenched out of context and treated as freestanding or universal principles, applicable to situations in which their justifications no longer operate. Because the generalizations are treated as freestanding or universal, their application seems obvious, and those who reject them appear morally obtuse, possibly even monstrous. I want to urge that the appearance is misleading and even productive of moral mistakes. There is nothing obtuse or monstrous about refusing to apply a generalization in contexts in which its rationale is absent.

Because Kahneman and Tversky were dealing with facts and elementary logic, they could demonstrate that the heuristics sometimes lead to errors. Unfortunately, that cannot easily be demonstrated here. In the moral and political domains, it is hard to come up with unambiguous cases in which the error is both highly intuitive and, on reflection, uncontroversial—cases in which people can ultimately be embarrassed about their own intuitions. Nonetheless, I hope to show that whatever one's moral commitments, moral heuristics exist and indeed are omnipresent. We should treat the underlying moral intuitions not as fixed points for analysis, but as unreliable and at least potentially erroneous. In the search for reflective equilibrium, understood as coherence among our judgments at all levels of generality,[4] it is important to see that some of our deeply held moral beliefs might be a product of heuristics that sometimes produce mistakes.

If moral heuristics are in fact pervasive, then people with diverse foundational commitments should be able to agree not that their own preferred theories are wrong, but that they are often applied in a way that reflects the use of heuristics. Utilitarians ought to be able to identify heuristics for the maximization of utility; deontologists should be able to point to heuristics for the proper discharge of moral responsibilities; those uncommitted to any large-scale theory should be able to specify heuristics for their own, more modest normative commitments. And if moral heuristics exist, blunders are highly likely not only in moral thinking but in legal and political practice as well. Conventional legal and political arguments are often a product of heuristics masquerading as universal truths. Hence I will identify a set of political and legal judgments that are best understood as a product of heuristics and that are often taken, wrongly and damagingly, as a guide to political and legal practice even when their rationale does not apply.

Ordinary Heuristics and an Insistent Homunculus

Heuristics and Facts

The classic work on heuristics and biases deals not with moral questions but with issues of fact. In answering hard factual questions, those who lack accurate information use simple rules of thumb. How many words, in four pages of a novel, will have *ing* as the last three letters? How many words, in the same four pages, will have *n* as the second-to-last letter? Most people will give a higher number in response to the first question than in response to the second[5]—even though a moment's reflection shows that this is a mistake. People err because they use an identifiable heuristic—the availability heuristic—to answer difficult questions about probability. When people use this heuristic, they answer a question of probability by asking whether examples come readily to mind. Lacking statistical knowledge, people try to think of illustrations. For people without statistical knowledge, it is far from irrational to use the availability heuristic; the problem is that this heuristic can lead to serious errors of fact in the form of excessive fear of small risks and neglect of large ones.

Or consider the representativeness heuristic, in accordance with which judgments of probability are influenced by assessments of resemblance (the extent to which A "looks like" B). The representativeness heuristic is famously exemplified by people's answers to questions about the likely career of a hypothetical woman named Linda, described as follows: "Linda is 31 years old, single, outspoken, and very bright. She majored in philosophy. As a student, she was deeply concerned with issues of discrimination and social justice and also participated in antinuclear demonstrations."[6] People were asked to rank, in order of probability, eight possible futures for Linda. Six of these were fillers (such as psychiatric social worker, elementary school teacher); the two crucial ones were "bank teller" and "bank teller and active in the feminist movement."

More people said that Linda was less likely to be a bank teller than to be a bank teller and active in the feminist movement. This is an obvious mistake, a conjunction error, in which characteristics A and B are thought to be more likely than characteristic A alone. The error stems from the representativeness heuristic: Linda's description seems to match "bank teller and active in the feminist movement" far better than "bank teller." In an illuminating reflection on the example, Stephen Jay Gould observes that "I know [the right answer], yet a little homunculus in my head continues to jump up and down, shouting at me—'but she can't just be a bank teller; read the description.'"[7] Because Gould's homunculus is especially inclined to squawk in the moral domain, I shall return to him on several occasions.

With respect to moral heuristics, existing work is suggestive rather than definitive; a great deal of progress remains to be made, above all through additional experimental work on moral judgments. Some of the moral heuristics that I shall identify might reasonably be challenged as subject to ad hoc rather than predictable application. One of my primary hopes is to help stimulate further research exploring when and whether people use moral heuristics that produce sense or nonsense in particular cases.

Attribute Substitution and Prototypical Cases

Kahneman and Shane Frederick suggest that heuristics are mental shortcuts used when people are interested in assessing a "target attribute" and substitute a "heuristic attribute" of the object, which is easier to handle.[8] Heuristics therefore operate through a process of *attribute substitution*. The use of heuristics gives rise to intuitions about what is true,[9] and these intuitions sometimes are biased, in the sense that they produce errors in a predictable direction. Consider the question whether more people die from suicides or homicides. Lacking statistical information, people might respond by asking whether it is easier to recall cases in either class (the availability heuristic). The approach is hardly senseless, but it might also lead to errors, a result of availability bias in the domain of risk perception. Sometimes heuristics are linked to affect, understood as an emotional reaction, and indeed affect has even been seen as a heuristic, by which people evaluate products or actions by reference to the affect that they produce.[10] But attribute substitution is often used for factual questions that lack an affective component.

Similar mechanisms are at work in the moral, political, and legal domains. Unsure what to think or do about a target attribute (what morality requires, what the law is), people might substitute a heuristic attribute instead—asking, for example, about the view of trusted authorities (a leader of the preferred political party, an especially wise judge, a religious figure). Often the process works by appeal to *prototypical cases*. Confronted by a novel and difficult problem, observers often ask whether it shares features with a familiar problem. If it seems to do so, then the solution to the familiar problem is applied to the novel and difficult one. It is possible that in the domain of values, as well as facts, real-world heuristics generally perform well in the real world—so that moral errors are reduced, not increased, by their use, at least compared to the most likely alternatives (see my remarks on rule utilitarianism below). The only claim here is that some of the time, our moral judgments can be shown to misfire.

The principal heuristics should be seen in light of dual-process theories of cognition.[11] Recall that System 1 is intuitive; it is rapid, automatic, and effortless (and it features Gould's homunculus). System 2, by contrast, is reflective; it is slower, self-aware, calculative, and deductive. System 1 proposes quick answers to problems of judgment; System 2 operates as a monitor, confirming or overriding those judgments. Consider, for example, someone who is flying from New York to London in the month after an airplane crash. This person might make a rapid, barely conscious judgment, rooted in System 1, that the flight is quite risky; but there might well be a System 2 override, bringing a more realistic assessment to bear. System 1 often has an affective component, but it need not; for example, a probability judgment might be made quite rapidly and without much affect at all.

There is growing evidence that people often make automatic, largely unreflective moral judgments for which they are sometimes unable to give good reasons.[12] Moral, political, or legal judgments often substitute a heuristic attribute for a target attribute; System 1 is operative here as well, and it may or may not be subject to System 2 override. Consider the incest taboo. People feel moral revulsion toward incest even in circumstances in which the grounds for that taboo seem to be absent; they are subject to "moral dumbfounding"[13]—that is, an inability to give an account for a firmly held intuition. It is plausible, at least, to think that System 1 is driving their judgments, without System 2 correction. The same is true in legal and political contexts as well.

Heuristics and Morality

To show that heuristics operate in the moral domain, we have to specify some benchmark by which we can measure moral truth. On these questions, I want to avoid any especially controversial claims. Whatever one's view of the foundations of moral and political judgments, I suggest, moral heuristics are likely to be at work in practice.

In this section, I begin with a brief account of the possible relationship between ambitious theories (understood as large-scale accounts of the right or the good) and moral heuristics. I suggest that for those who accept ambitious theories about morality or politics, it is tempting to argue that alternative positions are mere heuristics; but this approach is challenging, simply because any ambitious theory is likely to be too contentious to serve as the benchmark for measuring moral truth. (I will have more to say on this topic in the next chapter.) It is easiest to make progress not by opposing (supposedly correct) ambitious theories to (supposedly blundering) commonsense morality, but in two more modest ways: first, by showing that moral heuristics are at work on *any* view about what morality requires; and second, by showing that such heuristics are at work on a minimally contentious view about what morality requires.

Some people are utilitarians; they believe that the goal should be to maximize utility. At the outset, there are pervasive questions about the meaning of that idea. In Bentham's own words: "By utility is meant that property in any object, whereby it tends to produce benefit, advantage, pleasure, good, or happiness, (all this in the present case comes to the same thing) or (what comes again to the same thing) to prevent the happening of mischief, pain, evil, or unhappiness to the party whose interest is considered."[14] Admittedly, those words leave many questions unanswered; but it is not my goal to answer them here. Let us simply note that many utilitarians, including John Stuart Mill and Henry Sidgwick, have a more capacious understanding of utility than did Bentham, and argue that ordinary morality is based on simple rules of thumb that generally promote utility but that sometimes misfire.[15] For example, Mill emphasizes that human beings "have been learning by experience the tendencies of experience" so that the "corollaries from the principle of utility" are being progressively captured by ordinary morality.[16]

With the aid of modern psychological findings, utilitarians might be tempted to argue that ordinary morality is simply a series of heuristics for what really matters, which is utility. They might contend that ordinary moral commitments are a set of mental shortcuts that generally work well, but that also produce severe and systematic errors from the utilitarian point of view. Suppose that most people reject utilitarian approaches to punishment and are instead committed to retributivism (understood, roughly, as an approach that sees punishment as what is morally deserved, rather than as an effort to maximize utility); this is their preferred theory. Are they responding to System 1? Might they be making a cognitive error? (Is Kantianism a series of cognitive errors? See chapter 15.) Note that with respect to what morality requires, utilitarians frequently agree with their deontological adversaries about concrete cases; they can join in accepting the basic rules of criminal and civil law. When deontologists and others depart from utilitarian principles, perhaps they are operating on the basis of heuristics that usually work well but that sometimes misfire.

But it is exceedingly difficult to settle large-scale ethical debates in this way. In the case of many ordinary heuristics, based on availability and representativeness, a check of the facts or of the elementary rules of logic will show that people err. In the moral domain, this is much harder to demonstrate. To say the least, those who reject utilitarianism are not easily embarrassed by a demonstration that their moral judgments can lead to reductions in utility. For example, utilitarianism is widely challenged by those who insist on the importance of distributional considerations. It is far from clear that a moderate utility loss to those at the bottom can be justified by a larger utility gain for many at the top.

Emphasizing the existence of moral heuristics, those who reject utilitarianism might well turn the tables on their utilitarian opponents. They might contend that the rules recommended by utilitarians are consistent, much of the time, with what morality requires—but also that utilitarianism, taken seriously, produces serious mistakes in some cases. In this view, utilitarianism is itself a heuristic, one that usually works well but leads to systematic errors. And indeed, many debates between utilitarians and their critics involve claims, by one or another side, that the opposing view usually produces good results but also leads to severe mistakes and should be rejected for that reason.

These large debates are not easy to resolve, simply because utilitarians and deontologists are most unlikely to be convinced by the suggestion that their defining commitments are mere heuristics. Here there is a large difference between moral heuristics and the heuristics uncovered in the relevant psychological work, where the facts or simple logic provide a good test for whether people have erred. If people tend to think that more words in a given space end with the letters *ing* than have *n* in the next-to-last position, something has clearly gone wrong. If people think that Linda is more likely to be "a bank teller who is active in the feminist movement" than a "bank teller," there is an evident problem. If citizens of France think that New York University is more likely to have a good basketball team than St. Joseph's University because they have not heard of the latter, then a simple examination of the record might show that they are wrong. In the moral domain, factual blunders and simple logic do not provide such a simple test.

Neutral Benchmarks and Weak Consequentialism

My goal here is therefore not to show, with Sidgwick and Mill, that commonsense morality is a series of heuristics for the correct general theory, but more cautiously that in many cases, moral heuristics are at work—and that this point can be accepted by people with diverse general theories, or with grave uncertainty about which general theory is correct. I contend that it is possible to conclude that a moral heuristic is at work without accepting any especially controversial normative claims. In several examples, that claim can be accepted without accepting any contestable normative theory at all. Other examples will require acceptance of what I shall call *weak consequentialism*, in accordance with which the social consequences of the legal system are relevant, other things being equal, to what law ought to be doing.

Weak consequentialists insist that consequences are what matter, but they need not be utilitarians; they do not have to believe that law and policy should attempt to maximize utility. Utilitarianism is highly controversial, and many people, including many philosophers, reject it. For one thing, there are pervasive questions about the meaning of the idea of *utility*. Are we speaking only of maximizing pleasure and minimizing pain? Doesn't that seem to be a constricted account of what people do and should care about? Weak consequentialists think that it is. They are prepared to agree that whatever their effects on utility, violations of rights count among the consequences that ought to matter, so such violations play a role in the overall assessment of what should be done. Consider Amartya Sen's frequent insistence that consequentialists can insist that consequences count without accepting utilitarianism and without denying that violations of rights are part of the set of relevant consequences. Thus Sen urges an approach that "shares with utilitarianism a consequentialist approach (but differs from it in not confining attention to utility consequences only)" while also attaching "intrinsic importance to rights (but ... not giving them complete priority irrespective of other consequences)."[17] Weak consequentialism is in line with this approach. In evaluating decisions and social states, weak consequentialists might well be willing to give a great deal of weight to nonconsequentialist considerations.

Some deontologists, insistent on duties and rights, will reject any form of consequentialism altogether. They might believe, for example, that retribution is the proper theory of punishment and that the consequences of punishment are never relevant to the proper level of punishment. Some of my examples will be unpersuasive to deontologists who believe that consequences do not matter at all. But weak consequentialism seems to me sufficiently nonsectarian, and attractive enough to sufficiently diverse people, to make plausible the idea that in the cases at hand, moral heuristics are playing a significant role. And for those who reject weak consequentialism, it might nonetheless be productive to ask whether, from their own point of view, certain rules of morality and law are reflective of heuristics that sometimes produce serious errors.

Evolution and Rule Utilitarianism: Simple Heuristics That Make Us Good?

Two clarifications before we proceed. First, some moral heuristics might well have an evolutionary foundation.[18] Perhaps natural selection accounts for automatic moral revulsion against incest or cannibalism, even if clever experiments, or life, can produce situations in which the revulsion is groundless. In the case of incest, the point is straightforward: the automatic revulsion might be far more useful, from the evolutionary perspective, than a more fine-grained evaluation of contexts.[19] In fact an evolutionary account might be provided for most of the heuristics that I explore here. When someone has committed to a harmful act, evolutionary pressures might well have inculcated a sharp sense of outrage and a propensity to react in proportion to it. As a response to wrongdoing, use of an *outrage heuristic* might well be much better than an attempt at any kind of consequentialist calculus, weak or strong. Of course many moral commitments are a product not of evolution but of social learning and even cascade effects;[20] individuals in a relevant society will inevitably be affected by a widespread belief that it is wrong to tamper with nature, and evolutionary pressures need not have any role at all.

Second, and relatedly, some or even most moral heuristics might have a rule-utilitarian or rule-consequentialist defense.[21] The reason is that in most cases they work well despite their simplicity, and if people attempted a more fine-grained assessment of the moral issues involved, they might make more moral mistakes rather than fewer (especially because their self-interest is frequently at stake). Simple but somewhat crude moral principles might lead to less frequent and less severe moral errors than complex and fine-grained moral principles. Compare the availability heuristic. Much of the time, use of that heuristic produces speedy judgments that are fairly accurate, and those who attempt a statistical analysis might make more errors (and waste a lot of time in the process). If human beings use "simple heuristics that make us smart,"[22] then they might also use "simple heuristics that make us good." I will offer some examples in which moral heuristics seem to me to produce significant errors for law and policy, but I do not contend that we would be better off without them. On the contrary, such heuristics might well produce better results, from the moral point of view, than the feasible alternatives—a possibility to which I will return.

The Asian Disease Problem and Moral Framing

In a finding closely related to their work on heuristics, Kahneman and Tversky themselves find "moral framing" in the context of what has become known as "the Asian disease problem."[23] Framing effects do not involve heuristics, but because they raise obvious questions about the rationality of moral intuitions, they provide a valuable backdrop. Here is the first component of the problem:

Imagine that the US is preparing for the outbreak of an unusual Asian disease, which is expected to kill six hundred people. Two alternative programs to combat the disease have been proposed. Assume that the exact scientific estimates of the consequences are as follows:

If Program A is adopted, two hundred people will be saved.

If Program B is adopted, there is a one-third probability that six hundred people will be saved and a two-thirds probability that no people will be saved.

Which of the two programs would you favor?

Most people choose Program A.

But now consider the second component of the problem, in which the same situation is given but is followed by this description of the alternative programs:

If Program C is adopted, four hundred people will die.

If Program D is adopted, there is a one-third probability that nobody will die and a two-thirds probability that six hundred people will die.

Most people choose Problem D. But a moment's reflection should be sufficient to show that Program A and Program C are identical, and so too for Program B and Program D. These are merely different descriptions of the same programs. The purely semantic shift in framing is sufficient to produce different outcomes. Apparently people's moral judgments about appropriate programs depend on whether the results are described in terms of "lives saved" or "lives lost." What accounts for the difference? The most sensible answer begins with the fact that human beings are pervasively averse to losses (hence the robust cognitive finding of loss aversion).[24] With respect to either self-interested gambles or fundamental moral judgments, loss aversion plays a large role in people's decisions. But what counts as a gain or a loss depends on the baseline from which measurements are made. Purely semantic reframing can alter the baseline and hence alter moral intuitions (many examples involve fairness).[25]

This finding is usually taken to show a problem for standard accounts of rationality. But it has been argued that subjects are rationally responding to the information provided, or "leaked," by the speaker's choice of frame.[26] Certainly the speaker's choice might offer a clue about the desired response; some subjects in the Asian disease problem might be responding to that clue. But even if people are generally taking account of the speaker's clues,[27] that claim is consistent with the proposition that frames matter a great deal to moral intuitions, which is all I am stressing here.

Moral framing has been demonstrated in the important context of obligations to future generations,[28] a much-disputed question of morality, politics, and law.[29] To say the least, the appropriate discount rate for those yet to be born is not a question that most people have pondered, and hence their judgments are highly susceptible to different frames. From a series of surveys, Maureen Cropper and her coauthors suggest that people are indifferent about saving one life today versus saving forty-five lives in one hundred years.[30] They make this suggestion based on responses to asking people whether they would choose a program that saves one hundred lives now or a program that saves a substantially larger number one hundred years from now. It is possible, however, that people's responses depend on uncertainty about whether people in the future will otherwise die (perhaps technological improvements will save them?), and other ways of framing the same problem yield radically different results.[31] For example, most people consider a single death from pollution next year and a single death from pollution in one hundred years "equally bad." This finding implies no preference for members of the current generation. The simplest conclusion is that people's moral judgments about obligations to future generations are very much a product of framing effects.[32]

The same point holds for the question whether government should consider not only the number of lives but also the number of "life years" saved by regulatory interventions. If the government focuses on life years, a program that saves children will be worth far more attention than a similar program that saves senior citizens. Is this immoral? People's intuitions depend on how the question is framed.[33] People will predictably reject an approach that would count every old person as worth "significantly less" than what every young person is worth. But if people are asked whether they would favor a policy that saves 105 old people or 100 young people, many will favor the latter in a way that suggests a willingness to pay considerable attention to the number of life years at stake.

At least for unfamiliar questions of morality, politics, and law, people's intuitions are very much affected by framing. Above all, it is effective to frame certain consequences as "losses" from a status quo; when so framed, moral concern becomes significantly elevated. It is for this reason that political actors often phrase one or another proposal as "turning back the clock" on some social advance. The problem is that for many social changes, the framing does not reflect social reality but is simply a verbal manipulation.

Let's now turn to examples that are more controversial.

Moral Heuristics: A Catalogue

My principal interest here is the relationship between moral heuristics and questions of law and policy. I separate the relevant heuristics into four categories: those that involve morality and risk regulation; those that involve punishment; those that involve "playing God," particularly in the domains of reproduction and sex; and those that involve the act-omission distinction. The catalog is meant to be illustrative rather than exhaustive.

Morality and Risk Regulation

Cost-Benefit Analysis   An automobile company is deciding whether to take certain safety precautions for its cars. It conducts a cost-benefit analysis in which it concludes that certain precautions are not justified—because, say, they would cost $100 million and save only four lives, and because the company has a "ceiling" of $10 million per life saved (a ceiling that is, by the way, a bit higher than the amount the United States Environmental Protection Agency uses for a statistical life). How will ordinary people react to this decision? The answer is that they will not react favorably.[34] In fact they tend to punish companies that impose mortality risks on people after doing cost-benefit analysis, even if a high valuation is placed on human life.

By contrast, they impose less severe punishment on companies that are willing to impose a "risk" on people but that do not produce a formal risk analysis that measures lives lost and dollars and trades one against another.[35] The oddity here is that under tort law, it is unclear that a company should not be liable at all if it has acted on the basis of a competent cost-benefit analysis; such an analysis might even insulate a company from a claim of negligence. What underlies people's moral judgments, which are replicated in actual jury decisions?[36]

It is possible that when people disapprove of trading money for lives, they are generalizing from a set of moral principles that are generally sound, and even useful, but that work poorly in some cases. Consider the following moral principle: do not knowingly cause a human death. In ordinary life, you should not engage in conduct with the knowledge that several people will die as a result. If you are playing a sport or working on your yard, you ought not to continue if you believe that your actions will kill others. Invoking that idea, people disapprove of companies that fail to improve safety when they are fully aware that deaths will result. By contrast, people do not disapprove of those who fail to improve safety while believing that there is a risk but appearing not to know, for certain, that deaths will ensue. When people object to risky action taken after cost-benefit analysis, it seems to be partly because that very analysis puts the number of expected deaths squarely "on screen."[37]

Companies that fail to do such analysis but that are aware that a risk exists do not make clear, to themselves or to anyone else, that they caused deaths with full knowledge that this was what they were going to do. People disapprove, above all, of companies that cause death knowingly. There may be a kind of "cold-heart heuristic" here: those who know that they will cause a death, and do so anyway, are regarded as cold-hearted monsters.[38] In this view, critics of cost-benefit analysis should be seen as appealing to System 1 and as speaking directly to the homunculus: "Is a corporation or public agency that endangers us to be pardoned for its sins once it has spent $6.1 million per statistical life on risk reduction?"[39]

Note that it is easy to reframe a probability as a certainty and vice versa; if I am correct, the reframing is likely to have large effects. Consider two cases:

1. Company A knows that its product will kill ten people. It markets the product to its ten million customers with that knowledge. The cost of eliminating the risk would have been $100 million.
2. Company B knows that its product creates a one in one million risk of death. Its product is used by ten million people. The cost of eliminating the risk would have been $100 million.

I have not collected data, but I am willing to predict that Company A would be punished more severely than Company B, even though there is no difference between the two.

I suggest, then, that a moral heuristic is at work, one that imposes moral condemnation on those who knowingly engage in acts that will result in human deaths. And this heuristic does a great deal of good. The problem is that it is not always unacceptable to cause death knowingly, at least if the deaths are relatively few and an unintended byproduct of generally desirable activity. When government allows new highways to be built, it knows that people will die on those highways; when government allows new coal-fired power plants to be built, it knows that some people will die from the resulting pollution; when companies produce tobacco products, and when government does not ban those products, hundreds of thousands of people will die; the same is true for alcohol. Of course it would make sense, in all of these domains, to take extra steps to reduce risks. But that proposition does not support the implausible claim that we should disapprove, from the moral point of view, of any action taken when deaths are foreseeable.

There is a complementary possibility, involving the confusion between the ex ante and ex post perspective. If a life might have been saved by a fifty-dollar expenditure on a car, people are going to be outraged, and they will impose punishment. What they will not see or incorporate is the fact, easily perceived ex ante, that the fifty-dollar-per-car expenditure would have been wasted on millions of other people. It is hardly clear that the ex ante perspective is always preferable. But something has gone badly wrong if the ex post perspective leads people to neglect the trade-offs that are involved.

I believe that it is impossible to vindicate, in principle, the widespread social antipathy to cost-benefit balancing. But here too, "a little homunculus in my head continues to jump up and down, shouting at me" that corporate cost-benefit analysis, trading dollars for a known number of deaths, is morally unacceptable. The voice of the homunculus, I am suggesting, is not reflective, but instead a product of System 1 and a crude but quite tenacious moral heuristic.

Emissions Trading   In the last decades, those involved in enacting and implementing environmental law have experimented with systems of "emissions trading."[40] In those systems, polluters are typically given a license to pollute a certain amount, and the licenses can be traded on the market. The advantage of emissions-trading systems is that if they work well, they will ensure emissions reductions at the lowest possible cost.

Is emissions trading immoral? Many people believe so. (See Chapter 3.) Political theorist Michael Sandel, for example, urges that trading systems "undermine the ethic we should be trying to foster on the environment."[41] Sandel contends: "Turning pollution into a commodity to be bought and sold removes the moral stigma that is properly associated with it. If a company or a country is fined for spewing excessive pollutants into the air, the community conveys its judgment that the polluter has done something wrong. A fee, on the other hand, makes pollution just another cost of doing business, like wages, benefits and rent."

In the same vein, Sandel objects to proposals to open carpool lanes to drivers without passengers who are willing to pay a fee. Here, as in the environmental context, it seems unacceptable to permit people to do something that is morally wrong so long as they are willing to pay for the privilege.

I suggest that like other critics of emissions-trading programs, Sandel is using a moral heuristic; in fact, he has been fooled by his homunculus. The heuristic is this: people should not be permitted to engage in moral wrongdoing for a fee. You are not allowed to assault someone so long as you are willing to pay for the right to do so; there are no tradable licenses for rape, theft, or battery. The reason is that the appropriate level of these forms of wrongdoing is zero (putting to one side the fact that enforcement resources are limited; if they were unlimited, we would want to eliminate, not merely reduce, these forms of illegality). But pollution is an altogether different matter. At least some level of pollution is a byproduct of desirable social activities and products, including automobiles and power plants.

Certain acts of pollution, including those that violate the law or are unconnected with desirable activities, are morally wrong—but the same cannot be said of pollution as such. When Sandel objects to emissions trading, he is treating pollution as equivalent to a crime in a way that overgeneralizes a moral intuition that makes sense in other contexts. There is no moral problem with emissions trading as such. The insistent objection to emissions-trading systems stems from a moral heuristic.

Unfortunately, that objection has appeared compelling to many people, so much as to delay and to reduce the use of a pollution-reduction tool that is, in many contexts, the best available. Here, then, is a case in which a moral heuristic has led to political blunders, in the form of policies that impose high costs for no real gain.

Betrayals   To say the least, people do not like to be betrayed. A betrayal of trust is likely to produce a great deal of outrage. If a babysitter neglects a child or if a security guard steals from his employer, people will be angrier than if the identical acts are performed by someone in whom trust has not been reposed. So far, perhaps, so good: When trust is betrayed, the damage is worse than when an otherwise identical act has been committed by someone who was not a beneficiary of trust. And it should not be surprising that people will favor greater punishment for betrayals than for otherwise identical crimes.[42]

Perhaps the disparity can be justified on the ground that the betrayal of trust is an independent harm, one that warrants greater deterrence and retribution—a point that draws strength from the fact that trust, once lost, is not easily regained. A family robbed by its babysitter might well be more seriously injured than a family robbed by a thief. The loss of money is compounded and possibly dwarfed by the violation of a trusting relationship. The consequence of the violation might also be more serious. Will the family ever feel entirely comfortable with babysitters? It is bad to have an unfaithful spouse, but it is even worse if the infidelity occurred with your best friend, because that kind of infidelity makes it harder to have trusting relationships with friends in the future.

In this light it is possible to understand why betrayals produce special moral opprobrium and (where the law has been violated) increased punishment. But consider a finding that is much harder to explain: people are especially averse to risks of death that come from products (like airbags) designed to promote safety.[43] They are so averse to "betrayal risks" that they would actually prefer to face higher risks than do not involve betrayal. The relevant study involved two principal conditions. In the first, people were asked to choose between two equally priced cars, car A and car B. According to crash tests, there was a 2 percent chance that drivers of car A, with airbag A, would die in serious accidents as a result of the impact of the crash. With car B, and airbag B, there was a 1 percent chance of death, but also an additional one in ten thousand (0.01 percent) chance of death as a result of deployment of the airbag. Similar studies involved vaccines and smoke alarms.

The result was that most participants (over two-thirds) chose the higher-risk safety option when the less risky one carried a "betrayal risk." A control condition demonstrated that people were not confused about the numbers: when asked to choose between a 2 percent risk and a 1.01 percent risk, people selected the 1.01 percent risk so long as betrayal was not involved. In other words, people's aversion to betrayals is so great that they will increase their own risks rather than subject themselves to a (small) hazard that comes from a device that is supposed to increase safety. "Apparently, people are willing to incur greater risks of the very harm they seek protection from to avoid the mere possibility of betrayal."[44] Remarkably, "betrayal risks appear to be so psychologically intolerable that people are willing to double their risk of death from automobile crashes, fires, and diseases to avoid incurring a small possibility of death by safety device betrayal."[45]

What explains this seemingly bizarre and self-destructive preference? I suggest that a heuristic is at work: punish, and do not reward, betrayals of trust. The heuristic generally works well. But it misfires in some cases, as when those who deploy it end up increasing the risks they themselves face. An airbag is not a security guard or a babysitter, endangering those whom they have been hired to protect. It is a product, to be chosen if and only if it decreases aggregate risks. If an airbag makes people safer on balance, it should be used, even if in a tiny percentage of cases it will create a risk that would not otherwise exist. People's unwillingness to subject themselves to betrayal risks, in circumstances in which products are involved and they are increasing their likelihood of death, is the moral cousin to the use of the representativeness heuristic in the Linda case. Both stem from a generally sound rule of thumb that leads to systematic errors.

In a sense, the special antipathy to betrayal risks might be seen to involve not a moral heuristic but a taste. In choosing products, people are not making pure moral judgments; they are choosing what they like best, and it just turns out that a moral judgment, involving antipathy to betrayals, is part of what they like best. It would be useful to design a purer test of moral judgments, one that would ask people not about their own safety but about that of others—for example, whether people are averse to betrayal risks when they are purchasing safety devices for their friends or family members. There is every reason to expect that it would produce substantially identical results to those in the experiments just described.

Closely related experiments support that expectation.[46] In deciding whether to vaccinate their children against risks of serious diseases, people show a form of "omission bias." Many people are more sensitive to the risk of the vaccination than to the risk from diseases—so much so that they will expose their children to a greater risk from "nature" than from the vaccine. (There is a clear connection between omission bias and trust in nature and antipathy to "playing God," as discussed below.) The omission bias, I suggest, is closely related to people's special antipathy to betrayals. It leads to moral errors in the form of vaccination judgments, and undoubtedly others, by which some parents increase the fatality risks faced by their own children.

Morality and Punishment

Pointless Punishment   In the context of punishment, moral intuitions are sometimes disconnected with the consequences of punishment, suggesting that a moral heuristic may well be at work.[47] Suppose, for example, that a corporation has engaged in serious wrongdoing. People are likely to want to punish the corporation as if it were a person.[48] They are unlikely to inquire into the possibility that the consequences of serious punishment (say, a stiff fine) will not be to "hurt" corporate wrongdoers but instead to decrease wages, increase prices, or produce lost jobs. Punishment judgments are rooted in a simple heuristic, to the effect that penalties should be a proportional response to the outrageousness of the act. We have seen that in thinking about punishment, people use an *outrage heuristic*.[49] According to this heuristic, people's punishment judgments are a product of their outrage. This heuristic may produce reasonable results much of the time, but in some cases it seems to lead to systematic errors—at least if we are willing to embrace weak consequentialism.

Consider, for example, an intriguing study of people's judgments about penalties in cases involving harms from vaccines and birth control pills.[50] In one case, subjects were told that the result of a higher penalty would be to make companies try harder to make safer products. In an adjacent case, subjects were told that the consequence of a higher penalty would be to make the company more likely to stop making the product, with the result that less-safe products would be on the market. Most subjects, including a group of judges, gave the same penalties in both cases. "Most of the respondents did not seem to notice the incentive issue."[51] In another study, people said that they would give the same punishment to a company that would respond with safer products and one that would be unaffected because the penalty would be secret and covered by insurance (the price of which would not increase).[52] Here too the effects of the punishment did not affect judgments by a majority of respondents.

A similar result emerged from a test of punishment judgments that asked subjects, including judges and legislators, to choose penalties for dumping hazardous waste.[53] In one case, the penalty would make companies try harder to avoid waste. In another, the penalty would lead companies to cease making a beneficial product. Most people did not penalize companies differently in the two cases. Most strikingly, people preferred to require companies to clean up their own waste, even if the waste did not threaten anyone, instead of spending the same amount to clean up far more dangerous waste produced by another, now-defunct company.

How could this preference make sense? Why should a company be asked to engage in a course of action that costs the same but that does much less good? In these cases, it is most sensible to think that people are operating under a heuristic, mandating punishment that is proportional to outrageousness and requiring that punishment be based not at all on consequential considerations. As a general rule, of course, it is plausible to think that penalties should be proportional to the outrageousness of the act; utilitarians will accept the point as a first approximation, and retributivists will insist on it. But it seems excessively rigid to adopt this principle whether or not the consequence would be to make human beings safer and healthier. Weak consequentialists, while refusing to reject retributivism, will condemn this excessive rigidity. Those who seek proportional punishments might well disagree in principle. But it would be worthwhile for them to consider the possibility that they have been tricked by a heuristic—and that their reluctance to acknowledge the point is a product of the insistent voice of their own homunculus.

Probability of Detection   Now turn to closely related examples from the domain of punishment. On the economic account, the state's goal, when imposing penalties for misconduct, is to ensure optimal deterrence.[54] To increase deterrence, the law might increase the *severity* of punishment or instead increase the *likelihood* of punishment. A government that lacks substantial enforcement resources might impose high penalties, thinking that it will produce the right deterrent "signal" in light of the fact that many people will escape punishment altogether. A government that has sufficient resources might impose a lower penalty but enforce the law against all or almost all violators. These ideas lead to a simple theory in the context of punitive damages for wrongdoing: the purpose of such damages is to make up for the shortfall in enforcement. If injured people are 100 percent likely to receive compensation, there is no need for punitive damages. If injured people are 50 percent likely to receive compensation, those who bring suit should receive a punitive award that is twice the amount of the compensatory award. The simple exercise in multiplication will ensure optimal deterrence.

But there is a large question whether people accept this account and, if not, why not. (For the moment, let us put to one side the question whether they should accept it in principle.) Experiments suggest that people reject optimal deterrence and that they do not believe that the probability of detection is relevant to punishment. The reason is that they use the outrage heuristic. I participated in two experiments designed to cast light on this question.[55] In the first, subjects were given cases of wrongdoing, arguably calling for punitive damages, and also were provided with explicit information about the probability of detection. Different subjects saw the same case, with only one difference: the probability of detection was substantially varied. Subjects were asked about the amount of punitive damages that they would choose to award. The goal was to see if subjects would impose higher punishments when the probability of detection was low. In the second experiment, subjects were asked to evaluate judicial and executive decisions to reduce penalties when the probability of detection was high and to increase penalties when the probability of detection was low. Subjects were asked whether they approved or disapproved of varying the penalty with the probability of detection.

The findings were simple and straightforward. The first experiment found that varying the probability of detection had no effect on punitive awards. Even when people's attention was explicitly directed to the probability of detection, they were indifferent to it. The second experiment found that strong majorities of respondents rejected judicial decisions to reduce penalties because of a high probability of detection—and rejected executive decisions to increase penalties because of a low probability of detection. In other words, people did not approve of an approach to punishment that would make the level of punishment vary with the probability of detection. What apparently concerned them was the extent of the wrongdoing and the right degree of moral outrage—not optimal deterrence.

To be sure, many people have principled reasons for embracing retributivism and for rejecting utilitarian accounts of punishment. And some such people are likely to believe, on reflection, that the moral intuitions just described are correct—that what matters is what the defendant did, not whether his action was likely to be detected. But if we embrace weak consequentialism, we will find it implausible to suggest that the aggregate level of misconduct is *entirely* irrelevant to punishment. We will be unwilling to ignore the fact that if a legal system refuses to impose enhanced punishment on hard-to-detect wrongdoing, then it will end up with a great deal of wrongdoing. People's unwillingness to take any account of the probability of detection suggests the possibility that a moral heuristic is at work, one that leads to real errors. Because of the contested nature of the ethical issues involved, I cannot demonstrate this point. But those who refuse to consider the probability of detection might consider the possibility that System 1 has gotten the better of them.

Playing God: Reproduction, Nature, and Sex

Issues of reproduction and sexuality are prime candidates for the operation of moral heuristics. Consider human cloning, which most Americans reject and believe should be banned. Notwithstanding this consensus, the ethical and legal issues here are not so simple. To make progress, it is necessary to distinguish between reproductive and nonreproductive cloning; the first is designed to produce children, whereas the second is designed to produce cells for therapeutic use. Are the ethical issues different in the two cases? In any case, it is important to identify the grounds for moral concern. Do we fear that cloned children would be means to their parents' ends and, if so, why? Do we fear that they would suffer particular psychological harm? Do we fear that they would suffer from especially severe physical problems?

In a highly influential discussion of new reproductive technologies—above all, cloning—ethicist Leon Kass points to the "wisdom in repugnance."[56] He writes:

People are repelled by many aspects of human cloning. They recoil from the prospect of mass production of human beings, with large clones of look-alikes, compromised in their individuality, the idea of father-son or mother-daughter twins; the bizarre prospects of a woman giving birth to and rearing a genetic copy of herself, her spouse or even her deceased father or mother; the grotesqueness of conceiving a child as an exact replacement for another who has died; the utilitarian creation of embryonic genetic duplicates of oneself, to be frozen away or created when necessary, in case of need for homologous tissues or organs for transplantation; the narcissism of those who would clone themselves and the arrogance of others who think they know who deserves to be cloned or which genotype any child-to-be should be thrilled to receive; the Frankensteinian hubris to create human life and increasingly to control its destiny; man playing God. ... We are repelled by the prospect of cloning human beings not because of the strangeness or novelty of the undertaking, but because we intuit and feel, immediately and without argument, the violation of things that we rightfully hold dear. ... Shallow are the souls that have forgotten how to shudder.[57]

Kass is correct to suggest that revulsion toward human cloning might be grounded in legitimate concerns, and I mean to be agnostic here on whether human cloning is ethically defensible. But I want to suggest that moral heuristics, and System 1, are responsible for what Kass seeks to celebrate as "we intuit and feel, immediately and without argument." Kass's catalog of alleged errors seems to me an extraordinary exercise in the use of such heuristics. Availability operates in this context, not to drive judgments about probability but to call up instances of morally dubious behavior (e.g., "mass production of human beings, with large clones of look-alikes, compromised in their individuality"). The representativeness heuristic plays a similar role (e.g., "the Frankensteinian hubris to create human life and increasingly to control its destiny"). But I believe that Kass gets closest to the cognitive process here with three words: "man playing God."

We might well think that "do not play God" is the general heuristic here, with different societies specifying what falls in that category and with significant changes over time. As we saw in chapter 13, a closely related heuristic plays a large role in judgments of fact and morality: do not tamper with nature. This heuristic affects many moral judgments, though individuals and societies often become accustomed to various kinds of tampering (consider in vitro fertilization). An antitampering heuristic helps explain many risk-related judgments. For example, "human intervention seems to be an amplifier in judgments on food riskiness and contamination," even though "more lives are lost to natural than to man-made disasters in the world."[58] Studies show that people overestimate the carcinogenic risk from pesticides and underestimate the risks of natural carcinogens.[59] People also believe that nature implies safety, so much that they will prefer natural water to processed water even if the two are chemically identical.[60]

The moral injunction against tampering with nature plays a large role in public objections to genetic engineering of food, and hence legal regulation of such engineering is sometimes driven by that heuristic rather than by a deliberative, System 2 encounter with the substantive issues. For genetic engineering, the antitampering heuristic drives judgments even when the evidence of risk is slim.[61] In fact, companies go to great lengths to get a "natural" stamp on their products,[62] even though the actual difference between what counts as a natural additive and an artificial additive bears little or no relation to harms to consumers. So too in the domains of reproduction and sexuality, in which a pervasive objection is that certain practices are "unnatural." (With respect to sex, it is especially difficult to say what is "natural," and whether what is natural is good.) And for cloning, there appears to be a particular heuristic at work: do not tamper with natural processes for human reproduction. It is not clear that this heuristic works well—but it is clear that it can misfire.

Issues at the intersection of morality and sex provide an obvious place for the use of moral heuristics. Such heuristics are peculiarly likely to be at work in any area in which people are likely to think, "That's disgusting!" Any examples here will be contentious, but return to the incest taboo. We can easily imagine incestuous relationships—say, between first cousins or second cousins—that ought not give rise to social opprobrium but that might nonetheless run afoul of social norms or even the law.[63] The incest taboo is best defended by reference to coercion, psychological harm, and risks to children who might result from incestuous relationships. But in many imaginable cases, these concrete harms are not involved.

It is plausible to say that the best way to defend against these harms is by a flat prohibition on incest, one that has the disadvantage of excessive generality but the advantage of easy application. Such a flat prohibition might have evolutionary origins; it might also have strong rule-utilitarianism justifications. We would not like to have family members asking whether incest would be a good idea in individual cases, even if our underlying concern is limited to coercion and psychological harm. So defended, however, the taboo stands unmasked as a moral heuristic. Recall the phenomenon of *moral dumbfounding*—moral judgments that people "feel" but are unable to justify.[64] In the domain of sex and reproduction, many taboos can be analyzed in similar terms.

Acts and Omissions

To say the least, there has been much discussion of whether and why the distinction between acts and omissions might matter for morality, law, and policy. In one case, for example, a patient might ask a doctor not to provide life-sustaining equipment, thus ensuring the patient's death. In another case, a patient might ask a doctor to inject a substance that will immediately end the patient's life. Many people seem to have a strong moral intuition that a decision not to provide life-sustaining equipment, and even the withdrawal of such equipment, is acceptable and legitimate—but that the injection is morally abhorrent. And indeed, American constitutional law reflects judgments to exactly this effect: people have a constitutional right to withdraw equipment that is necessary to keep them alive, but they have no constitutional right to physician-assisted suicide.[65] But what is the morally relevant difference?

It is worth considering the possibility that the act-omission distinction operates as a heuristic for a more complex and difficult assessment of the moral issues at stake. From the moral point of view, harmful acts are generally worse than harmful omissions, in terms of both the state of mind of the wrongdoer and the likely consequences of the wrong. A murderer is typically more malicious than a bystander who refuses to come to the aid of someone who is drowning; the murderer wants his victim to die, whereas the bystander need have no such desire. In addition, a murderer typically guarantees death, whereas a bystander may do no such thing. (I put to one side some complexities about causation.) But in terms of either the wrong-doer's state of mind or the consequences, harmful acts are not *always* worse than harmful omissions.

The moral puzzles arise when life, or a clever interlocutor, comes up with a case in which there is no morally relevant distinction between acts and omissions, but moral intuitions (and the homunculus) strongly suggest that there must be such a difference. As an example, consider the vaccination question discussed earlier; many people show an omission bias, favoring inaction over statistically preferable action.[66] Here an ordinarily sensible heuristic, favoring omissions over actions, appears to produce moral error.

In such cases, we might hypothesize that moral intuitions reflect an overgeneralization of principles that usually make sense—but that fail to make sense in a particular case. Those principles condemn actions but permit omissions—a difference that is often plausible in light of relevant factors but that, in hard cases, cannot be defended. I believe that the persistent acceptance of withdrawal of life-saving equipment, alongside persistent doubts about euthanasia, is a demonstration of the point. There is no morally relevant difference between the two; the act-omission distinction makes a difference apparent or even clear when it is not real.

Exotic Cases, Moral Judgments, and Reflective Equilibrium

Some of these examples will seem more contentious than others. But taken as a whole, they seem to me to raise serious doubts about the wide range of work that approaches moral and political dilemmas by attempting to uncover moral intuitions about exotic cases of the kind never or rarely encountered in ordinary life. Should you shoot an innocent person if that is the only way to save twenty innocent people?[67] What is the appropriate moral evaluation of a case in which a woman accidentally puts cleaning fluid in her coffee, and her husband, wanting her dead, does not provide the antidote, which he happens to have handy?[68] If Martians arrived and told you that they would destroy the world unless you tortured a small child, should you torture a small child? Is there a difference between killing someone by throwing him into the path of a train and killing someone by diverting the train's path to send it in his direction?

I believe that in cases of this kind, the underlying moral intuitions ordinarily work well, but when they are wrenched out of familiar contexts their reliability, for purposes of moral and legal analysis, is unclear. Consider the following rule: do not kill an innocent person, even if doing so is necessary to save others. (I put to one side the contexts of self-defense and war.) In all likelihood, a society does much better if most people have this intuition, if only because judgments about necessity are likely to be unreliable and self-serving. But in a hypothetical case, in which it really is necessary to kill an innocent person to save twenty others, our intuitions might well turn out to be unclear and contested—and if our intuitions about the hypothetical case turn out to be very firm (do not kill innocent people, ever!), they might not deserve to be so firm simply because they have been wrenched out of the real-world context, which is where they need to be to make sense.

The use of exotic cases has been defended not on the ground that they are guaranteed to be correct but as a means of eliciting the structure of our moral judgments in a way that enables us to "isolate the reasons and principles" that underlie our responses.[69] But if those responses are unreliable, they might not help to specify the structure of moral judgments, except when they are ill-informed and unreflective. For isolating reasons and principles that underlie our responses, exotic cases might be positively harmful.

In short, I believe that some philosophical analysis, based on exotic moral dilemmas, is inadvertently and even comically replicating the early work of Kahneman and Tversky: uncovering situations in which intuitions, normally quite sensible, turn out to misfire. The irony is that while Kahneman and Tversky meant to devise cases that would demonstrate the misfiring, some philosophers develop exotic cases with the thought that the intuitions are likely reliable and should form the building blocks for sound moral judgments. An understanding of the operation of heuristics offers reason to doubt the reliability of those intuitions, even when they are very firm.

Now it is possible that the firmness of the underlying intuitions is actually desirable. Social life is almost certainly better, not worse, because of the large number of people who treat heuristics as moral rules and who believe, for example, that innocent people should never be killed. If the heuristic is treated as a universal and freestanding principle, perhaps some mistakes will be made, but only in highly unusual cases, and perhaps people who accept the principle will avoid the temptation to depart from it when the justification for doing so appears sufficient but really is not. In other words, a firm rule might misfire in some cases, but it might be better than a more fine-grained approach, which, in practice, would misfire even more. Those who believe that you should always tell the truth may do and be much better, all things considered, than those who believe that truth should be told only on the basis of case-specific, all-things-considered judgments in its favor.

To the extent that moral heuristics operate as rules, they might be defended in the way that all rules are—better than the alternatives even if productive of error in imaginable cases. I have noted that moral heuristics might show a kind of "ecological rationality," working well in most real-world contexts; recall the possibility that human beings live by simple heuristics that make us good. My suggestion is not that the moral heuristics, in their most rigid forms, are socially worse than the reasonable alternatives. It is hard to resolve that question in the abstract. I am claiming only that such heuristics lead to real errors and significant confusion. A great deal of experimental work remains to be done on this question; existing research has only scratched the surface.

Within philosophy, there is a large body of literature on the role of intuitions in moral argument, much of it devoted to their role in the search for reflective equilibrium.[70] In John Rawls' influential formulation, people's judgments about justice should be made via an effort to ensure principled consistency between their beliefs at all levels of generality.[71] Rawls emphasizes that during the search for reflective equilibrium, all beliefs are revisable in principle. But as Rawls also emphasizes, some of our beliefs, about particular cases and more generally, seem to us especially fixed, and it will take a great deal to uproot them. It is tempting to use an understanding of moral heuristics as a basis for challenging the search for reflection equilibrium, but I do not believe that anything said here supports that challenge. Recall that in Rawls' formulation, all of our intuitions are potentially revisable, including those that are quite firm.

What I am adding here is that if moral heuristics are pervasive, then some of our apparently fixed beliefs might result from them. We should be aware of that fact in attempting to reach reflective equilibrium. Of course some beliefs that are rooted in moral heuristics might turn out, on reflection, to be correct, perhaps for reasons that will not occur to people who use the heuristics mechanically. I am suggesting only that judgments that seem most insistent, or least revisable, may result from overgeneralizing intuitions that work well in many contexts but also misfire in others.

If this is harder to demonstrate in the domain of morality than in the domain of facts, it is largely because we are able to agree, in the relevant cases, about what constitutes factual error and often less able to agree about what constitutes moral error. With respect to the largest disputes about what morality requires, it may be too contentious to argue that one side is operating under a heuristic, whereas another side has it basically right. But I hope that I have said enough to show that in particular cases, sensible rules of thumb lead to demonstrable errors not merely in factual judgments, but in the domains of morality, politics, and law as well.

15 Rights

In political, moral, and legal theory, many of the largest debates pit consequentialists against deontologists. Recall that consequentialists believe that
the rightness of actions turns on their consequences, which are to be measured, aggregated, and ranked. (Utilitarianism is a species of consequentialism.) By contrast, deontologists believe that some actions are wrong even if
they have good consequences. Many deontologists think that it is wrong to
torture people or to kill them even if the consequences of doing so would be
good. Many deontologists also think that you should not throw someone
in the way of a speeding train even if that action would save lives on balance; that you should not torture someone even if doing so would produce
information that would save lives; that slavery is a moral wrong regardless
of the outcome of any utilitarian calculus; that the protection of free speech
does not depend on any such calculus; that the strongest arguments for
and against capital punishment turn on what is right, independent of the
consequences of capital punishment.

The disagreements between deontologists and consequentialists bear
directly on many issues in law and policy. Consequentialists believe that
constitutional rights, including the right to free speech, must be defended
and interpreted by reference to the consequences; deontologists disagree.
Consequentialists are favorably disposed to cost-benefit analysis in regulatory policy, but that form of analysis has been vigorously challenged on
broadly deontological grounds. Consequentialists favor theories of punishment that are based on deterrence, and they firmly reject retributivism,
which some deontologists endorse. For both criminal punishment and
punitive damage awards, consequentialists and deontologists have systematic disagreements. Consequentialists and deontologists also disagree about
the principles underlying the law of contract and tort.

In defending their views, deontologists often point to cases in which our intuitions seem very firm and hence to operate as "fixed points" against which we must evaluate consequentialism.[1] They attempt to show that consequentialism runs up against intransigent intuitions and is wrong for that reason. In the previous chapters, I explored weak consequentialism, which attempts to soften this disagreement. But it is true that in its usual forms, consequentialism seems to conflict with some of our deepest intuitions, certainly in new or unfamiliar situations.[2] For example, human beings appear to be intuitive retributivists; they want wrongdoers to suffer. With respect to punishment, efforts to encourage people to think in consequentialist terms do not fare at all well.[3]

In the face of the extensive body of philosophical work exploring the conflict between deontology and consequentialism, it seems reckless to venture a simple resolution, but let us consider one: deontology is a moral heuristic for what really matters, and consequences are what really matter. On this view, deontological intuitions are generally sound, in the sense that they usually lead to what would emerge from a proper consequentialist assessment. Protection of free speech and religious liberty, for example, is generally justified on consequentialist grounds. At the same time, however, deontological intuitions can sometimes produce severe and systematic errors in the form of suboptimal or bad consequences. The idea that deontology should be seen as a heuristic is consistent with a growing body of behavioral and neuroscientific research, which generally finds that deontological judgments are rooted in automatic, emotional processing.[4]

My basic claims here are twofold. First, the emerging research might serve to unsettle and loosen some deeply held moral intuitions and give us new reason to scrutinize our immediate and seemingly firm reactions to moral problems. Deontology may in fact be a moral heuristic, in the sense that it may be a mental shortcut for the right moral analysis, which is consequentialist. Thus Henry Sidgwick urges:

It may be shown, I think, that the Utilitarian estimate of consequences not only supports broadly the current moral rules, but also sustains their generally received limitations and qualifications: that, again, it explains anomalies in the Morality of Common Sense, which from any other point of view must seem unsatisfactory to the reflective intellect; and moreover, where the current formula is not sufficiently precise for the guidance of conduct, while at the same time difficulties and perplexities arise in the attempt to give it additional precision, the Utilitarian method solves these difficulties and perplexities in general accordance with the vague instincts of Common Sense, and is naturally appealed to for such solution in ordinary moral discussions.[5]

Sidgwick did not have the benefit of recent empirical findings, but he might have been willing to agree "that deontological philosophy is largely a rationalization of emotional moral intuitions."[6] But my second claim is that nothing in the emerging research is sufficient to establish that deontological judgments are wrong or false. Nonetheless, I am going to explore the possibility here.

Trolleys and Footbridges

A great deal of neuroscientific and psychological work is consistent with the view that deontological judgments stem from a moral heuristic, one that works automatically and rapidly. It bears emphasizing that if this view is correct, it is also possible—indeed, likely—that such judgments generally work well in the sense that they produce the right results (according to the appropriate standard) in most cases. The judgments that emerge from automatic processing, including emotional varieties, usually turn out the way they do for a reason. If deontological judgments result from a moral heuristic, we might end up concluding that they generally work well but misfire in systematic ways.

Consider in this regard the long-standing philosophical debate over two well-known moral dilemmas, which seem to test deontology and consequentialism.[7] The first, called the trolley problem, asks people to imagine that a runaway trolley is headed for five people, who will be killed if the trolley continues on its current course. The question is whether you would throw a switch that would move the trolley onto another set of tracks, killing one person rather than five. Most people would throw the switch. The second, called the footbridge problem, is the same as that just given, but with one difference: the only way to save the five is to throw a stranger, now on a footbridge that spans the tracks, into the path of the trolley, killing that stranger but preventing the trolley from reaching the others. Most people will not kill the stranger.

What is the difference between the two cases, if any? A great deal of philosophical work has been done on this question, much of it trying to suggest that our firm intuitions can indeed be defended, or rescued, as a matter of principle. The basic idea seems to be that those firm intuitions, separating the two cases, tell us something important about what morality requires, and an important philosophical task is to explain why they are essentially right.

Without engaging these arguments, consider a simpler answer. As a matter of principle, there is no difference between the two cases. People's different reactions are based on a deontological heuristic ("do not throw innocent people to their death") that condemns the throwing of the stranger but not the throwing of the switch. To say the least, it is desirable for people to act on the basis of a moral heuristic that makes it extremely abhorrent to use physical force to kill innocent people. But the underlying heuristic misfires in drawing a distinction between the two ingeniously devised cases. Hence people (including philosophers) struggle heroically to rescue their intuitions and to establish that the two cases are genuinely different in principle. But they are not. If so, a deontological intuition is serving as a heuristic in the footbridge problem, and it is leading people in the wrong direction. Can this proposition be tested? Does it suggest something more general about deontology?

Neuroscience

The Human Brain

How does the human brain respond to the trolley and footbridge problems? The authors of an influential study do not attempt to answer the moral questions in principle, but they find "that there are systematic variations in the engagement of emotions in moral judgment" and that brain areas associated with emotion are far more active in contemplating the footbridge problem than in contemplating the trolley problem.[8]

More particularly, the footbridge problem preferentially activates the regions of the brain that are associated with emotion, including the amygdala. By contrast, the trolley problem produces increased activity in parts of the brain associated with cognitive control and working memory. A possible implication of the authors' finding is that human brains distinguish between different ways of bringing about deaths; some ways trigger automatic, emotional reactions, whereas others do not. Other fMRI studies reach the same general conclusion.[9]

Actions and Omissions

People tend to believe that harmful actions are worse than harmful omissions; intuition strongly suggest a sharp difference between the two. Many people think that the distinction is justified in principle. They may be right, and the arguments offered in defense of the distinction might be convincing. But in terms of people's actual judgments, there is reason to believe that automatic (as opposed to deliberative or controlled) mechanisms help to account for people's intuitions. The provocative possibility is that the faster and more automatic part of the human brain regards actions as worse than omissions, but the slower and more deliberative part, focused on consequences, does not make such a sharp distinction between the two.[10]

In the relevant experiments, participants were presented with a series of moral scenarios, involving both actions and omissions. They judged active harms to be far more objectionable than inaction. As compared with harmful actions, harmful omissions produced significantly more engagement in the frontoparietal control network, an area that contributes to the ability to guide actions based on goals. Those participants who showed the *highest* engagement in that network while answering questions involving omissions also tended to show the *smallest* differences in their judgments of actions and omissions. This finding suggests that more controlled and deliberative processing does not lead to a sharp distinction between the two. A high level of such processing was necessary to override the intuitive sense that the two are different (with omissions seeming less troublesome). In the authors' words, there is "a role for controlled cognition in the elimination of the omission effect,"[11] meaning that such cognition leads people not to see actions as much worse than omissions.

The upshot is that lesser concern with omissions arises automatically, without the use of controlled cognition. People engage in such cognition to overcome automatic judgment processes in order to condemn harmful omissions. Hence "controlled cognition is associated not with conforming to the omission effect but with overriding it,"[12] and "the more a person judges harmful omissions on parity with harmful actions, the more they engage cognitive control during the judgment of omissions."[13]

Social Emotions and Utilitarianism

The ventromedial prefrontal cortex (VMPC) is a region of the brain that is necessary for social emotions, such as compassion, shame, and guilt.[14]

Patients with VMPC lesions show reductions in these emotions and reduced emotional receptivity in general. Researchers predicted that such patients would show an unusually high rate of utilitarian judgments in moral scenarios that typically trigger strong emotions—such as the footbridge problem. The prediction turned out to be correct.[15] Those with damage to the VMPC engaged in utilitarian reasoning in responding to problems of that kind.

This finding is consistent with the view that deontological reasoning is a product of negative emotional responses.[16] By contrast, consequentialist reasoning, reflecting a kind of cost-benefit analysis, is subserved by the dorsolateral prefrontal cortex, which shares responsibility for cognitive functions. Damage to the VMPC predictably dampens the effects of emotions and leads people to engage in an analysis of likely effects of different courses of action. Similarly, people with frontotemporal dementia are believed to suffer from "emotional blunting"—and they are especially likely to favor action in the footbridge problem.[17] According to an admittedly controversial interpretation of these findings, "patients with emotional deficits may, in some contexts, be the most pro-social of all."[18]

Behavioral Evidence and Deontology

A great deal of behavioral evidence also suggests that deontological thinking is associated with System 1 and in particular with emotions.

Words or Pictures?

People were tested to see if they had a visual or verbal cognitive style—that is, to see whether they performed better with tests of visual accuracy than with tests of verbal accuracy.[19] The authors hypothesized that because visual representations are more emotionally salient, those who do best with verbal processing would be more likely to support utilitarian judgments, and those who do best with visual processing would be more likely to support deontological judgments. The hypothesis was confirmed. Those with more visual cognitive styles were more likely to favor deontological approaches.

People's self-reports showed that their internal imagery—that is, what they visualized—predicted their judgments in the sense that those who "saw" pictures of concrete harm were significantly more likely to favor deontological approaches. In the authors' words, "visual imagery plays an important role in triggering the automatic emotional responses that support deontological judgments."[20]

The Effects of Cognitive Load

What are the effects of cognitive load? If people are asked to engage in tasks that are cognitively difficult, such that they have less "space" for complex processing, what happens to their moral judgments? The answer is clear: an increase in cognitive load interferes with consequentialist (utilitarian) moral judgment but has no such effect on deontological approaches.[21] This finding strongly supports the view that consequentialist judgments are cognitively demanding and that deontological judgments are relatively easy and automatic.[22]

Priming System 2

The cognitive reflection test (CRT) asks a series of questions that elicit answers that fit with people's intuitions but that turn out to be wrong. Here is one such question: A bat and a ball cost $1.10 in total. The bat costs a dollar more than the ball. How much does the ball cost? In response, most people do not give the correct answer, which is five cents. They are more likely to offer the intuitively plausible answer, which is ten cents. Those who take the CRT tend to learn that they often give an immediate answer that turns out, on reflection, to be incorrect. If people take the CRT before engaging in some other task, they will be "primed" to question their own intuitive judgments. What is the effect of taking the CRT on moral judgments?

The answer is clear: those who take the CRT are more likely to reject deontological thinking in favor of utilitarianism.[23] Consider the following dilemma:

John is the captain of a military submarine traveling underneath a large iceberg. An onboard explosion has caused the vessel to lose most of its oxygen supply and has injured a crewman who is quickly losing blood. The injured crewman is going to die from his wounds no matter what happens.

The remaining oxygen is not sufficient for the entire crew to make it to the surface. The only way to save the other crew members is for John to shoot dead the injured crewman so that there will be just enough oxygen for the rest of the crew to survive.

Is it morally acceptable for John to shoot the injured crewman? Those who took the CRT before answering that question were far more likely to find that action morally acceptable.[24] Across a series of questions, those who took the CRT became significantly more likely to support consequentialist approaches to social dilemmas.

Is and Ought

The evidence just outlined is consistent with the proposition that deontological intuitions are mere heuristics, produced by the automatic operations of System 1. The basic picture would be closely akin to the corresponding one for questions of fact. People use mental shortcuts, or rules of thumb, that generally work well but can also lead to systematic errors.

To be sure, the neuroscientific and psychological evidence is preliminary and suggestive but no more. Importantly, we do not have much cross-cultural evidence. Do people in diverse nations and cultures show the same kinds of reactions to moral dilemmas? Is automatic processing associated with deontological approaches only in certain nations and cultures? Do people in some nations show automatic moral disapproval (perhaps motivated by disgust) of practices and judgments that seem tolerable or even appropriate elsewhere? Where and how does deontology matter? There may not be simple answers to such questions; perhaps some deontological reactions are hardwired and others are not.

Moreover, deontological intuitions and judgments span an exceedingly wide range. They are hardly exhausted by the trolley and footbridge problems and by related hypothetical questions, and if deontological intuitions are confused or unhelpful in resolving such problems, deontology would not stand defeated by virtue of that fact. Consider, for example, retributive theories of punishment; autonomy-based theories of freedom of speech and religion; bans on slavery and torture, grounded in principles of respect for persons; and theories of tort law and contract law that are rooted in conceptions of fairness. We do not have neuroscientific or psychological evidence with respect to the nature and role of deontological thinking in the wide assortment of moral, political, and legal problems for which deontological approaches have been proposed or defended. Perhaps System 2, and not System 1, is responsible for deontological thinking with respect to some of those problems. It is certainly imaginable, however, that neuroscientific or psychological evidence will eventually find that automatic processing supports deontological thinking across a wide range of problems.

The Central Objection

Even if this is so, the proposition that deontology is a heuristic (in the sense in which I am using that term) runs into a serious and immediate objection. For factual matters, we have an independent standard by which to assess the question of truth. Suppose that people think that more people die as a result of homicide than suicide. The facts show that people's judgments, influenced by the availability heuristic, are incorrect. But if people believe that torture is immoral even if it has good consequences, we do not have a self-evidently correct independent standard to demonstrate that they are wrong.

To be sure, a great deal of philosophical work attempts to defend some version of consequentialism. But deontologists reject the relevant arguments. They do so for what they take to be good reasons, and they elaborate those reasons in great detail. With respect to facts, social scientists can show that certain rules of thumb produce errors; the same cannot be said for deontology. For this reason, deontological judgments may not be a mental shortcut at all. Even if automatic processing gives them a head start, they may ultimately be the product of a long and successful journey.

Or suppose that certain moral intuitions arise in part because of emotions and that some or many deontological intuitions fall into that category. Even if so, we would not have sufficient reason to believe that those intuitions are wrong. Some intuitions about states of the world arise from the emotion of fear, and they are not wrong for that reason. To be sure, people may be fearful when they are actually safe, but without knowing about the situations that cause fear, we have no reason to think that the emotion is leading people to make mistakes. The fact—if it is a fact—that some or many deontological intuitions are driven by emotions does not mean that those intuitions misfire.

If these points are right, then we might be able to agree that deontological thinking often emerges from automatic processing and that consequential thinking is often more calculative and deliberative. This might well be the right way to think about moral psychology, at least in many domains, and the resulting understanding of moral psychology certainly has explanatory power for many problems in law and politics; it helps us to understand why legal and political debates take the form that they do. But if so, we would not be able to conclude that deontological thinking is wrong. Consider in this regard the fact that in response to some problems and situations, people's immediate, intuitive responses are right, and a great deal of reflection and deliberation can produce mistakes. There is no reason to think that System 2 is always more accurate than System 1. Even if deontological judgments are automatic and emotional, they may turn out to be correct.

Two New Species

Here is a way to sharpen the point. Imagine that we discovered two new species of human beings: Kantians and Benthamites. Suppose that the Kantians are far more emotional than *Homo sapiens* and that Benthamites are far less so. Imagine that neuroscientists learn that Kantians and Benthamites have distinctive brain structures. Kantians have a highly developed emotional system and a relatively undeveloped cognitive system. By contrast, Benthamites have a highly developed cognitive system—significantly more developed than that in *Homo sapiens*. And true to their names, Kantians strongly favor deontological approaches to moral questions, whereas Benthamites are thoroughgoing consequentialists.

Impressed by this evidence, some people insist that we have new reason to think that consequentialism is correct. Indeed, anthropologists discover that Benthamites have written many impressive and elaborate arguments in favor of consequentialism. By contrast, Kantians have written nothing. (They do not write much.) With such discoveries, would we have new reason to think that consequentialism is right? Clearly not. Whether consequentialism is rights turns on the strength of the arguments offered on its behalf, not on anything about the brains of the two species.

To see the point, suppose that an iconoclastic Benthamite has written a powerful essay, contending that consequentialism is wrong and that some version of Kantianism is right. Wouldn't that argument have to be investigated on its merits? If the answer is affirmative, then we should be able to see that even if certain moral convictions originate in automatic processing, they may nonetheless be correct. Everything depends on the justifications that have been provided in their defense. A deontological conviction may come from System 1, but the Kantians might be right, and the Benthamites should listen to what they have to say.

Moral Reasoning and Moral Rationalization

Suppose that we agree that recent research shows that as a matter of fact, "deontological judgments tend to be driven by emotional responses"; a more provocative conclusion, consistent with (but not mandated by) the evidence, is that "deontological philosophy, rather than being grounded in moral *reasoning*, is to a large extent an exercise in moral *rationalization*."[25] Without denying the possibility that the intuitive system is right, Joshua Greene contends "that science, and neuroscience in particular, can have profound ethical implications by providing us with information that will prompt us to re-evaluate our moral values and our conceptions of morality."[26]

The claim seems plausible. But how exactly might scientific information prompt us to reevaluate our moral values? The best answer is that it might lead people to slow down and to give serious scrutiny to their immediate reactions. If you know that your moral judgment is a rapid intuition based on emotional processing, then you might be more willing to consider the possibility that it is wrong. You might be willing to consider the possibility that you have been influenced by irrelevant factors.

Suppose that you believe it is unacceptable to push someone into a speeding train even if you know that the result of doing so would be to save five people. Now suppose that you are asked whether it is acceptable to pull a switch that drops someone through a trapdoor when the result of doing so would also be to save five people. Suppose that you believe that it is indeed acceptable. Now suppose that you are asked to square your judgments in the two cases. You might decide that you cannot, that in the first case, physical contact is making all the difference to your moral judgments, but that on reflection it is irrelevant. If that is your conclusion, you might be moved in a more consequentialist direction.

And in fact, there is evidence to support this view.[27] Consider this case:

A major pharmaceutical company sells a desperately needed cancer drug. It decides to increase its profits by significantly increasing the price of the drug. Is this acceptable?

Many people believe that it is not. Now consider this case:

A major pharmaceutical company sells a desperately needed cancer drug. It decides to sell the right to market the drug to a smaller company; it receives

a lot of money for the sale and it knows that the smaller company will significantly increase the price of the drug. Is this acceptable?

Many people believe that it is. In a between-subjects design, in which
each person sees only one scenario, people regard the case of indirect harm
as far more acceptable than that of direct harm. But in a within-subjects
design, in which people see the two cases at the same time, the difference
evaporates. The apparent reason is that when people see the two cases at
once, they conclude that the proper evaluation of harmful actions should
not turn on the direct-indirect distinction. We could easily imagine the
same process in the context of other moral dilemmas, including the trolley
and footbridge problems. If System 1 and emotional processing are leading
to a rapid, intuitive conclusion that X is morally abhorrent or that Y is morally acceptable, a simultaneous encounter with cases A and B may weaken
that conclusion and show that it is based on morally irrelevant factors—or
at least factors that people come to see as morally irrelevant after reflection. It is also possible that when people see various problems at the same
time, they might conclude that certain factors are morally relevant that
they originally thought immaterial.

The same process may occur in straightforwardly legal debates. Suppose
that intuition suggests that punitive damages are best understood as a simple retributive response to wrongdoing and that theories of deterrence seem
secondary, unduly complex, or essentially beside the point.[28] If this is so,
people's judgments about appropriate punitive damage awards will not be
much influenced by the likelihood that the underlying conduct would be
discovered and punished—a factor that is critical to the analysis of optimal
deterrence. Critical reflection might lead people to focus on the importance
of deterrence and to conclude that a factor that they disregarded is in fact
highly relevant. Indeed, critical reflection—at least if it is sustained—might
lead people to think that some of their intuitive judgments about fairness
are not correct because they have bad consequences. Such reflection might
lead them to change their initial views about policy and law and even to
conclude that those views were rooted in a heuristic.

Even here, however, people's ultimate conclusions are not decisive. Let
us stipulate that people might well revisit their intuitions and come to a different (and perhaps more consistently consequentialist) point of view. Suppose that they do. Do we know that they are right? Not necessarily. Recall
that for some problems, people's immediate answers are more accurate

than those that follow from reflection. With respect to moral questions, a final evaluation would have to depend on the right moral theory. The fact that people have revised their intuitions does not establish that they have moved in the direction of that theory. It is evidence of what people think, under certain conditions, and surely some conditions are more conducive to good thinking than others. But the question remains whether what they think is right or true in principle.

Noisy Intuitions

We are learning a great deal about the psychology of moral judgment. It is increasingly plausible to think that many deontological intuitions are a product of rapid, automatic, emotional processing and that these intuitions play a large role in debates over public policy and law. But the relevant evidence is neither necessary nor sufficient to justify the conclusion that deontology is a mere heuristic (in the sense of a mental shortcut in the direction of the correct theory). What is required is a moral argument.

There is one qualification to this claim. It is well established that with respect to factual questions, rapid reactions, stemming from System 1, generally work well but can produce systematic errors. Deontological intuitions appear to have essentially the same sources as those rapid reactions. That point does not establish error, but it does suggest the possibility that, however firmly held, deontological intuitions are providing the motivation for elaborate justifications that would not be offered or have much appeal without the voice of Gould's homunculus, jumping up and down and shouting at us. The homunculus might turn out to be right. But it is also possible that we should be listening to other voices.

16   Partyism

With respect to prejudice and hostility, the English language has a number of isms: racism, sexism, classism, and speciesism are prominent examples. I aim to coin a new one here: *partyism*. The central idea is that those who identify with a political party often become deeply hostile to the opposing party and believe that its members have a host of horrific characteristics.[1] They might think that the opposing party is full of people who are ignorant, foolish, evil, corrupt, duped, out of touch, or otherwise awful.

My major suggestion here is that in the United States (and perhaps in other countries as well), partyism is real and on the rise, and that it has serious adverse consequences for governance, politics, and daily life. Sometimes it makes change possible and rapid, at least if one party controls the levels of power. Sometimes it leads to authoritarianism. Sometimes it makes change impossible or slow, at least when and because parties are able to block each other—and determined to do so.

I also offer a few words about the causes and consequences of partyism and make some suggestions about what might be done about it. Under conditions of severe partyism, it can become unusually difficult to address serious social problems, at least through legislation. To that extent, the system of separation of powers—which already imposes a series of barriers to legislative initiatives—is often an obstacle to desirable change. The executive branch might be able to produce change on its own—as both Barack Obama and Donald Trump discovered—but under conditions of partyism, unilateral change has problems of its own. It might not be legitimate; it might be ill-considered.

There is a great deal of evidence of partyism and its growth. Perhaps the simplest involves "thermometer ratings."[2] With those ratings, people are asked to rate a range of groups on a scale of 0 to 100, where 100 means that the respondent feels "warm" toward the group and 0 means that the respondent feels "cold." In-party rankings have remained stable over the last three decades, with both Democrats and Republicans ranking members of their own party around 70. By contrast, ratings of the other party have experienced a remarkable fifteen-point dip since 1988.[3] In 2008, the average out-party ranking was around 30—and it continues to decline. By contrast, Republicans ranked "people on welfare" in that year at 50, and Democrats ranked "big business" at 52. It is remarkable but true that negative affect toward the opposing party is not merely greater than negative affect toward unwelcome people and causes; it is much greater.

Implicit Association Test

Consider one of the most influential measures of prejudice: the implicit-association test (IAT).[4] The test is simple to take. Participants see words on the upper corners of a screen—for example, *white* paired with either *good* or *bad* in the upper-left corner, and *black* paired with one of those same adjectives in the upper right. Then they see a picture or a word in the middle of the screen—for example, a white face, an African American face, or the word *joy* or *terrible*. The task is to click on the upper corner that matches either the picture or the word in the middle.

Many white people quickly associate positive words like *joy*, or an evidently European American (Caucasian) face, with the upper-left corner when it says *white* and *good*—but have a much harder time associating *joy* with the left corner when the words there are *black* and *good*.[5] So too, many white people quickly associate *terrible* with the left corner when it says *black* and *bad*, but proceed a lot more slowly when the left corner says *white* and *bad*. And when the picture in the middle is evidently of a European American (Caucasian), white people are a lot faster in associating it with the word *good* than when the picture is evidently of an African American.

It is tempting to think that racial prejudice is deeply engrained and that nothing comparable can be found in the political domain, at least with respect to the two major parties in the United States. (To be sure, we might expect to see strongly negative implicit attitudes for Nazis or Communists.) To test for political prejudice, Shanto Iyengar and Sean Westwood, political scientists at Stanford University, conducted a large-scale implicit association test with two thousand adults.[6] They found people's political bias to be much larger than their racial bias. When Democrats see *joy*, it is much easier for them to click on a corner that says *Democratic* and *good* than on one that says *Republican* and *good*. Implicit bias across racial lines remains significant, but it is significantly greater across political lines.

Love and Marriage

If you are a Democrat, would you marry a Republican? Would you be upset if your sister did? Researchers have long asked such questions about race and have found that, along important dimensions, racial prejudice is decreasing.[7] At the same time, party prejudice in the United States has jumped, infecting not only politics but also decisions about marriage. In 1960, just 5 percent of Republicans and 4 percent of Democrats said that they would feel "displeased" if their son or daughter married outside their political party.[8] By 2010, those numbers had reached 49 percent and 33 percent.[9] Interestingly, comparable increases cannot be found in the relevant period in the United Kingdom.[10]

In 2009, by contrast, 6 percent of Americans reported that they "would be fine" if a member of their family married someone of any other race or ethnicity, a sharp change from as recently as 1986, when 65 percent of respondents said that interracial marriage was not fine for anyone or not fine for them.[11] Asked specifically about marriages between African American and white partners, only 6 percent of white respondents and 3 percent of African Americans recently said that "they could not accept a black-white interracial marriage in their family."[12] Similarly, a recent Gallup survey found that 87 percent of people approve of interracial marriage, compared to 4 percent in 1958: a dramatic shift in social norms, showing the opposite trend line from that observed for partyism.[13]

Hiring

The IAT measures attitudes, not behavior. Growing disapproval of marriage across political lines suggests an increase in prejudice and hostility, but it might not map to actual conduct. To investigate behavior, Iyengar and Westwood asked more than one thousand people to look at the resumes of several high school seniors and say which ones should be awarded a scholarship.[14] Some of these resumes contained explicitly racial cues ("president of the African American Student Association"), while others had explicitly political ones ("president of the Young Republicans").

In terms of ultimate judgments, race certainly mattered: African American participants preferred the African American scholarship candidates 73 percent to 27 percent. For their part, whites showed a modest preference for African American candidates as well, though by a significantly smaller margin. But party affiliation made a much larger difference. Both Democrats and Republicans selected their in-party candidate about 80 percent of the time.[15] Even when a candidate from the opposing party had better credentials, most people chose the candidate from their own party.[16] With respect to race, in contrast, merit prevailed.[17] It is worth underlining this finding: racial preferences were eliminated when one candidate was clearly better than the other; by contrast, party preferences led people to choose a clearly inferior candidate.

A similar study asked students to play the role of college admissions director and to decide which applicants to invite for an on-campus interview, based on both objective criteria (SAT scores, class rank) and subjective evidence (teacher recommendations).[18] Among partisans with strong party identification, there was significant evidence of partyism: 44 percent of the participants reviewing someone from the opposite party selected the stronger applicant, whereas 79 percent of the participants in the control (in which participants had no knowledge of the applicant's party affiliation) selected the stronger applicant.[19]

Trust

In a further test of the relationship between partyism and actual behavior, Iyengar and Westwood asked eight hundred people to play the trust game,[20] well-known among behavioral scientists. As the game is played, player 1 is given some money (say, ten dollars) and told that she can give some, all, or none of it to player 2. Player 1 is then told that the researcher will triple the amount that she allocates to player 2—and that player 2 can give some of that back to player 1. When player 1 decides how much money to give player 2, a central question is how well she trusts him to return an equivalent or greater amount. Higher levels of trust will result in higher initial allocations.

Are people less willing to trust people of a different race or party affiliation? Iyengar and Westwood found that race did not matter—but party did. People are significantly more trusting of others who share their party affiliation.

Partyism can motivate partisans to be especially inclined to share negative information about the opposing party—or even to avoid its members altogether when forming a group.[21] In one experiment, participants were asked to decide whether a strongly worded opinion piece, including hyperbole and name calling, that blamed congressional gridlock on one of the two political parties should be posted on a news organization's website.[22] The researchers found significant evidence of partyism: 65 percentage of people were willing to post the article if it was critical of the opposing party, but only 25 percent were willing to share it if it criticized its own party.[23] They also found that the intensity of a participant's partisan feelings correlated with their willingness to share a critical article.[24]

In a second experiment, the researchers asked participants to pick a team of three people out of a list of four to join them in completing a puzzle game.[25] Participants were informed of the partisan identities and education levels of the potential teammates; the least educated team member was always an independent. More than half the participants selected the least educated player for their team rather than choosing a better-educated member of the opposing party!

An Objection

From these studies and various others,[26] it seems clear that partyism is widespread and on the rise in the United States. We can imagine reasonable disputes about the precise magnitude of the phenomenon, but not about its existence and significance. But there is an obvious objection to the effort to compare racism to partyism, and indeed to the very effort to describe partyism as seriously troubling. The objection is that people have legitimate reasons for objecting to people because of their political beliefs. If we think that Fascism or Communism is hateful, we will not object to those who are unenthusiastic about Fascists or Communists.

For some people, a degree of suspicion and hostility across political lines is a product of legitimate disagreement, not of anything untoward. Racism and sexism result from devaluation of human beings on the basis of an immutable or at least irrelevant characteristic. Perhaps the same cannot be said for party affiliation. In fact the very idea of political prejudice, or any kind of corresponding ism, might seem badly misdirected. Perhaps we are speaking here not of any kind of prejudice but of a considered judgment about people who hold certain convictions. On certain assumptions, that is the precise opposite of prejudice.

To come to terms with this response, we need to begin by distinguishing between daily life and politics as such. It is hardly unreasonable to have a strong negative affect toward Fascists or Communists because of their political views. But if people dislike each other because of an affiliation with one of the major parties in the United States, something does seem badly amiss. To be sure, some characteristics or even commitments of one or another party might seem troublesome or worse. But both parties are large and diverse, and it is odd to think that outside of the political domain, members of one party should actually dislike members of another party as human beings.

Of course this judgment turns on substantive conclusions. If you believe that Republicans are essentially racists and sexists, antipathy toward Republicans is understandable, and so too if you believe that Democrats are unpatriotic socialists who seek to undermine the United States. But if you believe that across the two parties, good-faith disagreements are possible and pervasive, then partyism will be hard to defend, not least if it seeps into daily life.

In the political domain, of course, intensely held differences are common, and some kind of "we-they" attitude may be difficult or impossible to avoid. For members of Congress, such an attitude is, in a sense, built into the very structure of the two-party system. A degree of antipathy—at least if it is not personal—may reflect principled disagreement, not prejudice at all. It may be hard to avoid a measure of antipathy toward people with whom you intensely disagree, most of the time, in your day job. The problem is that good-faith disagreement is far from uncommon in politics, and in the face of such disagreement the task is to seek to identify ways to move forward (or not), rather than to discredit arguments because of their source. With respect to politics itself, something like partyism may be a product of principle, but it also has destructive consequences, as we shall shortly see.

Causes

What causes partyism? We do not yet know the answer, but some helpful clues have started to emerge.

From Ideological Disagreement to Partyism?

It is tempting to think that the growth in partyism is a product of the increasing intensity and visibility of ideological disagreements. Let us assume that at some point in the past—say, 1970—one or another of the two parties, or perhaps both, had a "wider tent." Let us assume, in fact, that the conservative wing of the Democratic party was more conservative than the liberal wing of the Republican party and thus the two parties had significant ideological overlap. If so, we would not expect to see much in the way of partyism.

This hypothesis could be tested in multiple ways. We could attempt to track ideological differences between the parties and test whether growth in ideological distance turned out to be correlated with increases in partyism. A strong correlation would not be definitive, but it would be at least suggestive. It would indicate that strong negative affect, across political lines, would have something to do with increasingly intense substantive disagreements. And if this turned out to be so, the rise of partyism would, in a sense, turn out to be rational, at least in the sense that prejudice and antipathy would be a product of something concrete and real. The role of partyism in the private domain would remain hard to defend, but in politics, at least, its recent increase would be comprehensible.

But a better way to test the hypothesis would be to see whether the intensity of people's policy preferences predicts partyism. In other words, when people have very strong views about political issues, and when those very strong views suggest clear divisions across party lines, are they more likely to show a negative affect toward the opposing party? Surprisingly, *the connection between ideological polarization and negative affect is relatively weak.*[27] As polarization between the parties grows, negative affect does not grow with it. It appears that people's partisan attachments are a product of their *identity* rather than their *ideology*. When Republicans dislike Democrats, or vice versa, it is largely because they are on the opposing side; substantive disagreements matter, to be sure, but they are not primary.

Campaigns

Do political campaigns create partyism? It is natural to suspect that they do, first because they make party differences salient, and second because part of the point is to cast the opposing side in a negative light. Iyengar and Westwood find strong support for this hypothesis. In particular, exposure to negative advertising contributes to a growth in partisan animus, and political campaigns themselves have that effect.[28] Apparently campaigns serve to "prime" partisan identity and to support stereotypical and negative perceptions of both supporters and opponents.

Your Media, My Media

In a fragmented media market, it is easy for people to segregate along partisan lines. Recall the phenomenon of group polarization (see chapter 2), which should increase with the presence of echo chambers and information cocoons. In the United States, Fox News has an identifiable conservative orientation; MSNBC has an identifiable liberal orientation. Some talk shows are easy to characterize in terms of the political commitments of the host. If a show or a station characterizes one group of people as "the other side," and if those on that side are described as malicious, foolish, or power-hungry, then viewers or listeners should experience a rise in partyism.

Social media can also be used for purposes of partisan self-sorting; many people end up in the equivalent of echo chambers as a result of Facebook and Twitter. That might well contribute to partyism. We do not have clear data on this speculation, but some is emerging.[29] It is reasonable to suspect a fragmented media market with clear political identifications contributes a great deal to partyism.

Political Polarization

Suppose that a society is divided on some proposition. The first group believes A, and the second group believes not-A. Suppose that the first group is correct. Suppose finally that truthful information is provided, not from members of the first group but from some independent source, in support of A. It would be reasonable to suppose that the second group would come to believe A. But in important settings, the opposite happens. The second group continues to believe not-A—and even more firmly than before. The result of the correction is to increase polarization.

The underlying studies do not involve party differences as such, but they explore something very close to that, and they suggest the following proposition: An important consequence of partyism is to ensure that *people with a strong political identification will be relatively immune from corrections, even on matters of fact, from people who do not share that identification*. Because agreement on matters of fact is often a precondition for political progress, this phenomenon can be extremely destructive.

In a relevant experiment, people were exposed to a mock news article in which President George W. Bush defended the Iraq war, in part by suggesting (as President Bush in fact did) that there "was a risk, a real risk, that Saddam Hussein would pass weapons or materials or information to terrorist networks."[30] After reading this article, they read about the Duelfer Report, which documented the lack of weapons of mass destruction in Iraq. Subjects were then asked to state their agreement, on a five-point scale (from "strongly agree" to "strongly disagree"), with the statement that Iraq "had an active weapons of mass destruction program, the ability to produce these weapons, and large stockpiles of WMD."[31]

The effect of the correction greatly varied by political ideology. For very liberal subjects, there was a modest shift in favor of disagreement with this statement; the shift was not significant, because very liberal subjects already tended to disagree with it.[32] But for those who characterized themselves as conservative, there was a statistically significant shift in the direction of *agreeing* with the statement. "In other words, the correction backfired— conservatives who received a correction telling them that Iraq did not have WMD were more likely to believe that Iraq had WMD than those in the control condition."[33] It follows that the correction had a polarizing effect; it divided people more sharply on the issue at hand than they had been divided before.

Another study confirmed the more general effect. People were asked to evaluate the proposition that cutting taxes is so effective in stimulating economic growth that it actually increases government revenue. They were then asked to read a correction. The correction actually increased people's commitments to the proposition in question. "Conservatives presented with evidence that tax cuts do not increase government revenues ended up believing this claim more fervently than those who did not receive a correction."[34]

Or consider a test of whether apparently credible media corrections alter the belief, supported and pressed by former Alaska Governor Sarah Palin, that the Affordable Care Act would create "death panels."[35] Among those who viewed Palin favorably but had limited political knowledge, the correction succeeded; it also succeeded among those who viewed Palin unfavorably.[36] But the correction actually backfired among Palin supporters with a high degree of political knowledge. After receiving the correction, they became *more* likely to believe that the Affordable Care Act contained death panels.[37]

Liberals (and Democrats) are hardly immune to this effect. In 2005, many liberals wrongly believed that President George W. Bush had imposed a ban on stem cell research.[38] Presented with a correction from the New York Times or FoxNews.com, liberals generally continued to believe what they did before.[39] By contrast, conservatives accepted the correction.[40] Hence the correction produced an increase in polarization.

As noted, the relevant experiments involve people with clear ideological (rather than partisan) convictions, and there appears to be no clear evidence on the specific question whether the same effects would be observed for party. But in light of the general evidence of partyism, there is every reason to believe that they would. Indeed, an important and related study shows that people will follow the views of their party even when those views diverge from their independent judgments—and that they are blind to the effects of party influence.[41]

In the relevant study, people—both Democrats and Republicans—were asked their views about an assortment of political issues. As a result, it was possible to obtain a sense of how members of both parties thought about those issues. Otherwise identical groups were then asked about the same issues, but with one difference: they were informed of the views of party leadership. The effect of that difference was significant. Armed with that information, people departed from the views that they would have held if they had not been so armed. Stunningly, the effect of the information "overwhelmed the impact of both the policy's objective impact and participants' ideological beliefs."[42] At the same time, people were blind to that impact; they actually said that their judgments were based solely on the merits, not on the effects of learning about the beliefs of party leaders. Here, then, is clear evidence of the consequences of partyism for people's judgments—and of people's unawareness of that fact.

Gridlock

How does partyism affect the likelihood of social change? In terms of enacted law, the conclusion is simple: Under circumstances of partyism, legislation will be difficult to enact. At least this is so when one or another party has the power to block initiatives. If legislators themselves suffer from partyism, this conclusion should seem self-evident. And even if they do not—even if they feel no antagonism to members of the opposing party and are fully willing to work with them—constituent pressures should push in this direction. In the United States, partyism has been contributing to a highly unusual degree of inactivity in Congress.

There is a legitimate question whether gridlock is good or bad. If an active Congress would reduce social welfare, there would be a good argument for an inactive Congress. Social welfare is the guide, not the volume of activity. In the relevant period, activity might produce welfare-reducing change. A blocked national legislature is something to lament only if the result, all things considered, is to diminish social welfare. One issue is whether and to what extent the legislative status quo is wanting; if it is not, new enactments are not so desirable. Another issue is whether new enactments would be improvements; if they would not be, then gridlock is a blessing, not a curse.

A full account of any particular state of affairs would require a theory of optimal deadlock. This is not the place for any such theory. But it seems reasonable to think that if a nation faces a range of serious problems, if imaginable initiatives would reduce or solve those problems, and if partyism makes it difficult to undertake those initiatives, then something is badly amiss. Under imaginable conditions, all of those assumptions are eminently reasonable.

Solutions

My principal goal here has been descriptive rather than normative. It is possible to believe that partyism is growing and real but that nothing should be done about it. But the increase in partyism has produced serious problems for American government. If some change is desirable, and if pressing challenges remain unaddressed, how might institutions respond?

It is tempting to urge that we should aim at its causes, to the extent that we are able to identify them. That would certainly be the most direct and ambitious response. But James Madison's words in Federalist No. 10, applied to the related phenomenon of faction, are highly relevant here: "Liberty is to faction what air is to fire, an aliment without which it instantly expires. But it could not be less folly to abolish liberty, which is essential to political life, because it nourishes faction, than it would be to wish the annihilation of air, which is essential to animal life, because it imparts to fire its destructive agency."[43]

With Madison's caution in mind, we should acknowledge that it would be folly to attempt to abolish partyism. To be sure, the nature and degree of partyism are not static. As we have seen, partyism has increased significantly in recent decades, and it might turn out to be much lower twenty years hence than it is now. But changes of that kind cannot easily be engineered. They are more likely to be a function of an array of social forces, including emerging technologies, invisible-hand mechanisms, and the decentralized decisions of a wide range of private and public actors.

The real solutions lie not in aiming at the causes of partyism but in working to counteract its effects. Consider three possibilities.

Timing Is Everything

For obvious reasons, partyism is likely to be most intense before a presidential or midterm election. At that point, negative campaigning will be heightened, and politicians might well be at risk if they attempt to make common cause with those from the opposing party. By contrast, partyism is likely to be reduced in the immediate aftermath of a presidential campaign, when the newly elected commander in chief enjoys a "honeymoon period." The term is a good one, because it captures a central feature of the immediate aftermath of an election, which is that a new relationship is created with a kind of warm glow. In the presence of that glow, partyism is diminished, at least for a time, and it may be possible to accomplish a great deal.

The point suggests the immense importance of the period of presidential transition and the need for a president-elect to focus carefully on the top priorities of her or his first term. Clear identification of those priorities, alongside a strategy for bringing them to fruition, has long been exceedingly important. But under conditions of partyism, it is essential to any president-elect—and potentially to the nation as a whole.

Precommitment

Under creatively designed laws, significant reform can happen as a result of congressional inaction. Consider, for example, the Defense Base Realignment and Closure Act of 1990,[44] which enables the president to appoint the nine members of a base-closing commission. The commission produces a list of recommended military base closures, and if the president approves, they happen—unless Congress enacts a resolution of disapproval within forty-five days. If Congress does nothing, the closures go into effect.

A more controversial example is known as the sequester.[45] In 2011, Congress and President Obama completed a difficult negotiation by agreeing that unless Congress enacted new legislation, automatic (and aggressive) spending cuts would go into effect in 2013.[46] At the time, few people favored the automatic cuts; they saw them as a mechanism to force Congress to do its job. But the sequester did go into effect, and for better or worse, it has had major effects on federal spending. The power of the 2011 decision was that it established a drastic outcome if Congress failed to act. The noteworthy surprise was that as a result of partyism, the default outcome actually went into effect.

If the goal is to improve infrastructure, reform Social Security, make significant changes in fiscal policy, or achieve any other large-scale reform, it is possible to imagine a strategy of this kind. With or without the help of a commission, Congress could allow specified changes to occur on a specified date unless a future Congress says otherwise. Of course there is a serious challenge to efforts of this kind: solutions to the problem of partyism might be defeated by partyism. But in some cases, some kind of precommitment strategy or an alteration of the status quo has sufficient appeal to be feasible.

Delegation, Change, and Technocracy

In many cases, the best response to partyism lies in delegation, and in particular in strengthening the hand of technocratic forces within government. I am aware that this conclusion will strike many people as jarring. In response, I suggest that the resolution of many political questions should not turn on politics, at least not in any simple or crude sense. Partyism is unhelpful because partisan differences are irrelevant or nearly so. What most matters are facts, and facts do not turn on political affiliation. Consider these problems:

1. Should EPA reduce the permissible level of ozone in the ambient air from seventy-five parts per billion (ppb) to 70 ppb, 65 ppb, or 60 pbb?
2. Should OSHA issue a new rule to control exposure to silica in the construction industry?
3. Should the Department of Transportation require rearview cameras to be installed in new automobiles?
4. Should the FDA ban asthma inhalers that emit CFCs?

All of these questions are highly technical. They cannot possibly be answered without careful engagement with empirical issues. Policymakers need to know the benefits of imaginable policies in terms of health and safety. They also need to know the costs, monetary and otherwise. Would a new rule for silica cost $100 million, or $500 million, or $1 billion? What would be the consequences of those costs? Would they result in fewer jobs or in reduced wages? What are the actual harms associated with exposure to silica at various levels? With proposed regulations, how many lives would be saved?

To be sure, judgments of value may turn out to play a role in controversies of this kind, but with imaginable empirical projections there may be sufficient consensus to ensure agreement on particular outcomes, even amid significant differences in value and across party lines. If, for example, a silica regulation would cost $1 billion and save merely two lives per year, few people would support it, whatever their party affiliation. And if it would cost $100 million and save seven hundred lives per year, few people would reject it. In any event, it is hopeless to try to answer many of the central questions by reference to one's party identification.

No one denies that Republicans and Democrats have different attitudes toward the EPA and OSHA, and those different attitudes might well lead to disagreements about particular initiatives. What I am urging here is that many disagreements are not really about values or partisan commitments but about facts, and when facts are sufficiently engaged, disagreements across party lines will often melt away.

At least this is so when technocrats, not rigidly bound to ideological convictions, are involved. Many social reforms call for close attention to matters of fact, and questions of value turn out to be secondary. What I am suggesting here is that to choose among reforms, it makes sense to give authority to those who know how to resolve disputes of fact.

The Fragility of Institutional Judgments

Although the main goal here has been descriptive rather than normative, we have seen that an understanding of the problem of partyism fortifies the case for certain forms of executive action and for receptivity to a degree of discretion on the part of the executive branch (at least if it is in reasonable hands). It is important to acknowledge, however, that, in practice, people's judgments about the authority of the executive are greatly and even decisively affected by their approval or disapproval of the incumbent president. Under a Republican president, Democrats do not approve of the idea of a discretion-wielding chief executive, enabled by deferential courts. Under a Democratic president, Republicans tend to have, and even to voice, the same cautions and concerns.

In this respect, some of the most important institutional judgments are fragile and even unstable. They are weakly held in the sense that they predictably "flip" with changes in the allocation of political power. We could even see institutional judgments as victims of partyism itself. Questions of institutional authority are, in a sense, overwhelmed by short-term assessments of the particular people who are currently occupying relevant offices. For this reason, it is possible that evaluations of arguments in favor a receptive approach to presidential power in light of partyism will be dominated by one factor: evaluation of the current occupant of the Oval Office.

The aspiration, of course, is that institutional claims can be evaluated behind a kind of veil of ignorance and that short-term considerations about the immediate winners and losers might be put to one side. For political actors, adoption of a veil of ignorance is extremely challenging because short-term electoral considerations often argue against any such veil. If, for example, a Republican politician argues for acceptance of presidential discretion when the president is a Democrat, she might seriously endanger her political prospects. Even for observers, the challenge is real because short-term political considerations have such salience.

Partyism is real, and it is increasing, and it has serious adverse effects both in daily life and in the political domain. It makes governance more difficult and in some cases even impossible. Even when legislators are aware that a bipartisan agreement would be sensible, they might well be under severe electoral pressure not to enter into it because they might face some kind of reprisal from constituents or colleagues.

Even under current conditions, the effects of partyism have been far more serious in some periods than in others. On the eve of a midterm election, for example, those effects are likely to be heightened. In the six months after a presidential election, they are likely to be reduced. But for structural reasons, large-scale reductions in partyism are unlikely, certainly in the short term.

Is this a problem? If the status quo is pretty good and if further action from the national government would likely make things worse, then there would little reason to lament the existence of partyism. In such circumstances, partyism might turn out to be a valuable safeguard. But if a nation faces serious problems and if imaginable initiatives would helpfully address them, then partyism might turn out to create significant dangers for both peace and prosperity.

At least in the immediate future, it seems unlikely that the United States will be able to make significant progress in reducing the causes of partyism. If such reductions are to occur, they probably will be a product of spontaneous forces rather than of any kind of self-conscious design. The best hope lies in reducing partyism's effects. I suggest that the most promising approaches include precommitment strategies and a renewed emphasis on the use of technocratic expertise.

Closing Words

Human beings like patterns. Our minds work by seeing them, whether or not they are really there. When an individual life has taken a particular shape, and when a society has gone in specific direction, we tend to think that it was all inevitable—as if various pieces fit together. After the fact, we can see that they do. John was destined to be a lawyer. From birth, it was clear that that Susan would go into medicine. Thomas and Linda were bound to break up. Joan and Eric were made for each other. If same-sex marriage came to certain countries in the second decade of the twenty-first century, the time was right. If a certain musician or film suddenly became spectacularly popular, that was essentially inevitable; it connected with the culture. If #MeToo exploded in 2017, and if there was new attention to sexual harassment and sexual assault in that year, then that was bound to happen, especially in light of what happened in 2016.

Because history is only run once, it is hard to show that these claims are false. Some marriages cannot be saved, and some social movements certainly seem inevitable. But small shocks make all the difference. John meets a terrific teacher in college, who inspires him to think about law school; without that teacher, he would never have done that. (That is what actually happened to me.) A musician or film gets the right break at the exactly the right time—a sudden burst of enthusiasm from the right person or group—and that changes everything.

Some political movements are beneficiaries of tipping points and cascade effects. Some are not. Some norm entrepreneurs are skilled, lucky, or both. Some are not. After the fact, we find patterns, and they are there. But if things had gone otherwise, we would have found different patterns, and they too would have been there. A movement that seems inevitable in one year or in one period may have been a beneficiary of a critical nudge or push at a particular moment. Without that, it might have developed later, or perhaps not at all.

Consider in this regard the 2013 Oscar winner for best documentary, *Searching for Sugar Man*, a stunning film about an unsuccessful Detroit singer-songwriter named Sixto Rodriguez, who released two long-forgotten albums in the early 1970s. Almost no one bought his albums, and his label dropped him. Rodriguez stopped making records and worked as a demolition man. What Rodriguez did not know, while working in demolition, was that he had become a spectacular success in South Africa—a giant, a legend, comparable to the Beatles and the Rolling Stones. Describing him as "the soundtrack to our lives," South Africans bought hundreds of thousands of copies of his albums, starting in the 1970s. *Searching for Sugar Man* is about the contrast between the failed career of Detroit's obscure demolition man and the renown of South Africa's mysterious rock icon.

It is tempting to think that Rodriguez resonated with South Africa's culture, that the cultural link made him a spectacular success there, and that the absence of such a link produced failure elsewhere. Don't believe it. He was the beneficiary of early popularity in South Africa, and that fueled a cascade. With a little luck, the same thing could have happened to him in the United States, the United Kingdom, Australia, or France. It didn't.

One of my major claims involves the constraining effects of social norms. People often do as they do, say what they say, and maintain silence only because of the pressure imposed by norms. We might take those norms for granted and have no particular attitude toward them. They are part of life's furniture. We might approve of them. We might dislike them or even deplore them; those are among the most interesting cases. If people live in accordance with norms they abhor, the circumstances are right for sudden change. People can be unleashed. Whether that is desirable depends on what exactly they are unleashed to do.

By contrast, some social movements inculcate beliefs and values that did not exist before. Sometimes preferences have adapted to existing practices and norms; nothing has been suppressed, and there is nothing to unleash. In those circumstances, large-scale change may be more difficult and also slower. But in such circumstances, cascades are possible as well. Serendipitous interactions and enclave deliberation, featuring people determined to fuel cascades, can be essential. They produce stunning surprises.

Acknowledgments

This book reflects decades of thinking, and I owe a great debt to a lot of people. I hope I may be forgiven for singling out just a few.

Special thanks to Richard Thaler, my collaborator on all issues relating to nudging, for that collaboration and, even more, his friendship. Heartfelt thanks too to Jon Elster, Eric Posner, Lucia Reisch, and Edna Ullmann-Margalit for help with many of the ideas here. Emily Taber, my editor, did a terrific, careful job; she is also a joy to work with. Thanks as well to Sarah Chalfant, my agent, for wisdom and support; Madeleine Joseph for truly exceptional research assistance; Melinda Rankin for a careful and superb copyedit; and the Program on Behavioral Economics and Public Policy at Harvard Law School for financial support.

The chapters here draw on earlier work, though there have been substantial revisions. For permission, I am grateful to the relevant publications: chapter 1, *Unleashed*, 85 Soc. Res. 73 (2018); chapter 2, *Deliberative Trouble? Why Groups Go to Extremes*, 110 Yale L. J. 71 (2000); chapter 3, *On the Expressive Function of Law*, 144 U. Pa. L. Rev. 2021 (1996); chapter 4, *Nudging: A Very Short Guide*, 37 J. Consumer Pol'y 583 (2014); chapter 5, *Forcing People to Choose Is Paternalistic*, 82 Missouri L. Rev. 643 (2017); chapter 7, *Nudges That Fail*, 1 Behav. Pub. Pol'y 4 (2017); chapter 9, *The Ethics of Nudging*, 32 Yale J. Reg. 413 (2015); chapter 10, *"Better Off, as Judged by Themselves": A Comment on Evaluating Nudges*, Int'l Rev. Econ. (2017); chapter 11, *Nudges vs. Shoves*, 127 Harv. L. Rev. F. 210 (2014); chapter 11, *On Preferring A to B, While Also Preferring B to A*, 30 Rationality and Politics 305 (2018); chapter 12, *Output Transparency vs. Input Transparency*, in *Troubling Transparency* (David Pozen and Michael Schudson eds. 2018); chapter 13, *Beyond the*

Precautionary Principle, 151 U. Pa. L. Rev. 1003 (2004); chapter 14, *Moral Heuristics*, 28 Behav. & Brain Sci. 531 (2005); chapter 15, *Is Deontology a Heuristic? On Psychology, Neuroscience, Ethics, and Law*, 63 Iyyun: The Jerusalem Philosophical Quarterly 83 (2014) (special memorial issue for Edna Ullmann-Margalit); chapter 16, *Partyism*, 2015 U. Chi. Legal F. 1 (2015).

Notes

Epigraphs

1. Milton Mayer, They Thought They Were Free 93 (1955/2017).

2. James Miller, "Democracy Is in the Streets": From Port Huron to the Siege of Chicago 52 (1987).

3. Herbert A. Simon, Models of My Life 281 (1991).

1 Unleashed

1. See Timur Kuran, Private Truths, Public Lies (1998).

2. For a broadly consistent account, see Catharine MacKinnon, Sexual Harassment of Working Women (1978). Of course it is true that some harassers were and are women, and some objects of harassment were and are men. For simplicity of exposition, and to capture what mostly has happened and does happen, I bracket this point.

3. See Lawrence Lessig, *The Regulation of Social Meaning*, 62 U. Chi. L. Rev. 943 (1995).

4. See Meritor Savings Bank v. Vinson, 477 US 57 (1986); Oncale v. Sundowner Offshore Services, 523 US 75 (1998).

5. See Richard McAdams, The Expressive Powers of Law: Theories and Limits (2015), and in particular at 148: "When the perception of public attitudes falls seriously out of line with reality, legislators gain by enacting legislation corresponding to actual attitudes (and actual future votes), which produces a dramatic revelation—a 'wake up call'—of actual attitudes."

6. See P. Wesley Schultz et al., *The Constructive, Destructive, and Reconstructive Power of Social Norms*, 18 Psych. Sci. 429 (2007).

7. That point is not meant to deny that the objections to "political correctness" as a way of silencing dissenters are often quite right.

8. Leonardo Bursztyn et al., Misperceived Social Norms: Female Labor Force Participation in Saudi Arabia (2018), http://www.nber.org/papers/w24736.

9. Timur Kuran, *Sparks and Prairie Fires: A Theory of Unanticipated Political Revolution*, 61 Public Choice 41 (1989).

10. See id.; Duncan Watts, Everything Is Obvious (2011); Susanne Lohmann, *The Dynamics of Social Cascades*, 47 World Pol. 42 (1994). Note, however, that it would be possible to attempt to measure hidden preferences, beliefs, and values—for example, by guaranteeing anonymity. For an instructive finding that anonymity matters because of the role of social norms, see Leonardo Bursztyn et al., From Extreme to Mainstream: How Social Norms Unravel (2017), http://www.nber.org/papers/w23415, discussed below. For a demonstration that people are more willing to acknowledge discrimination online than on the phone, see Timur Kuran and Edward McCaffery, *Expanding Discrimination Research: Beyond Ethnicity and to the Web*, 85 Soc. Sci. Q. 713 (2004).

Even if we obtain a sense of hidden preferences, we might not be able to predict change because of the importance of social dynamics, which cannot be anticipated in advance. See Susanne Lohmann, *I Know You Know He or She Knows We Know You Know They Know: Common Knowledge and the Unpredictability of Informational Cascades*, in Political Complexity: Nonlinear Models of Politics 137 (Diana Richards ed. 2000); see also the discussion below.

11. Anna Collar, Religious Networks in the Roman Empire: The Spread of New Ideas (2013).

12. Kuran, supra note 1.

13. Merouan Mekouar, Protest and Mass Mobilization: Authoritarian Collapse and Political Change (2016).

14. See Duncan Watts, The Non-Inevitability of Donald Trump (and Almost Everything) (2017), https://medium.com/@duncanjwatts/the-non-inevitability-of-donald-trump-and-almost-everything-2a78e764183f.

15. Timur Kuran, *Ethnic Norms and Their Transformation through Reputational Cascades*, 27 J. Legal Stud. 623 (1998).

16. See Volker Ullrich, Hitler: Ascent, 1889–1939 (2016). A highly controversial account is found in Daniel Jonah Goldhagen, Hitler's Willing Executioners (1997); a counterpoint appears in Christopher Browning, Ordinary Men (rev. ed. 2017).

17. Martin Mayer, They Thought They Were Free: The Germans, 1933–45 (1955/2017).

18. Id. at 124.

19. See Edna Ullmann-Margalit, *Considerateness*, 60 Iyyun 205 (2011).

20. See Philip O'Leary, The Prose Literature of the Gaelic Revival, 1881–1921 (2005).

21. See Collar, supra note 11.

22. Jon Elster, *Rationality, Emotions, and Social Norms*, 98 Synthese 21, 23 (1994).

23. I do not deal here with norms that solve collective action problems. For the defining account, see Edna Ullmann-Margalit, The Emergence of Norms (1977); see also Edna Ullmann-Margalit, Normal Rationality (2017). The analysis here could be adapted to that context, but with several wrinkles. The most important is that while such norms constrain people from doing as they wish (by preventing defection), they also operate to their mutual advantage, and so maintenance of the norm is in people's interest. For that reason, the leash that such norms impose should be quite welcome, at least on reflection.

24. The classic account is found in Mark Granovetter, *Threshold Models of Collective Behavior*, 83 Am. J. Soc. 1420 (1978); the idea is productively extended in Kuran, supra note 1.

25. See Cass R. Sunstein, *Social Roles and Social Norms*, 96 Colum. L. Rev. 903 (1996); see Cristina Bicchieri, Norms in the Wild 163–207 (2016). Both discriminators and objects of discrimination can of course serve as norm entrepreneurs. In the context of sexual harassment, Taylor Swift served as a norm entrepreneur in 2017, with her highly publicized objection to an act of unwanted touching. See Melena Ryzik, *Taylor Swift Spoke Up. Sexual Assault Survivors Were Listening*, New York Times (August 15, 2017), https://www.nytimes.com/2017/08/15/arts/music/taylor-swift-sexual-assault .html?_r=0.

26. There are many accounts. For especially good ones, see Kuran, supra note 1; D. Garth Taylor, *Pluralistic Ignorance and the Spiral of Silence: A Formal Analysis*, 46 Pub. Opinion Q. 311 (1982). A valuable account, with special reference to law, is Richard McAdams, The Expressive Powers of Law 136–162 (2015).

27. See id.; Sushil Bikhshandani et al., *A Theory of Fads, Fashion, Custom, and Cultural Change as Informational Cascades*, 100 J. Polit. Econ. 992 (1992).

28. An intriguing wrinkle is that when a cascade gets going, people might underrate the extent to which those who join it are reacting to the signals of others, and not their own private signals. For that reason, they might see the cascade as containing far more informational content than it actually does. See Erik Eyster & Matthew Rabin, *Naïve Herding in Rich-Information Settings*, 2 Am. Econ. J.: Microeconomics 221 (2010); Eric Eyster et al., An Experiment on Social Mislearning (2015), https://papers .ssrn.com/sol3/papers.cfm?abstract_id=2704746. Norm entrepreneurs have a strong interest in promoting this mistake.

29. See Amos Tversky & Daniel Kahneman, *Availability: A Heuristic for Judging Frequency and Probability*, 5 Cognitive Psychol. 207 (1973).

30. See Timur Kuran & Cass R. Sunstein, *Availability Cascades and Risk Regulation*, 51 Stan. L. Rev. 683 (1999).

31. Gordon Wood, The Radicalism of the American Revolution 29 (rev. ed. 1998).

32. Id. at 29–30.

33. Id. at 169.

34. Id.

35. Thomas Paine, "Letter to the Abbe Raynal," in *Life and Writings of Thomas Paine*, 242 (Daniel Edwin Wheeler ed. 1908). Quoted in Gordon Wood, The Creation of the American Republic, 1776–1787 68 (rev. ed. 1998).

36. See Lawrence Lessig, *The Regulation of Social Meaning*, 62 U. Chi. L. Rev. 943 (1995). See also Richard H. McAdams, *Cooperation and Conflict: The Economics of Group Status Production and Race Discrimination*, 108 Harv. L. Rev. 1003, 1065–1085 (1995).

37. Lessig, supra note 36, at 966.

38. See Leonardo Bursztyn et al., From Extreme to Mainstream: How Social Norms Unravel (2017), http://www.nber.org/papers/w23415.

39. Id.

40. Helpful discussion can be found in Timur Kuran, *Ethnic Norms and Their Transformation through Reputational Cascades*, 27 J. Legal Stud. 623 (1998).

41. George Orwell, Nineteen Eighty-Four (1949).

2   The Law of Group Polarization

1. See John Turner et al., Rediscovering the Social Group 142 (1987).

2. See Roger Brown, Social Psychology 222 (2d ed. 1983). These include the United States, Canada, New Zealand, India, Bangladesh, Germany, and France. See, e.g., Johannes Zuber et al., *Choice Shift and Group Polarization*, 62 J. Personality & Social Psychol. 50 (1992); Dominic Abrams et al., *Knowing What to Think by Knowing Who You Are*, 29 British J. Soc. Psychol. 97, 112 (1990). Of course it is possible that some cultures would show a greater or lesser tendency toward polarization; this would be an extremely interesting area for empirical study.

3. See D. G. Myers, *Discussion-Induced Attitude Polarization*, 28 Hum. Rel. 699 (1975).

4. Brown, supra note 2, at 224.

5. D. G. Myers & G. D. Bishop, *The Enhancement of Dominant Attitudes in Group Discussion*, 20 J. Personality & Soc. Psychol. 286 (1976).

6. Id.

7. See J. A. F. Stoner, A Comparison of Individual and Group Decisions Including Risk, unpublished master's thesis, Sloan School of Management, Massachusetts Institute of Technology (1961), available as J. A. F. Stoner, Risky and Cautious Shifts in Group Decisions: The Influence of Widely Held Values (2017); J. A. F. Stoner, *Risky and Cautious Shifts in Group Decisions: The Influence of Widely Held Values*, 4 J. Experimental Soc. Psychol. 442 (1968).

8. See Brown, supra note 2, at 208–210, for an overview.

9. Paul Cromwell et al., *Group Effects on Decision-Making by Burglars*, 69 Psychol. Rep. 579, 586 (1991).

10. Brown, supra note 2, at 211.

11. Most of the work was done with Daniel Kahneman and David Schkade. For a collection, see Cass R. Sunstein et al., Punitive Damages: How Juries Decide (2007).

12. See David Schkade et al., *Deliberating About Dollars: The Severity Shifts* 100 Colum. L. Rev. 1139 (2000).

13. Brown, supra note 2, at 210–225, reviews this literature; see also Turner et al., supra note 1, at 142–170, for an overview and an attempt to generate a new synthesis.

14. A. I. Teger & D. G. Pruitt, *Components of Group Risk-Taking*, 3 J. Experimental Soc. Psychol. 189 (1967).

15. See Robert S. Baron et al., *Social Corroboration and Opinion Extremity*, 32 J. Experimental Soc. Psychol. 537–560 (1996); Chip Heath & Richard Gonzales, *Interaction with Others Increases Decision Confidence but Not Decision Quality: Evidence against Information Collection Views of Interactive Decision Making*, 61 Org. Behav. & Hum. Decision Processes 305–326 (1997).

16. See Hans Brandstatter, *Social Emotions in Discussion Groups*, in Dynamics of Group Decisions (Hans Brandstatter et al. ed. 1978). Turner et al., supra note 1, at 154–159, attempt to use this evidence as a basis for a new synthesis, one that they call "a self-categorization theory of group polarization" (id. at 154). In this account, "persuasion is dependent upon self-categorizations which create a common identity within a group," and polarization occurs "because group members adjust their opinion in line with their image of the group position (conform) and more extreme, already polarized, prototypical responses determine this image" (id. at 156). The key point here is that when a group is tending in a certain direction, the perceived "prototype" is determined by where the group is leaning, and this is where individuals will shift (id. at 156). As Turner et al. suggest, their account shows "overlap with

many aspects of social comparison and persuasive arguments models"; because of the overlap, I do not discuss it as a separate account here. For possible differences in predictions, and supporting evidence, see id. at 158–170. An especially interesting implication is that a group of comparative extremists will show a comparatively greater shift toward extremism (id. at 158).

17. See Turner et al., supra note 1, at 153.

18. See Russell Spears, Martin Lee, & Stephen Lee, *De-Individuation and Group Polarization in Computer-Mediated Communication*, 29 British J. Soc. Psychol. 121 (1990); Dominic Abrams et al., *Knowing What to Think by Knowing Who You Are*, 29 British J. Soc. Psychol. 97, 112 (1990); Patricia Wallace, The Psychology of the Internet 73–76 (1999).

19. See Lee Roy Beach, The Psychology of Decision Making in Organizations (1997).

20. See H. Burnstein, *Persuasion as Argument Processing*, in Group Decision Making (H. Brandstetter, J. H. Davis, & G. Stocker-Kreichgauer eds. 1982).

21. Brown, supra note 2, at 225.

22. Amiram Vinokur & Eugene Burnstein, *The Effects of Partially Shared Persuasive Arguments on Group-Induced Shifts*, 29 J. Personality & Soc. Psychol. 305 (1974).

23. Id.

24. See David G. Myers, *Polarizing Effects of Social Interaction*, in Group Decision Making 125, 137–138 (Hermann Barndstatter et al. eds 1982).

25. See R. T Riley & T. F. Pettigrew, *Dramatic Events and Attitude Change*, 34 J. Personality & Soc. Psychol 1004, (1976).

26. Myers, supra note 24, at 135.

27. See Lois Marie Gibbs, Love Canal: The Story Continues 26–124 (1998).

28. See Callahan v. US, 364 US 487, 493–494 (1961) ("Concerted action … decreases the probability that the individuals will depart from their path of criminality"). I am grateful to Dan Kahan for pressing this point.

29. See Timur Kuran, *Ethnic Norms and Their Transformation through Reputational Cascades*, 27 J. Legal Stud. 623, 648 (1998).

30. Id.

31. See Caryn Christensen & Ann S. Abbott, *Team Medical Decision Making*, in Decision Making in Health Care 267, 273–276 (Gretchen Chapman & Frank Sonnenberg eds. 2000).

32. Id. at 274.

33. C. Kirchmeyer and A. Cohen, *Multicultural Groups: Their Performance and Reactions with Constructive Conflict*, 17 Group & Org. Mgmt. 153 (1992).

34. See Letter to Madison (January 30, 1798), reprinted in The Portable Thomas Jefferson 882 (M. Peterson ed. 1975).

35. See Speech to the Electors (November 3, 1774), reprinted in Burke's Politics 116 (R. Hoffman & P. Levack eds. 1949).

36. Id.

37. See The Federalist No. 10.

38. See Heather Gerken, *Second-Order Diversity*, 118 Harv. L. Rev. 1099 (2005).

3 The Expressive Function of Law

1. 163 US 537, 544 (1896) (noting that segregation laws "do not necessarily imply the inferiority of either race to the other").

2. 347 US 483 (1954).

3. See Bernard Williams, *A Critique of Utilitarianism*, in Utilitarianism: For and Against 108–109 (J. J. C. Smart & Bernard Williams eds. 1973).

4. Herbert A. Simon, Models of My Life 281 (1991).

5. Robert C. Ellickson, Order without Law: How Neighbors Settle Disputes 167 (1991) ("Members of tight social groups ... informally encourage each other to engage in cooperative behavior"); Edna Ullmann-Margalit, The Emergence of Norms 22–60 (1977).

6. See Edna Ullmann-Margalit, Normal Rationality (2017).

7. See Elijah Anderson, Streetwise: Race, Class, and Change in an Urban Community (1990).

8. Cass R. Sunstein, *Social Norms and Social Roles*, 96 Colum. L. Rev. 903 (1996).

9. See Viviana A. Zelizer, The Social Meaning of Money (1994).

10. Joel Waldfogel, *The Deadweight Loss of Christmas*, 83 Am. Econ. Rev. 1328 (1993). Waldfogel's engaging book on the subject is Scroogenomics (1998).

11. See Margaret J. Radin, *Market-Inalienability*, 100 Harv. L. Rev. 1849, 1871 (1987).

12. See Ullmann-Margalit, supra note 5, at 134–197 (discussing norms involving partiality and inequality).

13. See Steven Kelman, What Price Incentives? Economists and the Environment 27–28 (1981) (arguing that a society "fails to make a statement stigmatizing pollut-

ing behavior" when it relies upon economic incentives to carry out environmental policies).

4 Nudging

1. Louis D. Brandeis, Other People's Money 92 (1914).

5 Forcing Choices

1. See Daniel Kahneman, Thinking, Fast and Slow 20–21 (2011). The idea of two "systems" is controversial in some circles, and nothing here depends on accepting that idea.

2. See Sarah Conly, Against Autonomy (2012); Ryan Bubb & Richard Pildes, *How Behavioral Economics Trims Its Sails and Why*, 127 Harv. L. Rev. 1593, 1659 (2014).

3. See Sendhil Mullainathan & Eldar Shafir, Scarcity: Why Having Too Little Means So Much 39–66 (2013).

4. For a demonstration, see Björn Bartling & Urs Fischbacher, *Shifting the Blame: On Delegation and Responsibility*, 79 Rev. Econ. Stud. 67 (2012). On people's preference for flipping a coin as a way of avoiding responsibility, see Nadja Dwenger, Dorothea Kübler & Georg Weizsäcker, Flipping a Coin: Theory and Evidence, unpublished manuscript (2013), https://www.wzb.eu/sites/default/files/%2Bwzb/mp/vam/flipping _2014-01-21.pdf. Consider this suggestion:

The cognitive or emotional cost of deciding may outweigh the benefits that arise from making the optimal choice. For example, the decision-maker may prefer not to make a choice without having sufficient time and energy to think it through. Or, she may not feel entitled to make it. Or, she may anticipate a possible disappointment about her choice that can arise after a subsequent resolution of uncertainty. Waiving some or all of the decision right may seem desirable in such circumstances even though it typically increases the chance of a suboptimal outcome. (id. at 1)

5. See *Pandora Can Predict How You Vote Based on Your Favorite Stations*, Huffington Post, February 18, 2014, https://www.huffingtonpost.com/2014/02/18/pandora-democrat-republican-_n_4809401.html.

6. See, e.g., Paternalism: Theory and Practice (Christian Coons & Michael Weber eds., 2013); Gerald Dworkin, The Theory and Practice of Autonomy (1988).

7. See F. A. Hayek, The Market and Other Orders 384–386 (Bruce Caldwell ed., 2014).

8. John Stuart Mill, *On Liberty*, in On Liberty 5, 76 (Stefan Collini ed., 1859/1989) (1859).

9. Id at 76.

10. See George Loewenstein et al., *Warning: You Are About to Be Nudged*, 1 Behav. Sci. & Pol'y 35, 37, 40 (2015).

11. See Hendrik Bruns et al., *Can Nudges Be Transparent and Yet Effective?* 16–17 (WiSo-HH Working Paper Series, Working Paper No. 33, 2016), https://papers.ssrn .com/sol3/papers.cfm?abstract_id=2816227; Mary Steffel, Elanor F. Williams, & Ruth Pogacar, *Ethically Deployed Defaults: Transparency and Consumer Protection through Disclosure and Preference Articulation*, 53 J. Marketing Res. 865, 872 (2016).

12. Simona Botti & Christopher Hsee, *Dazed and Confused by Choice*, 112 Org. Behav. & Hum. Decision Processes 161 (2010).

6 Welfare

1. Richard Thaler & Cass Sunstein, *Nudge: Improving Decisions about Health, Wealth, and Happiness* 5 (2008); italics in original.

2. Robert Sudgen, *Do People Really Want to Be Nudged toward Healthy Lifestyles?*, 64 Int'l Rev. Econ. 113 (2006).

3. For data from various sources, see Cass R. Sunstein & Lucia A. Reisch, *Trusting Nudges: An International Survey* (forthcoming 2019); Janice Y. Jung & Barbara A. Mellers, *American Attitudes toward Nudges*, 11 Judgment and Decision Making 62 (2016); Cass R. Sunstein, *The Ethics of Influence* (2016); Lucia A. Reisch & Cass R. Sunstein, *Do Europeans Like Nudges?* 11 Judgment and Decision Making 310 (2016); Cass R. Sunstein, Lucia A. Reisch, & Julius Rauber, Behavioral Insights All Over the World? Public Attitudes toward Nudging in a Multi-Country Study, https://papers .ssrn.com/sol3/papers.cfm?abstract_id=2921217.

4. Jung & Mellers, supra note 3.

5. Amos Tversky & Richard H. Thaler, *Anomalies: Preference Reversals*, 4 Journal of Economic Perspectives 201, 211 (1990).

6. Jacob Goldin, *Which Way to Nudge? Uncovering Preferences in the Behavioral Age*, 125 Yale L. J. 226 (2015); Jacob Goldin & Nicholas Lawson, *Defaults, Mandates, and Taxes: Policy Design with Active and Passive Decision-Makers*, 18 Am. J. L. & Eco. 438 (2016).

7 Nudges That Fail

1. See Albert Hirschman, The Rhetoric of Reaction (1991).

2. See Lauren E. Willis, *When Defaults Fail: Slippery Defaults*, 80 U. Chi. L. Rev. 1155 (2012), for an excellent discussion. I deal only glancingly here with the risk of *counterproductive* nudges—Hirschman's category of "perversity"—though that is an important topic. See, e.g., George Loewenstein et al., *The Unintended Consequences of*

Conflict of Interest Disclosure, 307 JAMA 669 (2012); Ryan Bubb & Richard Pildes, *How Behavioral Economics Trims Its Sails and Why*, 127 Harv. L. Rev. 1593 (2014); Sunita Sah et al., *Effect of Physician Disclosure of Specialty bias on Patient Trust and Treatment Choice*, PNAS (2016), http://www.pnas.org/content/early/2016/06/16/1604908113 .full.pdf.

3. For a good discussion, Gabriel D. Carroll et al., *Optimal Defaults and Active Decisions*, 124 Q. J. Econ. 1639, 1641–1643 (2009). For an overview, with citations to the relevant literature, see Cass R. Sunstein, Choosing Not to Choose (2015).

4. Eyal Zamir, Law, Psychology, and Morality: The Role of Loss Aversion (2014).

5. See generally Elizabeth F. Emens, *Changing Name Changing: Framing Rules and the Future of Marital Names*, 74 U. Chi. L. Rev. 761 (2007).

6. Id. at 786.

7. Young Eun Huh, Joachim Vosgerau, & Carey K. Morewedge, *Social Defaults: Observed Choices Become Choice Defaults*, 41 J. Consumer Res. 746 (2014).

8. John Beshears et al., The Limitations of Defaults, unpublished manuscript (September 15, 2010), http://www.nber.org/programs/ag/rrc/NB10-02,%20Beshears,%20 Choi,%20Laibson,%20Madrian.pdf.

9. See Erin Todd Bronchetti et al., When a Default Isn't Enough: Defaults and Saving among Low-Income Tax Filers 28–29 (Nat'l Bureau of Econ. Research, Working Paper No. 16887, 2011), http://www.nber.org/papers/w16887 (explaining that default manipulation did not have an impact on tax refund allocation to a savings bond where an individual previously intended to spend the refund). Note, however, that the "default" in this study consisted of a mere statement on a form with the option to opt out. Id. at 17–18. In such a case, the line between the use of such a "default" and active choosing is relatively thin.

10. See Zachary Brown et al., *Testing the Effects of Defaults on the Thermostat Settings of OECD Employees*, 39 Energy Econ. 128 (2013).

11. Aristeidis Theotokis & Emmanouela Manganari, *The Impact of Choice Architecture on Sustainable Consumer Behavior: The Role of Guilt*, 131 J. Bus. Ethics 423 (2014).

12. René A. de Wijk et al., An In-Store Experiment on the Effect of Accessibility on Sales of Wholegrain and White Bread in Supermarkets (2016), http://journals.plos. org/plosone/article?id=10.1371%2Fjournal.pone.0151915.

13. David J. Just & Brian Wansink, *Smarter Lunchrooms: Using Behavioral Economics to Improve Meal Selection* (2009), http://www.choicesmagazine.org/UserFiles/file/ article_87.pdf.

14. Lauren E. Willis, *Why Not Privacy by Default?*, 29 Berkeley Tech. L. J. 62 (2014)— and in particular this suggestion: "Firms surround defaults they favor with a power-

ful campaign to keep consumers in the default position, but meet defaults set contrary to their interests with an equally powerful campaign to drive consumers to opt out. Rather than giving firms an incentive to facilitate consumer exercise of informed choice, many defaults leave firms with opportunities to play on consumer biases or confuse consumers into sticking with or opting out of the default."

15. Requirements for Overdraft Services, 45 § C.F.R. 205.17 (2010).

16. See Lauren E. Willis, When Defaults Fail: Slippery Defaults, 80 U. Chi. L. Rev. 1155, 1174–1175 (2012).

17. Id. at 1186–1187.

18. Id. at 1192.

19. See id.

20. See id.

21. Id. at 130.

22. See Tatiana Homonoff, Essays in Behavioral Economics and Public Policy (September 2013), https://dataspace.princeton.edu/jspui/bitstream/88435/dsp01jw 827b79g/1/Homonoff_princeton_0181D_10641.pdf.

23. See Willis, supra note 16, for an excellent discussion.

24. See Punam Anand Keller et al., *Enhanced Active Choice: A New Method to Motivate Behavior Change*, 21 J. Consumer Psychol. 376, 378 (2011).

25. Ariel Porat & Lior J. Strahilevitz, *Personalizing Default Rules and Disclosure with Big Data*, 112 Mich. L. Rev. 1417 (2014).

26. For a short discussion, full of implications, see Lauren Willis, *The Financial Education Fallacy*, 101 Am. Econ. Rev. 429 (2011).

27. See Sharon Brehm & Jack Brehm, Psychological Reactance: A Theory of Freedom and Control (1981); Louisa Pavey & Paul Sparks, *Reactance, Autonomy and Paths to Persuasion: Examining Perceptions of Threats to Freedom and Informational Value*, 33 Motivation & Emotion 277 (2009).

28. See Erin Frey & Todd Rogers, *Persistence: How Treatment Effects Persist after Interventions Stop*, 1 Pol'y Insights from Behav. & Brain Sci. 172 (2014), exploring four "persistence pathways" that "explain how persistent treatment effects may arise: building psychological habits, changing what and how people think, changing future costs, and harnessing external reinforcement."

29. Hunt Allcott & Todd Rogers, *The Short-Run and Long-Run Effects of Behavioral Interventions: Experimental Evidence from Energy Conservation*, 104 Am. Econ. Rev. 3003 (2014); Henrik Crongvist et al., *When Nudges Are Forever: Inertia in the Swedish Premium Pension Plan*, 108 Am. Econ. Rev. 153 (2018).

8 Ethics

1. David Foster Wallace, Commencement Address, Kenyon College, Gambier, Ohio, May 21, 2005; for the text of his address, see David Foster Wallace, in His Own Words, September 19, 2008, https://www.1843magazine.com/story/david-foster -wallace-in-his-own-words.

2. Meghan R. Busse et al., Projection Bias in the Car and Housing Markets (Nat'l Bureau of Econ. Research, Working Paper No. 18212, 2012), http://www.nber.org/ papers/w18212.

3. See Daniel Kahneman, Thinking, Fast and Slow (2011).

4. See Lauren Willis, *The Financial Education Fallacy*, 101 Am. Econ. Rev. 429 (2011).

5. Friedrich Hayek, *The Market and Other Orders*, in The Collected Works of F. A. Hayek 384 (Bruce Caldwell ed., 2013); italics added.

6. See Sarah Conly, Against Autonomy (2012).

7. See Stephen Darwell, *The Value of Autonomy and the Autonomy of the Will*, 116 Ethics 263, 269 (2006).

8. See T. M. Wilkinson, *Nudging and Manipulation*, 61 Pol. Stud. 341, 347 (2013).

9. Id. at 351.

10. See Conly, supra note 6.

11. Wilkinson, supra note 8, at 345.

9 Control

1. See *"Don't Tell Me What I Can't Do!" Lost Compilation*, YouTube (May 4, 2009), https://www.youtube.com/watch?v=JAsp4rn9QnM.

2. Sharon Brehm and Jack L. Brehm, Psychological Reactance: A Theory of Freedom and Control (1981).

3. Alexis de Tocqueville, The Ancien Regime and the French Revolution 151 (Jon Elster ed., 2007).

4. See The Federalist No. 10:

The two great points of difference between a democracy and a republic are: first, the delegation of the government, in the latter, to a small number of citizens elected by the rest; secondly, the greater number of citizens, and greater sphere of country, over which the latter may be extended. The effect of the first difference is, on the one hand, to refine and enlarge the public views, by passing them through the medium of a chosen body of citizens, whose wisdom may best discern the true interest of their country, and whose patriotism and love of justice will be least likely to sacrifice it to temporary or partial considerations. Under such a regulation, it may well happen that the public voice, pronounced by the representatives of the people, will be more consonant to the public good than if pronounced by the people themselves, convened for the purpose.

5. See Oren Bar-Gill and Cass R. Sunstein, *Regulation as Delegation*, 7 J. Legal Analysis 1 (2015).

6. For illuminating discussion, see Edna Ullmann-Margalit & Sidney Morgenbesser, *Picking and Choosing*, 44 Soc. Res. 757 (1977); Edna Ullmann-Margalit, Normal Rationality (Avishai Margalit & Cass R. Sunstein eds. 2017).

7. See, for example, Tali Sharot et al., *How Choice Reveals and Shapes Expected Hedonic Outcome*, 29 J. Neuroscience, 3760 (2009), http://doi.org/10.1523/JNEUROSCI .4972-08.2009.

8. Nicola J. Bown et al., *The Lure of Choice*, 16 J. Behav. Decision Making 297 (2003).

9. See David Owens et al., *The Control Premium: A Preference for Payoff Autonomy*, 6 Am. Econ. J.: Microeconomics 138 (2014), http://doi.org/10.1257/mic.6.4.138.

10. Suzanne C. Thompson, *Illusions of Control: How We Overestimate Our Personal Influence*, 8 Current Directions Psychol. Sci. 187 (1999), http://doi.org/10.1111/ 1467-8721.00044.

11. Sebastian Bobadilla-Suarez et al., *The Intrinsic Value of Control: The Propensity to Under-Delegate in the Face of Potential Gains and Losses*, 54 J. Risk & Uncertainty 187 (2017). I draw on our joint work for several of the following paragraphs here; many thanks to my coauthors, from whom I have learned a great deal.

12. David Owens, Zachary Grossman, & Ryan Fackler, *The Control Premium: A Preference for Payoff Autonomy*, 6 Am. Econ. J.: Microeconomics 138 (2014), http://doi .org/10.1257/mic.6.4.138; Björn Bartling, Ernst Fehr, & Holger Herz, *The Intrinsic Value of Decision Rights*, 82 Econometrica 2005 (2013), http://doi.org/10.3982/ ECTA11573.

13. John Stuart Mill, *On Liberty*, in On Liberty 5, 76 (Stefan Collini ed. 1859/1989).

10 Coercion

1. See Sarah Conly, Against Autonomy (2012); Ryan Bubb & Richard Pildes, *How Behavioral Economics Trims Its Sails and Why*, 127 Harv. L. Rev. 1593 (2014).

2. I am bracketing the question of definition, but note that freedom of choice is, by any reasonable account, an important ingredient in social welfare. See Daniel Benjamin et al., *Beyond Happiness and Satisfaction: Toward Well-Being Indices Based on Stated Preference*, 104 Am. Econ. Rev. 2698 (2014); Björn Bartling et al., *The Intrinsic Value of Decision Rights* (U. of Zurich, Dept. of Econ. Working Paper No. 120, 2013), http:// papers.ssrn.com/sol3/papers.cfm?abstract_id=2255992. For valuable discussion of foundational issues, see Matthew Adler, Well-Being and Fair Distribution: Beyond Cost–Benefit Analysis (2011).

3. Nat'l High. Traf. Safety Administration, *Final Regulatory Impact Analysis: Corporate Average Fuel Economy for MY 2017–MY 2025*, August 2012, table 13.

4. See Xavier Gabaix & David Laibson, *Shrouded Attributes, Consumer Myopia, and Information Suppression in Competitive Markets*, 121 Q. J. Econ. 505, 511 (2006).

5. See Light-Duty Vehicle Greenhouse Gas Emission Standards and Corporate Average Fuel Economy Standards; Final Rule, Part II, 75 Fed. Reg. 25,324, 25,510–25,511 (May 7, 2010), https://www.gpo.gov/fdsys/pkg/FR-2010-05-07/pdf/2010-8159.pdf.

6. Hunt Allcott & Michael Greenstone, *Is There an Energy Efficiency Gap?*, 26 J. Econ. Persp. 3 (2012).

11 On Preferring A to B, While Also Preferring B to A

1. The initial discovery was in 1992. See Max Bazerman et al., *Reversals of Preference in Allocation Decisions: Judging an Alternative versus Choosing among Alternatives*, 37 Admin. Sci. Q. 220 (1992). For a valuable overview, see Christopher Hsee et al., *Preference Reversals between Joint and Several Evaluations of Options*, 125 Psychol. Bull. 576 (1999). For a recent treatment with helpful additional complexity, see Yin-Hui Cheng et al., *Preference Reversals between Joint and Separate Evaluations with Multiple Alternatives and Context Effects*, 120 Psychol. Rep. 1117 (2017).

There is extensive literature on other kinds of preference reversals not discussed here. See, for example, Amos Tversky & Richard Thaler, *Preference Reversals*, 4 J. Econ. Persp. 201 (1990); Amos Tversky et al., *The Causes of Preference Reversal*, 80 Am. Econ. Rev. 204 (1990). The best explanation of some such reversals—"scale compatibility"—belongs, I think, in the same general family as those explored here, though I cannot establish that proposition in this space.

2. Christopher Hsee, *The Evaluability Hypothesis: An Explanation for Preference Reversals between Joint and Separate Evaluations of Alternatives*, 67 Organizational Behav. & Hum. Decision Processes 247, 248 (1996).

3. See id.; Christopher K. Hsee, *Attribute Evaluability: Its Implications for Joint-Separate Evaluation Reversals and Beyond*, in Choices, Values, and Frames 543–565 (Daniel Kahneman & Amos Tversky eds. 2000). Other explanations are explored in Max H. Bazerman et al., *Explaining How Preferences Change across Joint versus Separation Evaluation*, 39 J. Econ. Behav. & Org. 41 (1999).

4. Compare the important finding of "comparison friction" in Jeffrey R. Kling et al., *Comparison Friction: Experimental Evidence from Medicare Drug Plans*, 127 Q. J. Econ. 199 (2012). In brief, Kling and his coauthors describe comparison friction as "the wedge between the availability of comparative information and consumers' use of it." Id. at 200. They find that the wedge is significantly larger than people think, in the sense that even when information is readily available, people do not use it. There is a clear relationship between comparison friction and preference reversals of

the kind on which I focus here; in real markets, and in politics, it is because of comparison friction that in separate evaluation, people do not obtain the information that they could readily obtain.

5. See Shane Frederick et al., *Opportunity Cost Neglect*, 36 J. Consumer Res. 553 (2009).

6. See Ted O'Donoghue & Matthew Rabin, *Doing It Now or Later*, 89 Am. Econ. Rev. 103 (1999).

7. Hsee, supra note 2, at 253.

8. Id.

9. John A. List, *Preferences Reversals of a Different Kind: The "More Is Less" Phenomenon*, 92 Am. Econ. Rev. 1636 (2002).

10. Id. at 1641.

11. George Loewenstein, Exotic Preferences: Behavioral Economics and Human Motivation 261 (2007).

12. A methodological note: At several points, I will offer some speculations about what imaginable groups would do, without collecting data. My hope is that the speculations will be sufficiently plausible, a logical necessity (given the assumptions), or even self-evident, so that the absence of data is not a problem. But I emphasize that some of the speculations are only that, and that data would be much better.

13. For evidence in this vein, see Cheng et al., supra note 1.

14. See Christopher Hsee et al., *Magnitude, Time, and Risk Differ Similarly between Joint and Single Evaluations*, 40 J. Consumer Res. 172 (2013).

15. See Max H. Bazerman et al., *Explaining How Preferences Change across Joint versus Separate Evaluation*, 39 J. Econ. Behav. & Org. 41 (1999).

16. See Mark Kelman, Yuval Rottenstreich, & Amos Tversky, *Context- Dependence in Legal Decision-Making*, 25 J. Legal Stud. 287 (1996).

17. See Christopher Hsee & Jiao Zhang, *Distinction Bias: Misprediction and Mischoice Due to Joint Evaluation*, 86 J. Personality and Social Psych. 680 (2004).

18. See Daniel Kahneman & Richard Thaler, *Utility Maximization and Experienced Utility*, 20 J. Econ. Persp. 221 (2006); Daniel Kahneman et al., *Back to Bentham? Explorations of Experienced Utility*, 112 Q. J. Econ. 376 (1997).

19. Timothy Wilson & Daniel Gilbert, *Affective Forecasting*, 35 Advances Experimental Soc. Psychol. 345 (2003), http://homepages.abdn.ac.uk/c.n.macrae/pages/dept/HomePage/Level_3_Social_Psych_files/Wilson%26Gilbert(2003).pdf.

20. See Hsee & Zhang, supra note 17.

21. This suggestion can be found in Max Bazerman et al., *Negotiating With Yourself and Losing: Making Decisions With Competing Internal Preferences*, 23 Acad. Mgmt. Rev. 225, 231 (1998).

22. See Max Bazerman et al., *Joint Evaluation as a Real-World Tool for Managing Emotional Assessments of Morality*, 3 Emotion Rev. 290 (2011).

23. See Max Bazerman et al., *Explaining How Preferences Changes across Joint versus Separate Evaluation*, 39 J. Econ. Behav. & Org. 41 (1999).

24. I borrow here from id. at 46, which uses a VCR instead of a cell phone.

25. Xavier Gabaix & David Laibson, *Shrouded Attributes, Consumer Myopia, and Information Suppression in Competitive Markets*, 121 Q. J. Econ. 505 (2006).

26. True, this is based on a personal mistake. I love the old 11-inch MacBook Air, but I bought the new MacBook, with its terrific screen and its awful keyboard. (I am writing this on the former. The latter is in some drawer somewhere.)

27. Max Bazerman et al., *Explaining How Preferences Change across Joint versus Separate Evaluation*, 39 J. Econ. Behav. & Org. 41 (1999).

28. See Hsee, supra note 2.

29. Iris Bohnet et al., *When Performance Trumps Gender Bias: Joint vs. Separate Evaluation*, 62 Mgmt. Sci. 1225 (2015).

30. Id.

31. State Farm Mutual Automobile Insurance Co. v. Campbell, 538 US 408 (2003); TXO Production Corp. v. Alliance Resources, 509 US 443 (1993).

32. Cass R. Sunstein, Daniel Kahneman, Ilana Ritov, & David Schkade, *Predictably Incoherent Judgments*, 54 Stan. L. Rev. 1153 (2002).

33. Id.

34. Id.

35. See Daniel Kahneman et al., *Shared Outrage and Erratic Awards: The Psychology of Punitive Damages*, 16 J. Risk & Uncertainty 49 (1998).

36. See Daniel Kahneman & Cass R. Sunstein, *Cognitive Psychology of Moral Intuitions*, in Neurobiology of Human Values: Research and Perspectives in Neurosciences 91 (Jean-Pierre Changeux et al. eds. 2005).

37. See Kahneman et al., supra note 35.

38. See David Schkade et al., *Do People Want Optimal Deterrence?*, 29 J. Legal Stud. 237 (2000).

39. See Netta Barak-Corren et al., *If You're Going to Do Wrong, At Least Do It Right: Considering Two Moral Dilemmas At the Same Time Promotes Moral Consistency*, 64 Mgmt. Sci. 1528 (2017).

40. See Cass R. Sunstein, *How Do We Know What's Moral?*, N.Y. Rev. Books (Apr. 24, 2014).

41. See J. A. Hausman, Contingent Valuation: A Critical Assessment (2012); Handbook on Contingent Valuation (Anna Albertini & James Kahn eds. 2009).

42. See, e.g., Peter A. Diamond, *Contingent Valuation: Is Some Number Better Than No Number?*, 8 J. Econ. Persp. 45 (1994).

43. Daniel Kahneman, Ilana Ritov, & David Schkade, *Economic Preferences or Attitude Expressions? An Analysis of Dollar Responses to Public Issues*, 19 J. Risk & Uncertainty 220 (1999).

44. Id.

45. Id.

46. Janice Y. Jung & Barbara A. Mellers, *American Attitudes toward Nudges*, 11 Judgment & Decision Making 62 (2016).

47. See id.; Cass R. Sunstein, The Ethics of Influence (2016).

48. See Jung & Mellers, supra note 46.

49. See Shai Davidai & Eldar Shafir, *Are Nudges Getting A Fair Shot? Joint Versus Separate Evaluations*, 3 Behav. Pub. Pol'y (forthcoming 2018).

50. Id.

12 Transparency

1. See Amartya Sen, Poverty and Famines (1981).

2. See Amartya Sen, Development as Freedom (1999).

3. Transparency and Open Government, 74 Fed. Reg. 4685 (January 29, 2009).

4. For a 2016 account, see Corey Zarek, *Agencies Continue to Deliver on Day-One Commitment to Open Government*, White House Blog (July 14, 2016), https://www .whitehouse.gov/blog/2016/07/14/agencies-continue-deliver-day-one-commitment -open-government.

5. Louis D. Brandeis, Other People's Money 92 (1914).

6. For evidence, see Archon Fung et al., Full Disclosure (2008).

7. Archon Fung & Dana O'Rourke, *Reinventing Environmental Regulation from the Grassroots Up: Explaining and Expanding the Success of the Toxics Release Inventory*, 25 Envtl. Mgmt. 115 (2000).

8. See Partha Deb & Carmen Vargas, *Who Benefits from Calorie Labeling? An Analysis of Its Effects on Body Mass* (Nat'l Bureau of Econ. Research, Working Paper No. 21992, 2016), http://www.nber.org/papers/w21992.

9. See Fung et al., supra note 6.

10. Senator Elizabeth Warren, Speech at Administrative Conference of the United States: Regulatory Capture Forum (March 3, 2016), https://www.warren.senate.gov/files/documents/2016-3-3_Warren_ACUS_Speech.pdf.

11. Samantha Power, "A Problem from Hell": America and the Age of Genocide (2002). By the way, I like this book a lot, and I have learned a great deal from its author.

12. Max Farrand, The Records of the Constitutional Convention of 1787, vol. 3, 367 (1911)

13. See United States v. Nixon, 418 US 683 (1974).

14. 44 USC §§ 2201–2207 (2012).

13 Precautions

1. The literature is vast. See, for general discussion, The Precautionary Principle in the 20th Century: Late Lessons from Early Warnings (Poul Harremoes et al. eds. 2002); Arie Trouwborst, Evolution and Status of the Precautionary Principle in International Law (2002); Interpreting the Precautionary Principle (Tim O'Riordan & James Cameron eds., 2002); Precaution, Environmental Science and Preventive Public Policy (Joel Tickner ed., 2002); Protecting Public Health and the Environment: Implementing the Precautionary Principle (Carolyn Raffensberger & Joel Tickner eds. 1999).

2. Benny Joseph, Environmental Studies 254 (2005).

3. Final Declaration of the First European "Seas At Risk" Conference, Annex 1, Copenhagen, 1994.

4. Alan McHughen, Pandora's Picnic Basket (2000).

5. See Ling Zhong, *Note, Nuclear Energy: China's Approach toward Addressing Global Warming*, 12 Geo. Int'l Envtl. L. Rev. 493 (2000). Of course, it is reasonable to urge that nations should reduce reliance on either coal-fired power plants or nuclear power and move instead toward environmentally preferred alternatives, such as solar power. For general discussion, see Renewable Energy: Power for a Sustainable Future (Godfrey Boyle ed., 1996); Allan Collinson, Renewable Energy (1991); Dan E.

Arvizu, *Advanced Energy Technology and Climate Change Policy Implications*, 2 Fla. Coastal L. J. 435 (2001). But these alternatives pose problems of their own, involving feasibility and expense.

6. See Testimony of Vice Admiral Charles W. Moore, Deputy Chief of Naval Operations for Readiness and Logistics, before the House Resources Committee, Subcommittee on Fisheries Conservation, Wildlife and Oceans, June 13, 2002.

7. Paul Rozin & Carol Nemeroff, *Sympathetic Magical Thinking: The Contagion and Similarity "Heuristics,"* in Heuristics and Biases: The Psychology of Intuitive Judgment (Thomas Gilovich, Dale Griffin, & Daniel Kahneman eds. 2002).

8. Id.

9. See Paul Slovic, The Perception of Risk 291 (2000).

10. See James P. Collman, Naturally Dangerous (2001).

11. See Daniel B. Botkin, *Adjusting Law to Nature's Discordant Harmonies*, 7 Duke Envtl. L. & Pol'y F. 25, 27 (1996).

12. Id., 33.

13. See Collman, supra note 10.

14. Id., 31.

15. See Richard H. Thaler, *The Psychology of Choice and The Assumptions of Economics*, in Quasi-rational Economics 137, 143 (1991) (arguing that "losses loom larger than gains"); Daniel Kahneman, Jack L. Knetsch, & Richard H. Thaler, *Experimental Tests of the Endowment Effect and the Coase Theorem*, 98 J. Pol. Econ. 1325, 1328 (1990); Colin Camerer, *Individual Decision Making*, in The Handbook of Experimental Economics 587, 665–670 (John H. Kagel & Alvin E. Roth eds. 1995).

16. See Slovic, supra note 9, at 140–143.

17. See Amos Tversky & Daniel Kahneman, *Judgment under Uncertainty: Heuristics and Biases*, in id., 3, 11–14.

18. Id., 11.

19. Id.

20. Id.

21. Slovic, supra note 9, at 40.

22. For an especially good discussion of this point, see Daniel Steel, Philosophy and the Precautionary Principle: Science, Evidence, and Environmental Policy (2014).

23. See Frank H. Knight, Risk, Uncertainty, and Profit 19–20 (1921/1985) (distinguishing measurable uncertainties, or "'risk' proper," from unknowable uncertainties, called uncertainty); Paul Davidson, *Is Probability Theory Relevant for Uncertainty? A Post Keynesian Perspective*, 5 J. Econ. Persp. 129, 129–131 (1991) (describing the difference between true uncertainty and risk); Cass R. Sunstein, *Irreversible and Catastrophic*, 91 Cornell L. Rev. 841, 848 (2006) (noting that for risk, "probabilities can be assigned to various outcomes," while for uncertainty, "no such probabilities can be assigned"). For a technical treatment of the possible rationality of maximin, see generally Kenneth J. Arrow & Leonid Hurwicz, *An Optimality Criterion for Decision-Making under Ignorance*, in Uncertainty and Expectations in Economics: Essays in Honor of G.L.S. Shackle 1 (C. F. Carter & J. L. Ford eds., 1972). For a nontechnical overview, see Jon Elster, Explaining Technical Change app. 1 at 185–207 (1983).

24. A distinctive argument, ventured by Nassim Nicholas Taleb et al., refers to a "ruin" problem, involving a low probability of catastrophically high costs. Nassim Nicholas Taleb et al., The Precautionary Principle (with Application to the Genetic Modification of Organisms) 10 (Extreme Risk Initiative—NYU Sch. of Eng'g Working Paper Series, 2014), http://www.fooledbyrandomness.com/pp2.pdf (arguing that by "manipulat[ing] large sets of interdependent factors at the same time," GMOs have the potential to upset the entire food system).

25. See Cass R. Sunstein, Worst-Case Scenarios (2009); Cass R. Sunstein, Irreparability as Irreversibility, 2018 Supreme Court Review 93.

26. See Aaron Wildavsky, But Is It True? (1995), 433.

14 Moral Heuristics

1. Amos Tversky & Daniel Kahneman, *Judgment under Uncertainty: Heuristics and Biases*, 185 Science 1124 (1974).

2. See Jonathan Baron, *Nonconsequentialist Decisions*, 17 Behav. & Brain Sci. 1 (1994); Jonathan Baron, Judgment Misguided: Intuition and Error in Public Decision Making (1998); David Messick, *Equality as a Decision Heuristic*, in Psychological Perspectives on Justice (B. Mellers & J. Baron eds. 1993).

3. See Jonathan Baron, *Nonconsequentialist Decisions*, 17 Behav. & Brain Sci. 1 (1994).

4. John Rawls, A Theory of Justice (1971); Norman Daniels, Justice and Justification: Reflective Equilibrium in Theory and Practice (1996).

5. Daniel Kahneman & Amos Tversky, *Choices, Values, and Frames*, 39 Am. Psychol. 341 (1984).

6. See Daniel Kahneman & Shane Frederick, *Representativeness Revisited: Attribute Substitution in Intuitive Judgment*, in Heuristics and Biases: The Psychology of Intuitive Judgment 49, 62 (Thomas Gilovich, Dale Griffin, & Daniel Kahneman eds.

2002); Barbara Mellers, Ralph Hertwig, & Daniel Kahneman, *Do Frequency Representations Eliminate Conjunction Effects?*, 12 Psychol. Sci. 469 (2001).

7. Stephen J. Gould, Bully for Brontosaurus: Reflections in Natural History 469 (1991).

8. Kahneman & Frederick, supra note 6, at 63.

9. See D. G. Myers, Intuition: Its Powers and Perils (2002).

10. Paul Slovic et al., *The Affect Heuristic*, in Heuristics and Biases: The Psychology of Intuitive Judgment 397 (Thomas Gilovich, Dale Griffin, & Daniel Kahneman eds. 2002).

11. Kahneman & Frederick, supra note 6.

12. Joshua D. Greene & Jonathan Haidt, *How (and Where) Does Moral Judgment Work?*, 6 Trends in Cognitive Sci. 517 (2002); Jonathan Haidt & Matthew Hersh, *Sexual Morality: The Cultures and Emotions of Conservatives and Liberals*, 31 J. Applied Soc. Psychol. 191 (2002). Compare David A. Pizarro & Paul Bloom, *The Intelligence of the Moral Intuitions: Comment on Haidt*, 110 Psychol. Rev. 193 (2001).

13. Jonathan Haidt et al., Moral Dumbfounding: When Intuition Finds No Reason, unpublished manuscript, University of Virginia (2004).

14. Jeremy Bentham, An Introduction to the Principles of Morals and Legislation 12 (J. H. Burns & H. L. A. Hart eds. 1970).

15. See John Stuart Mill, Utilitarianism 28–29 (1861/1971); Henry Sigdwick, The Methods of Ethics 199–216 (1874); R. M. Hare, Moral Thinking: Its Levels, Method and Point (1981); J. J. C. Smart, *An Outline of a System of Utilitarian Ethics*, in Utilitarianism: For and Against (J. J. C. Smart & B. Williams eds. 1973).

16. See Mill, supra note 15, at 29. In a widely held view, a primary task of ethics is to identify the proper general theory and to use it to correct intuitions in cases in which they go wrong. B. Hooker, Ideal Code, Real World: A Rule-Consequentialist Theory of Morality (2000). Consider here the provocative claim that much of everyday morality, nominally concerned with fairness, should be seen as a set of heuristics for the real issue, which is how to promote utility. See J. Baron, Judgment Misguided: Intuition and Error in Public Decision Making (1998), https://www.sas.upenn.edu/~baron/vbook.htm. To the same general effect, with numerous examples from law, see L. Kaplow & S. Shavell, Fairness versus Welfare (2002).

17. Amartya Sen, *Fertility and Coercion*, 63 U. Chi. L. Rev. 1035, 1038 (1996).

18. Frans de Waal, Good Natured: The Origins of Right and Wrong in Humans and Other Animals (1996); Elliot Sober & David Sloan Wilson, Unto Others: The Evolution and Psychology of Unselfish Behavior (1999); Leonard D. Katz, Evolutionary Origins of Morality: Cross-Disciplinary Perspectives (2000).

19. Ethics and Evolution: The MIT Encyclopedia of the Cognitive Sciences (R. A. Wilson & F. C. Weil eds. 2001).

20. See Cass R. Sunstein, Why Societies Need Dissent (2003).

21. See Brad Hooker, Ideal Code, Real World: A Rule-Consequentialist Theory of Morality (2000).

22. Gerd Gigerenzer et al., Simple Heuristics that Make Us Smart (1999).

23. Daniel Kahneman & Amos Tversky, *Choices, Values, and Frames*, 39 Am. Psychol. 341 (1984).

24. Amos Tversky & Daniel Kahneman, *Loss Aversion in Riskless Choice: A Reference-Dependent Model*, 106 Q. J. Econ. 1039 (1991).

25. See Daniel Kahneman, Jack L. Knetsch, & Richard H. Thaler, *Fairness as a Constraint on Profit-Seeking: Entitlements in the Market*, 76 Am. Econ. Rev. 728 (1986).

26. Craig R. McKenzie, *Framing Effects in Inference Tasks—and Why They Are Normatively Defensible*, 32 Memory & Cognition 874 (2004).

27. Note also that loss aversion is quite robust in the real world. Colin Camerer, *Prospect Theory in the Wild: Evidence from the Field*, in Choices, Values and Frames (Daniel Kahneman & Amos Tversky eds. 2000); Shlomo Benartzi & Richard H. Thaler, *Myopic Loss Aversion and the Equity Premium Puzzle*, in Choices, Values and Frames (Daniel Kahneman & Amos Tversky eds. 2000). And it has not been shown to be solely or mostly a result of the speaker's clues. Note also that the nature of the cue, when there is one, depends on the speaker's appreciation of the existence of framing effects; otherwise, the clue would be ineffective.

28. See Shane Frederick, *Measuring Intergenerational Time Preference: Are Future Lives Valued Less?*, 26 J. Risk & Uncertainty 39 (2003).

29. Richard Revesz, *Environmental Regulation, Cost–Benefit Analysis, and the Discounting of Human Lives*, 99 Colum. L. Rev. 941 (1999); Edward R. Morrison, *Comment, Judicial Review of Discount Rates Used in Regulatory Cost–Benefit Analysis*, 64 U. Chi. L. Rev. 1333 (1998).

30. Maureen L. Cropper et al., *Preferences for Life-Saving Programs: How the Public Discounts Time and Age*, 8 J. Risk & Uncertainty 243 (1994).

31. Shane Frederick, *Measuring Intergenerational Time Preference: Are Future Lives Valued Less?*, 26 J. Risk & Uncertainty 39 (2003).

32. For a similar result, see Jonathan Baron, *Can We Use Human Judgments to Determine the Discount Rate?*, 20 Risk Analysis 861 (2000). Here, too, the frame may indicate something about the speaker's intentions, and subjects may be sensitive to the degree of certainty in the scenario (assuming, for example, that future deaths

may not actually occur). While strongly suspecting that these explanations are not complete, see Shane Frederick, *Measuring Intergenerational Time Preference: Are Future Lives Valued Less?*, 26 J. Risk & Uncertainty 39 (2003). I mean not to reject them, but only to suggest the susceptibility of intuitions to frames. For skeptical remarks, see Frances Kamm, *Moral Intuitions, Cognitive Psychology, and the Harming-versus-Not-Aiding Distinction*, 108 Ethics 463 (1998).

33. See Cass R. Sunstein, *Lives, Life-Years, and Willingness to Pay*, 104 Colum. L. Rev. 205 (2004).

34. See W. Kip Viscusi, *Corporate Risk Analysis: A Reckless Act?*, 52 Stan. L. Rev. 547, 547, 558 (2000).

35. See id; Phillip E. Tetlock et al., *The Psychology of the Unthinkable: Taboo Trade-Offs, Forbidden Base Rates, and Heretical Counterfactuals*, 78 J. Personality & Soc. Psychol. 853 (2000).

36. See Viscusi, supra note 34.

37. Phillip E. Tetlock et al., *The Psychology of the Unthinkable: Taboo Trade-Offs, Forbidden Base Rates, and Heretical Counterfactuals*, 78 J. Personality & Soc. Psychol. 853–870 (2000).

38. I am grateful to Jonathan Haidt for this suggestion.

39. Frank Ackerman & Lisa Heinzerling, Priceless: On Knowing the Price of Everything and the Value of Nothing (2004).

40. Cass R. Sunstein, Risk and Reason: Safety, Law, and the Environment (2002).

41. Michael Sandel, *It's Immoral to Buy the Right to Pollute*, New York Times (December 15, 1997); see also Steven Kelman, What Price Incentives? Economists and the Environment (1981).

42. See Jonathan J. Koehler & Andrew D. Gershoff, *Betrayal Aversion: When Agents of Protection Become Agents of Harm*, 90 Org. Behav. & Hum. Decision Processes 244 (2003).

43. See id.

44. Id. at 244.

45. Id.

46. Ilana Ritov & Jonathan Baron, *Reluctance to Vaccinate: Omission Bias and Ambiguity*, 3 J. Behav. Decision Making 263 (1990).

47. John Darley et al., *Incapacitation and Just Deserts as Motives for Punishment*, 24 L. & Hum. Behav. 659 (2000); Kevin M. Carlsmith et al., *Why Do We Punish? Deterrence and Just Deserts as Motives for Punishment*, 83 J. of Personality & Soc. Psychol. 284 (2000).

48. See Daniel Kahneman, David Schkade, & Cass R. Sunstein, *Shared Outrage and Erratic Awards: The Psychology of Punitive Damages*, 16 J. of Risk & Uncertainty 49 (1998); Cass R. Sunstein et al., Punitive Damages: How Juries Decide (2002).

49. See Kahneman & Frederick, supra note 6, at 63.

50. Ilana Ritov & Jonathan Baron, *Reluctance to Vaccinate: Omission Bias and Ambiguity*, 3 J. Behav. Decision Making 263 (1990).

51. See Jonathan Baron, Morality and Rational Choice 108, 123 (1993).

52. Id.

53. Jonathan Baron & Ilana Ritov, *Intuitions about Penalties and Compensation in the Context of Tort Law*, 7 J. Risk & Uncertainty 17 (1993).

54. Mitchell A. Polinsky & Steven S. Shavell, *Punitive Damages: An Economic Analysis*, 111 Harv. L. Rev. 869 (1998).

55. Cass R. Sunstein, David Schkade, & Daniel Kahneman, *Do People Want Optimal Deterrence?*, 29 J. Legal Stud. 237, 248–249 (2000).

56. L. Kass, *The Wisdom of Repugnance*, in The Ethics of Human Cloning 17–19 (L. Kass & J. Q. Wilson eds. 1998).

57. Id.

58. P. Rozin, *Technological Stigma: Some Perspectives from the Study of Contagion*, in Risk, Media, and Stigma: Understanding Public Challenges to Modern Science and Technology 31, 38 (J. Flynn, P. Slovic, & H. Kunreuther eds. 2001).

59. Id.

60. Id.

61. A. McHughen, Pandora's Picnic Basket (2000).

62. E. Schlosser, Fast Food Nation: The Dark Side of the All-American Meal (2002).

63. J. Haidt & M. Hersh, *Sexual Morality: The Cultures and Emotions of Conservatives and Liberals*, 31 J. Applied Soc. Psychol. 191–221.

64. Haidt et al., supra note 13.

65. See Washington v. Glucksberg 1997, 724–725.

66. J. Baron & I. Ritov, *Intuitions about Penalties and Compensation in the Context of Tort Law*, 7 J. Risk & Uncertainty 17–33.

67. B. Williams, *A Critique of Utilitarianism*, in Utilitarianism: For and Against (J. J. C. Smart & B. Williams eds. 1973).

68. J. J. Thomson, *The Trolley Problem*, in Rights, Restitution and Risk: Essays in Moral Theory 31 (J. J. Thomson & W. Parent eds. 1986).

69. F. Kamm, Morality, Mortality, Vol. 1: Death and Whom to Save from It 8 (1993); see generally R. Sorenson, Thought Experiments (1992).

70. B. Hooker, Ideal Code, Real World: A Rule-Consequentialist Theory of Morality (2000); J. Raz, *The Relevance of Coherence*, in Ethics in the Public Domain 277–326 (J. Raz ed. 1994).

71. J. Rawls, A Theory of Justice (1971).

15 Rights

1. Frances Kamm, Intricate Ethics (2006); Bernard Williams, *A Critique of Utilitarianism*, in Utilitarianism: For and Against (J. C. Smart and Bernard Williams eds. 1973).

2. An important effort to explore differences among the leading ethical theories, and to suggest that they converge, is Derek Parfit, On What Matters, vol. 1 (2013). Throughout I oppose consequentialism and deontology in the conventional way.

3. C. R. Sunstein, D. Schkade, & D. Kahneman, *Do People Want Optimal Deterrence?*, 29 J. Legal Stud. 237–253.

4. Note, however, that the relevant findings cover only a very small portion of the domain in which deontological judgments are and might be made and that some evidence does not support the view that such judgments are distinctly associated with automatic processing. Andrea Manfrinati et al., *Moral Dilemmas and Moral Principles: When Emotion and Cognition Unite*, 27 Cognition & Emotion 1276 (2013). Note also that learning and culture certainly matter and we do not have much cross-cultural evidence, which would be highly informative about the relationships among deontology, automatic processing, and culture.

5. Henry Sidgwick, The Methods of Ethics 425–426 (1981).

6. Joshua D. Greene, *Reply to Mikhail and Timmons*, in Moral Psychology: The Neuroscience of Morality: Emotion, Brain Disorders, and Development 3 (Walter-Sinnott-Armstrong ed. 2007).

7. Judith Jarvis Thomson, *The Trolley Problem*, in Rights, Restitution and Risk: Essays in Moral Theory (J. J. Thomson & W. Parent eds. 1986).

8. Joshua D. Greene, Brian R. Somerville, Leigh E. Nystrom, John M. Darley, & Jonathan D. Cohen, *An fMRI Investigation of Emotional Engagement in Moral Judgment*, 293 Science 2105, 2106 (2001). Various questions have been raised about the methodology in Greene et al.'s paper, in particular the difficulty of inferring causation: Selim Berker, *The Normative Insignificance of Neuroscience*, 37 Phil. & Public Affairs 293, 305–313 (2009); I bracket those questions here.

9. Joshua D. Greene, *The Cognitive Neuroscience of Moral Judgment*, in The Cognitive Neurosciences (M. S. Gazzaniga ed., 4th ed., 2009).

10. Fiery Cushman, Dylan Murray, Shauna Gordon-McKeon, Sophie Wharton, & Joshua D. Greene, *Judgment before Principle: Engagement of the Frontoparietal Control Network*, 7 Soc. Cognitive & Affective Neuroscience 888 (2011).

11. Id., 893.

12. Id., 894.

13. Id., 893.

14. Michael L. Koenigs, Liane Young, Ralph Adolphs, Daniel Tranel, Fiery Cushman, Marc Hauser, & Antonio Damasio, *Damage to the Prefrontal Cortex Increases Utilitarian Moral Judgments*, 446 Nature 908, 909 (2007).

15. Id., 909–910.

16. Joshua D. Greene, *Why Are VMPFC Patients More Utilitarian? A Dual-Process Theory of Moral Judgment Explains*, 11 Trends in Cognitive Sci. 322 (2007).

17. Mario Mendez, Eric Anderson, & Jill S. Shapira, *An Investigation of Moral Judgment in Frontotemporal Dementia*, 18 Cognitive & Behav. Neurology 193 (2005).

18. Id. Note that on their own, fMRI studies suggest only correlations and cannot distinguish cause and effect. If region X is active when we make decision Y, it is not necessarily the case that X is causing decision Y. Y may be causing X, or both may be caused by something else altogether. For example, the act of making a deontological judgment may cause an emotional reaction that may be processed by the amygdala and/or VMPC. By contrast, lesions studies may suggest cause and effect. (I am grateful to Tali Sharot for clarifying this point.)

19. Elinor Amit & Joshua D. Greene, *You See, The Ends Don't Justify the Means: Visual Imagery and Moral Judgment*, 23 Psychol. Sci. 861, 862 (2012).

20. Id., 866.

21. Joshua D. Greene, Sylvia A. Morelli, Kelly Lowenberg, Leigh E. Nystrom, & Jonathan D. Cohen, *Cognitive Load Selectively Interferes with Utilitarian Moral Judgment*, 107 Cognition 1144, 1151 (2008).

22. Contrary evidence, suggesting that deontological thinking can actually take longer than consequentialist thinking and that "cognitive and emotional processes participate in both deontological and consequentialist moral judgments," can be found in Andrea Manfrinati et al., *Moral Dilemmas and Moral Principles*, 27 Cognition & Emotion 1276 (2013).

23. Joseph M Paxton, Leo Ungar, & Joshua D. Greene, *Reflection and Reasoning in Moral Judgment*, 36 Cognitive Science 163, 171–172 (2012).

24. Id., 166.

25. Joshua D. Greene, *The Secret Joke of Kant's Soul*, in 3 Moral Psychology: The Neuroscience of Morality: Emotion, Brain Disorders, and Development 36 (W. Sinnott-Armstrong ed. 2007); italics in original.

26. Joshua D. Greene, *From Neural "Is" to Moral "Ought": What Are the Moral Implications of Neuroscientific Moral Psychology?*, 4 Nature Reviews Neuroscience 847–850, 847 (2003); for critical evaluation, see R. Dean, *Does Neuroscience Undermine Deontological Theory?*, 3 Neuroethics 43–60 (2010). An especially valuable overview, from which I have learned a great deal, is Joshua D. Greene, *Beyond Point-and-Shoot Morality: Why Cognitive (Neuro)Science Matters for Morality*, 124 Ethics 695 (2014).

27. N. Paharia, K. S. Kassamb, J. D. Greene, and M. H. Bazerman, *Dirty Work, Clean Hands: The Moral Psychology of Indirect Agency*, 109 Organizational Behav. & Hum. Decision Processes 134–141, 140 (2009); S. Berker, *The Normative Insignificance of Neuroscience*, 37 Phil. & Pub. Aff. 293–329, 327–329 (2009).

28. Cass R. Sunstein, David Schkade, & Daniel Kahneman, *Do People Want Optimal Deterrence?*, 29 J. Legal Stud. 237, 248–249 (2000).

16 Partyism

1. Shanto Iyengar, Guarav Sood, & Yphtach Lelkes, *Affect, Not Ideology: A Social Identity Perspective on Polarization*, 76 Pub. Opinion Q. 405 (2012), http://pcl.stanford.edu/research/2012/iyengar-poq-affect-not-ideology.pdf.

2. Id.

3. Id.

4. See, e.g., Anthony Greenwald, Debbie E. McGhee, & Jordan L. K. Schwartz, *Measuring Individual Differences in Implicit Cognition: The Implicit Association Test*, 74 J. Personality & Soc. Psychol. 1464 (1998); N. Sriram & Anthony G. Greenwald, *The Brief Implicit Association Test*, 56 Experimental Psychol. 283 (2009) ("In eleven years since its introduction, the Implicit Association Test ... has been used in several hundred studies to provide measures of association strengths.").

5. E.g., Greenwald, McGhee, & Schwartz, supra note 4, at 1474; Scott A. Ottaway, Davis C. Hayden, & Mark A. Oakes, *Implicit Attitudes and Racism: Effects of Word Familiarity and Frequency on the Implicit Association Test*, 19 Soc. Cognition 97, 130 (2001); Shanto Iyengar & Sean J. Westwood, *Fear and Loathing across Party Lines: New Evidence on Group Polarization*, 59 Am. J. Polit. Sci. 690 (2015).

6. Iyengar & Westwood, supra note 5.

7. See Iyengar, Sood, & Lelkes, supra note 1, at 416 (showing a steady decrease in racial polarization from 1964 to 2008).

8. Id. at 415–418.

9. Id.

10. Id.

11. Paul Taylor et al., The Rise of Intermarriage, Pew Social & Demographic Trends 7 (February 16, 2012), http://www.pewsocialtrends.org/files/2012/02/SDT -Intermarriage-II.pdf.

12. Id. at 36.

13. Frank Newport, In U.S., 87% Approve of Black-White Marriage, vs. 4% in 1958, Gallup (July 25, 2013), http://www.gallup.com/poll/163697/approve-marriage-blacks -whites.aspx.

14. Iyengar & Westwood, supra note 5.

15. Id. at 15–16.

16. Id. at 16–17.

17. Id. at 18.

18. Geoffrey D. Munro, Terell P. Lasane, & Scott P. Leary, *Political Partisan Prejudice: Selective Distortion and Weighting of Evaluative Categories in College Admissions Applications*, 40 J. Applied Soc. Psych. 2434, 2440 (2010).

19. Id. at 2444–2445.

20. Iyengar & Westwood, supra note 5.

21. Yphtach Lelkes & Sean J. Westwood, *The Nature and Limits of Partisan Prejudice* (Working Paper, 2014).

22. Id. at 9.

23. Id. at 10.

24. Id. at 11.

25. Id. at 14.

26. See Lilliana Mason, *"I Disrespectfully Agree": The Differential Effects of Partisan Sorting on Social and Issue Polarization*, 59 Am. J. Pol. Sci. 128 (2015); Adrian Furnham, *Factors Relating to the Allocation of Medical Resources*, 11 J. Soc. Behav. & Personality 615, 620 (1996).

27. See Iyengar, Sood, & Lelkes, supra note 1, at 422–423; Mason, supra note 26.

28. See Iyengar, Sood, & Lelkes, supra note 1, at 425–427 (finding that residence in a battleground state during an election year correlates significantly with inten-

sity of partisan affect and that partisan affect increases significantly over the course of a campaign, especially in battleground states); Guarav Sood, Shanto Iyengar, & Kyle Dropp, *Coming to Dislike Your Opponents: The Polarizing Impact of Political Campaigns* (Working Paper, April 2013) (finding that over the course of a campaign, partisans form more negative views of the opposing party, and the most strongly correlated feature is exposure to televised political advertising, especially negative ads).

29. See Yphtach Lelkes, Shanto Iyengar, & Gaurav Sood, *The Hostile Audience: Selective Exposure to Partisan Sources and Affective Polarization* (Working Paper, 2013) (finding that for partisans who pay attention to politics, cable access is correlated with greater partisan affect in years when cable carries partisan content, and further finding that the preference of partisans for choosing, between MSNBC and Fox News, the news sources amenable to their party "in and of itself—is sufficient to predict partisan animus, greater affect for in-party elites vis-à-vis out-party elites, greater social distance between partisans, and a preference for attack-oriented campaign rhetoric").

30. Brendan Nyhan & Jason Reifler, *When Corrections Fail: The Persistence of Political Misperceptions*, 32 Pol. Behav. 303, 312 (2010).

31. Id. at 312–313.

32. Id. at 314.

33. Id. at 314–315.

34. Id. at 320. An important set of qualifications of these findings can be found in Thomas Wood & Ethan Porter, *The Elusive Backfire Effect: Mass Attitudes' Steadfast Factual Adherence* (2018), Political Behavior (forthcoming), available at https:// papers.ssrn.com/sol3/papers.cfm?abstract_id=2819073. Wood and Porter show that in multiple domains, corrections do not backfire, even when they challenge preexisting political convictions. Their findings suggest that we need to know the boundary conditions for the phenomenon of backfiring corrections. An intense commitment to the original belief will of course make corrections less likely to work (and potentially backfire); distrust of the source is also relevant.

35. Brendan Nyhan, Jason Reifler, & Peter A. Ubel, *The Hazards of Correcting Myths about Health Care Reform*, 51 Med. Care 127, 127 (2013).

36. Id. at 129–130.

37. Id.

38. Id.

39. Nyhan & Reifler, supra note 30, at 321.

40. Id. at 321–322.

41. See Geoffrey Cohen, *Party over Policy*, 85 J. Persp. Soc. Psychol. 808 (2003).

42. Id.

43. See The Federalist No. 10 (James Madison).

44. Pub. L. 101-510, 104 Stat. 1485 (1990).

45. The Budget Control Act of 2011, Pub. L. 112-25, S. 365, 125 Stat. 240 (2011).

46. Id.

Index